Stained Glass

THE DIAL PRESS | NEW YORK

STAINED GLASS

TRADITIONS
AND
TECHNIQUES

Plus a Design Workbook

and 10 Projects

Illustrations and Original Designs

by Barbara Sablow

By Joan M. Scobey

Published by The Dial Press
1 Dag Hammarskjold Plaza
New York, New York 10017

All photographs not otherwise credited were taken by
the author.

Manufactured in the United States of America

First printing

Library of Congress Cataloging in Publication Data
Scobey, Joan.
Stained glass.
Bibliography: p.
Includes index.
1. Glass craft.   2. Glass painting and staining—
History.   I. Title.
TT298.S36   748.5   78-17265

ISBN 0-8037-7926-0
ISBN 0-8037-7925-x pbk.

To Rafe

Acknowledgments

Of the many people who have guided me through the fascinating world of stained glass, I want first to thank Joe Castagna who tutored me in the intricacies of the craft and gave me a sense of what could be accomplished with the materials. With unfailing good humor he shared his knowledge, his talents, and most precious of all, his time, and always made me welcome in his New York Art Glass Studio.

There were other artists who were generous with their photographs, and I regret that space prevents me from using all the pictures they made available: Kathie Bunnell, Kenneth Potter, Narcissus Quagliata, Elizabeth Quantock, Beverly Reiser, Ludwig Schaffrath, Penelope Comfort Starr, and Fred Varney.

My pleasant search for historical information and photographs was aided by many people and institutions, among them All Saints' Church, York, the Reverend Alban C. M. Howard; Mr. and Mrs. Joseph S. Blank, Caisse Nationale des Monuments Historiques, Paris, Mme. G. Gareau; Center for the Visual Arts, Oakland, California, Rita Gardner; Council for Places of Worship, London, Alison Knight and David Williams; Mary D'Arth, Coventry Cathedral; M. Roger Doe, Atelier Simon, Travaux d'Art Decoratif, Reims; Friends of Canterbury Cathedral, F. W. Cole; Friends of Salisbury Cathedral, Lt. Col. G. F. Woolnough, M. C.; Hadassah, New York, Marion Berg; Sonia Halliday, Bucks, England; Clive Hicks, London; Dena Justin, San Francisco; Isaac Kleinerman, New York; C. & R. Loo, Inc., Emeryville, California, C. Y. Loo and Molly Stone; Metropolitan Museum of Art, New York; Malcolm B. Miller, Syndicat d'Initiativ, Chartres; Gerald M. Philips; Sy and Theo Portnoy; Royal Commission on Historical Monuments, London, Cecil Farthing; Sotheby & Co., London; Steuben Glass, New York; Victoria and Albert Museum, London; Mrs. Bryan Wallace, Chateau de Champigny-sur-Veude, France; Westminster Abbey, N. H. MacMichael, Keeper of the Muniments.

And not least there are my professional colleagues and friends who saw me through my long apprenticeship—Warren Wallerstein, Martha Schwerin, Jack Ribik, and Jane Wilson—and my delightful and talented young illustrator, Barbara Sablow.

Contents

Introduction

The pleasures of learning any craft are several. First there is the joy of translating newly learned skills into artifacts and objects that you can use and enjoy. Then, especially if it is a craft practiced long and honorably, there is the sense of continuity—of heritage and tradition. And most assuredly there is the quickening pleasure that comes with an understanding of the technique, enhancing one's view of great examples. A painter, no matter how poor his talents, brings a special quality to his enjoyment of paintings; a rugmaker has a special appreciation for a great carpet; and a stained glass craftsman will walk through a cathedral with a new eye to the glazed windows and a heightened awareness of the intimate relationship between stained glass—be it religious or secular—and the architecture that contains it. More than that, however, is the sense that stained glass is somehow a primal medium, combining earth, sea, fire, and sky in its creation. From the earth and the sea come the raw materials—the silica; from fire, the heat to transform it into glass, and from the sky the glow to illuminate it.

For a novice stained glass may be an altogether unfamiliar medium. It is usually mounted high in a wall, far beyond close inspection and certainly reach. And its tools are more industrial than hobby—the tools of the glazier and the metal worker. This book is designed to bring the craft close at hand, to explain the techniques simply, and to put stained glass art in its historical context.

In Part I you can follow the story of stained glass from its early beginnings in the Middle East, through the glorious religious windows of the Middle Ages, to its contemporary, often secular, vigorous life today. In Part II you will see how to work in stained glass, using the two basic techniques of leading and copper foil. You will find richly illustrated explanations of how to design for stained glass, how to make working drawings, how to handle and cut glass, and how to work with solder. Part III offers a variety of stained glass designs with which you can make your first projects. And in Part IV are the projects themselves, which utilize a variety of assembly techniques.

These techniques are readily adaptable to other kinds of stained glass work. For example, after you have made the cigarette box—or at least studied its assembly carefully—you will know how to join four sides to a bottom and add a hinged top. This will put a fish tank or a terrarium or any other box-like object within easy grasp. Likewise, the methods for assembling the wall light can be readily transferred to a living room or kitchen valance. Once you know how to make the window panel, you not only can fill the windows in your home with glorious light, but you can also lay a panel horizontally on legs and produce a table top, or stand it vertically for a fire screen, or hang it on nylon thread from the ceiling in front of a window.

The designs as well as the techniques are flexible. The face of the clock, for instance, would make a lovely mirror (eliminating the hands, of course), the rose a charming belt buckle. So approach both the stained glass designs and the projects with some abandon, and use the step-by-step assembling and finishing information to mix-and-match them.

A word about the absence of lamp shades, a deliberate omission. Whole books are devoted to steering you through the complexities of shade making, and the limited space in this book could not do justice to what is an ambitious project, especially for beginners. Once you have mastered the basic skills for working in stained glass, you may want to consider one of the many lamp shade kits that are available; some even duplicate the patterns of Tiffany lamps, and some are accompanied by actual molds on which to assemble the three-dimensional shade. They are helpful in making one's first shade.

With a grounding in the basic techniques of stained glass craft, and an understanding of its great traditions, you can join craftsmen—both novice and professional—who have discovered the pleasures of working in this vigorous medium. And then, perhaps, you may even want to push your glass horizons still further and investigate the newer techniques of working with epoxy res-ins, fusing, laminating, even bending glass to your will in new ways.

Stained glass, once the educational tool for teaching the Bible to illiterate worshipers, has become purely pleasurable, as often secular as religious. Moreover, it is becoming a very personal form of expression, freeing itself of its architectural bonds and finding new places in the home. This book is offered to introduce you to new skills and pleasures, with the hope that you will enter a joyous new world of visual delights.

PART 1

THE STORY OF STAINED GLASS

The Origins of Stained Glass

For eons glass has been formed naturally when silica—sand, flint, or quartz crystals—and potash or soda become hot enough to fuse into a vitreous form, thus creating natural glass substances like obsidian, which provided early man with his cutting tools and arrowheads. The Roman historian Pliny the Elder credits the Phoenicians with the discovery of glass, and places the site on a beach at the foot of Mount Carmel in present Israel, where all the necessary materials existed.

However, it was the genius of man that somehow, at least four to five millennia ago, accidentally or intentionally, he found a way of producing glass himself. In any event, by 1500 B.C.E., glassmaking was certainly a skill of Egyptian artisans, who made glass perfume bottles and cosmetic jars. Indeed, Egyptians considered glass artifacts so precious that they fashioned beads, amulets, and other jewelry from glass in imitation of precious and semiprecious jewels. The glass was almost opaque; any color came from the accidental presence of impurities—probably metal oxides—in the raw materials. Further evidence of early glassmaking was found on seventh-century tablets found at Nineveh in descriptions that anticipate many of the techniques used in the Middle Ages.

From the Middle East glassmaking spread throughout the Mediterranean world. Traders carried glass, and the methods for producing it, from Alexandria, a glassmaking center, to Greece and to Rome. Alexander the Great's conquest of Egypt brought Greek artisans and craftsmen to Alexandria to work. The Romans refined the art of glassmaking considerably. They were able to make transparent glass, and then to color it intentionally. Sometimes they are credited with inventing glassblowing—although that important technique was probably already known to the Egyptians and Syrians—by which they produced decorative and commercial glass containers with prodigious skill and formed sheets of glass for windows. The latter were commonly small panes set in a wood or bronze lattice, and were popular with Romans who could afford them. Caligula had glass windows in his palace, and archaeologists have uncovered some at Herculaneum and Pompeii, buried under volcanic ash, and in the ruins of the Roman–British town at Silchester, England. Clearly, the Romans dispersed both glass artifacts and the techniques to make them throughout the Roman Empire—to Gaul, Spain, and northern Europe, where windows were a welcome defense against a sometimes hostile climate.

At the eastern end of the Empire, meanwhile, one of the influential antecedents of stained glass—mosaics—was becoming an important decorative form. After the Roman Emperor Constantine moved his capital to Byzantium and built Constantinople as a Christian city, all the building arts glorified the new city, not least among them mosaics. For centuries, mosaics of stone, marble, or ceramic pieces had been used in floors. Now mosaics of colored glass began to cover the vertical surfaces, bringing gloriously colored pictorial scenes to the walls, columns, arches, and domes of basilicas. In the sixth century, during the reign of Justinian and Theodora, the art of mosaics reached its peak with the decoration of the Church of Santa Sophia in Constantinople and the Church of San Vitale in Ravenna.

Just as mosaics suggest one of the techniques of stained glass in its fitting together of small pieces of glass to form a design, so the sister art of enameling, especially cloisonné enameling, suggests another: the metal framework that holds these glass pieces together. In cloisonné enameling, narrow strips of metal, called *cloisons,* are soldered to a metal base and the sections formed by the metal bands are filled with colored powdered enamel, which fuses into areas of color when the piece is fired. The result is remarkably similar to stained glass sections that are held in place by narrow strips of lead. One can reasonably assume that once the technique of casting grooved strips of lead had been perfected, the glaziers borrowed this assembly technique from the enamelers.

The skills of the mosaicist and the enameler, so influential in the development of stained glass, eventually found their way to Western Europe, where the earliest stained glass windows were made. They were first brought by artisans who moved from Constantinople to Rome to avoid religious and political persecution when the break occurred between the Eastern and the Western Church, and later into central France when a group of Venetian artisans settled in Limoges in A.D. 959.

Somehow the art of stained glass church windows evolved, joining methods and ideas borrowed from its sister art forms—mosaics, enameling, even fresco painting and illuminated manuscripts—with the techniques of glazing that had been in limited use in Roman and Byzantine homes, although just when and where the first stained glass window was made is not known. Even before the time of Charlemagne, glazed windows were believed to have been installed in churches. Tantalizing fragments from a German abbey of the ninth or tenth century remain. Yet without evidence of a logical progression in the art of stained glass, we are unprepared for the impact of the earliest extant windows—for the simplicity and strength of the eleventh-century head of Christ from Wissembourg, or the glorious colors and design of the five prophets in the Augsburg Cathedral in Germany, or the twelfth-century "Ascension" window in Le Mans Cathedral in France. By a process we can cheer, if not fully trace, the Venetians must have transmitted the ideas and skills of Byzantine decorative conventions to the West, where a glorious ecclesiastical art form sprang virtually full-blown from what were its ornamental secular roots.

Medieval Techniques

Almost as interesting as the virtually unheralded appearance of extraordinary stained glass church windows in northern Europe was the manner of their making—a technique so successful that it has survived essentially intact. And if our knowledge of the origins of these windows is sketchy, our information about their fabrication is remarkably complete—thanks to the reporting of a German monk who called himself Theophilus. A painter and metal craftsman, Theophilus

Opposite: In Le Mans Cathedral, the twelve apostles and the Virgin look upward to Christ's Ascension. The round Romanesque arch is characteristic of twelfth-century windows.
Photo courtesy Caisse Nationale des Monuments Historiques et des Sites, Archives Photographiques, Paris

lived in northwest Germany during the early part of the twelfth century and wrote a treatise—called "The Various Arts" in translation—that described several medieval crafts, including stained glass. The techniques he recorded in detail for assembling a stained glass window are so similar to present-day methods that the contemporary instructions given in a later chapter, "Working with Lead," could almost describe a medieval workshop—save for the substitution of a modern glass-cutting wheel and an electric soldering iron for the original heated iron rod.

Likewise, the medieval methods for making glass resemble modern techniques for hand-blown glass (but not, of course, for machine-rolled glass). Medieval glass was made in two ways—by the muff and the crown methods. In the muff method, a glassblower gathered a blob of molten glass on the end of his blow pipe, blew it into a ball, then swung and rotated the pipe until the glass sphere formed an elongated cylindrical bubble. After cutting off both ends of the bubble, the glassblower split the resulting tube, or muff, lengthwise with a hot iron, then cooled it slowly in an annealing oven where it flattened into a sheet of glass about 15 by 24 inches, the same general size as sheets of contemporary hand-blown glass. In the crown method, which is not often used today, the molten glass was blown into a bubble and the pipe twirled rather than swung from side to side to spin the glass bubble into a flattened disk about 24 inches in diameter.

Colored glass was made by both methods. Color came from the addition to the molten glass of metallic salts or oxides, with the metal and the temperature of the hot glass varying for different colors. Impurities in the metals and in the silica produced the imperfections of color that make hand-blown glass so dazzling. Glass colored throughout its thickness was called pot metal. Clear glass covered with a thin layer of colored glass during manufacture was called flashed glass. Both terms are still used.

An Architectural Art

Like frescoes and mosaics, stained glass is an architectural art. It depends for its existence on a structure with apertures to fill and on transmitted light. So the story of stained glass is inextricably bound up with the story of architecture and of the kinds of spaces that are hospitable to stained glass. From the first these buildings were ecclesiastical, in part because only the Church could afford the expense of stained glass, and in part because stained glass required the skills of many artisans—glassblowers, glaziers, masons, ironworkers—and only the Church could inspire, or command, this cooperative undertaking.

Early Christian churches were based on the rectangular basilica of the Romans, an easily constructed building that could accommodate the large numbers of new converts. It had a large central space, or nave, that rose taller than the side aisles. It was the basis for most church plans to follow, and was as important for its lavishly decorated walls of marble, mosaics, and frescoes as for its architecture. When Constantine the Great moved the capital of the Roman Empire to Constantinople in A.D. 330, the Roman concept of large space was happily joined with the Byzantine love of ornament. It was an architectural marriage that culminated in the sixth-century Church of Santa Sophia, in which glorious glass mosaics sheathed the upper parts of the walls and the interior of the vaults, and windows were relatively small.

In Europe the style that evolved from the early Christian basilica was the Romanesque, characterized by thick walls and round-headed arches. To accommodate the growing number of congregants and clergy, a cross arm containing north and south transepts was added, which intersected the long arm with nave, chancel, and altar. At the crossing, a central tower called the lantern illuminated the dim intersection. Later a second, shorter transept expanded space still further.

Most churches in Western Europe were built on this cruciform plan, and from about the sixth century the building was placed so its head—the altar end—faced the east and the rising sun. The west end became the entrance, from which the entering worshiper had an exalting prospect of the nave, leading to the chancel and to the intimate recesses of the altar beyond. The placement of the walls, and the stained glass windows they contained, came to have symbolic meaning in the complex ecclesiastical iconography that developed.

In the story of stained glass, however, the most significant feature of the Romanesque church was the stone vaulting that for safety reasons replaced the highly flammable timbered roof of the early basilicas. The thrust of these stone barrel vaults required thick walls for counterbalance, and since any aperture weakened the walls, windows were small. Consequently, Romanesque churches were fairly dark. This led to a constant search—especially in northern Europe, where days were short and often dark—to enlarge window openings, to let in as much light as possible.

As the size of the Romanesque windows gradually increased, they began to accommodate stained glass windows. Now color, always an important decorative element in church design, moved from walls to windows, from mosaics and frescoes lit by reflected light to jewellike colored glass illuminated by transmitted light from the outside, bathing the interior in radiant splendor. The glory of light and color that the newly glazed windows introduced into churches intensified the search to find methods of construction to support still larger windows. This was the problem that architects of Romanesque buildings could not solve satisfactorily, as long as they were wedded to the barrel vault, and the challenge that Gothic architects met so brilliantly that eventually Gothic structures were able to support entire walls of glass.

The genius of Gothic architecture rested on three new structural forms—the pointed arch, which could span larger and higher areas than ever before, the ribbed vault, which was stronger than the barrel vault, and the flying buttress, which could absorb the thrust of the higher vaults and support high clerestory windows as well as large apertures at ground level. These three interlocking structural elements were first used in the Abbey Church of Saint-Denis, outside Paris, a seminal structure rebuilt in 1140 that linked Romanesque and Gothic architecture. As the buttressing structure became more sophisticated, walls became ever narrower and the glass in them covered an increasingly larger area until only thin stone mullions separated the windows. The quintessential example is Sainte-Chapelle in Paris, a tiny crystal palace whose structure seems to exist only to frame and support the walls of glass.

The great Gothic period of church building and decoration that flourished at such a creative level during the Middle Ages was followed by a decline in the art of stained glass that was due in part to architectural forms—Renaissance, Baroque, Rococo—that were less hospitable to glazed windows. In the classical forms of the Renaissance, for example, windows were to illuminate interior decoration and not to transmit their own images. Not until the Gothic Revival of the nineteenth century was there renewed interest in medieval art and in the traditions and techniques of stained glass. And by the twentieth century new methods of construction—particularly steel and reinforced concrete—could again provide whole walls of glass for glazing, an opportunity that has become as challenging to modern architects and glass artists as Gothic windows were to their medieval counterparts, and that may well produce another great era of stained glass art.

A Christian Art

From its early beginnings to the Renaissance, stained glass was a Christian art. In every sense it was a creature of the Church. The Church was its chief patron: it employed the artisans, dictated the subject matter and the forms of expression, and displayed the finished windows. Its principal aim was simple—to educate an illiterate congregation and at the same time inspire a sense of devotion. This would be accomplished by explaining the festivals of the Church, visualizing the life of Christ and the saints, and illuminating the points of the sermons—all through the engagingly simple device of colored glass windows that shone with an apparent light from heaven as the congregation worshiped. As Abbé Suger, the father of stained glass, wrote, "The pictures in the windows are there for the purpose of showing simple people, who cannot read the Holy Scriptures, what they must believe." During each Mass, the message reached thousands at a time—often the entire population of a town.

That these glorious glass texts were beautiful and decorative, a resplendent glory of Gothic art, may be pure serendipity, or it may be due to the fortunate convergence of several strands: the great age of ecclesiastical construction from the middle of the eleventh to the middle of the fourteenth century; the splendid Gothic spaces that could house the monumental windows that exalted God and diminished man; the religious zeal of all people—high- and lowborn—who supported the Church in the hope that their generosity would ease their passage through this life and the next. Perhaps only in an age of faith, when a universal church united noble and serf in obedience to its authority and inspired in them great devotion, could a central institution command the energies and the resources required to produce great ecclesiastical art.

Stained Glass Sources

Because the purpose of church windows was instructive, not surprisingly the texts from which they drew their inspiration were religious. The Vulgate Bible, translated by Saint Jerome and in wide use during the Middle Ages, was the primary but not the only source; the writings of scholars and early Church fathers, apocryphal gospels, and medieval mystics also contributed subjects. The

development of printing with wooden blocks produced devotional books like the *Poor Man's Bible* and *Mirror of Man's Salvation*, which gained wide circulation, and the subsequent development of movable type and the printing press made religious texts even more accessible. These were the sources that supplied the central themes of stained glass art: the Old Testament stories—the Creation, the Flood, Adam and Eve, Abraham and the patriarchs—scenes from the life of Christ and the Virgin, the genealogy of Christ, the lives and miracles of special saints.

The Symbolic Language of Stained Glass

To tell these stories to an illiterate congregation required a precise, instantly recognizable language of symbols that everyone could understand. For this universal iconography the Church borrowed the imagery and rich symbolism of the Bible and other texts to compile a visual language, and with it the Church, through its stained glass artisans, addressed its members. Congregants viewing a stained glass panel immediately understood

Some universal symbols in stained glass. *Top:* A bunch of grapes, signifying the fertility of the Promised Land, is carried back to Moses by the two scouts sent ahead to reconnoiter, in a thirteenth-century medallion, Canterbury Cathedral. Photo courtesy Council for Places of Worship, London. *Center:* A lamb, symbolizing Christ's sacrifice, appears in the thirteenth-century Good Samaritan window in Sens Cathedral. *Bottom:* Wavy lines represent water in a fourteenth-century scene in Bourges Cathedral showing Mary the Egyptian going to Jerusalem.

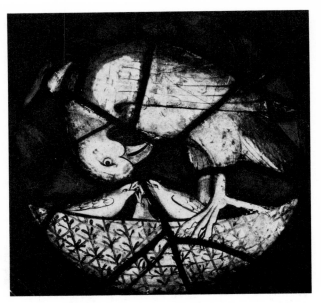

Above: Christ raises two fingers of his right hand in blessing in a fourteenth-century window in All Saints' Church, York; at bottom left is a Roman soldier, traditionally asleep at Christ's tomb. *Above right:* "Pelican in Her Piety," a fifteenth-century English medallion, symbolizes redemption through sacrifice. This common symbol probably comes from the tradition that the pelican feeds her young with the blood from her breast, which in turn derives from the bird's rosy breast feathers and red-tipped beak.
Photo courtesy Victoria and Albert Museum, Crown Copyright, London

that the presence of a fish or lamb represented Christ; the dove stood for the Holy Ghost; and a hand meant the hand of God. When Christ raised the first two fingers of his right hand, he was giving a benediction. Upright or supine, the Magi always wore crowns and the Bishop a mitre. White stood for purity, blue for heaven, and red for the blood of the martyrs. Furthermore, the placement, symmetry, grouping, and number of the symbols all conveyed further meaning in what became a sophisticated iconography.

The placement of windows within the church was also significant. The most important sides of the church were the east—site of the altar—and the west, the ceremonial entrance; their windows were correspondingly important in subject and size. Windows of the Old Testament were usually assigned to the north side (dark and cold) and the New Testament to the south side (light and warm). The west end often related the history of the Church.

Types of Stained Glass Windows

Through most of the Middle Ages, the wealth of subjects sorted themselves out into two general types of windows—figure windows and narrative, or medallion, windows.

Figure windows were filled with a single large figure—a saint, one of the twelve apostles or prophets, a patriarch from the Old Testament, a king. They were placed high in the clerestory windows, as befits a saint, a prophet, or a patriarch, and they were monumental in scale, so they could be seen easily by the worshipers below. In many churches, a popular group were figures from the Old Testament that illustrated the ancestry of Christ, among them Adam, Noah, Moses, Aaron, David, Solomon, Daniel.

Left: Solomon and Aaron are two of the Old Testament figures that stand below the north rose window in Chartres Cathedral. *Above:* The figures of French kings occupy canopied niches in the Basilica of St.-Denis, where French royalty was buried for over 600 years, to the French Revolution.

Medallion, or narrative, windows tell stories. The tall narrow windows were divided into smaller areas—they could be diamonds, circles, quatrefoils, for example—and separate scenes were glazed in each frame or medallion. From the Old Testament came the stories of the Creation and the histories of the patriarchs. From the New Testament were the stories based on the life of Christ and the Virgin. One type of medallion window called "typological," or "type and antitype," contrasted one scene from the Old Testament (type) with one from the New Testament (antitype) to make an instructive point. Narrative windows were set at the lowest level along the aisles of the church so the congregation could "read" them.

The Tree of Jesse, often called a Jesse window, combined features of both figure and picture windows, and was a popular subject for stained glass in every country and period. It pictured Jesse reclining at the bottom of the window, with a tree or vine springing from his body, its branches twining upward around the figures of Jesse's descendents—the kings and the prophets—and culminating at the top in the figure of Mary. Although the tree suggests a tree of life or the tree of knowledge, it is actually a family tree, tracing the genealogy of Christ back to Jesse, the father of David. It took its inspiration from Isaiah's prophecy of the Messiah: ''And there shall come forth a rod out of the stem of Jesse, and a branch shall grow out of his roots.''

Although ecclesiastical subjects inspired virtually all medieval stained glass, there

Medallion windows in a variety of shapes. The four large circles (far left) of one of the Miracle Windows at Canterbury Cathedral are subdivided into individual scenes. See detail (top center) and color insert 3. The thirteenth-century window (left) is in a chapel of Bourges Cathedral; its bottom right section (top right) shows a scene from the life of the apostle James.

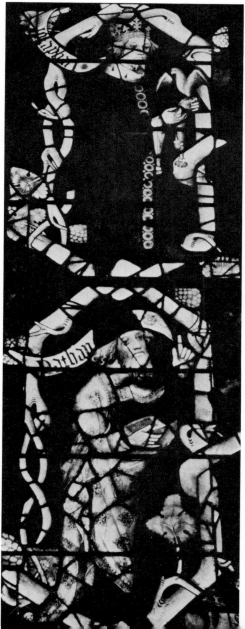

Tree of Jesse windows over the centuries. *Top left:* A detail of a thirteenth-century Jesse window at Canterbury Cathedral; reading from the bottom, Jesse flanked by Jonah and Amos, David flanked by Osiah and Isaiah, Rehoboam. *Bottom left:* A detail of a fourteenth-century Jesse window in Winchester College Chapel. *Top right:* A sixteenth-century Jesse window in Sens Cathedral includes a donkey sitting on a tree, a reference to a satiric festival ridiculing religious ceremonies that took place annually in the town. *Above:* A detail of a twentieth-century Jesse window by Marc Chagall in Reims Cathedral that shows the Virgin holding the Child.

were two interesting nonreligious ones—donor figures and heraldry. The first presented a portrait of the benefactor, the second identified him by his coat of arms, in addition to or instead of the figure. Although the cost of stained glass was high, and only the Church could be relied on to pay for it, occasionally a noble or rich merchant would try to ensure his immortality by giving funds for

Below: The figure of the donor holds a replica of the window he is giving to Evreux Cathedral.
Right: A heraldic window in Ste.-Chapelle, Paris, prominently displays the castles of Blanche of Castile and, in the border, the fleur-de-lis of France and her son, King Louis IX.

a window. For his generosity, the portrait of the benefactor would be included in the window, usually in an attitude of piety and sometimes attended by his family.

Rose windows often represented Christ and the Virgin, or Christ as the Apocalyptic Judge. They were also the place for secular designs like the signs of the zodiac or the twelve labors of the months. The tracery lights—those odd-shaped sections that fill the wall space above the main windows—often displayed the nine orders of angels and occasionally even the heads of donors, probably because only small figures would fit into the irregular spaces.

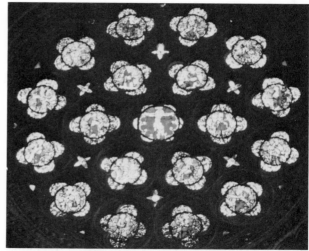

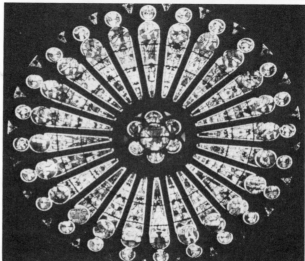

Rose windows take many forms. *Top left:* A ring of figures revolves around a seated Christ in the thirteenth-century south rose in Troyes Cathedral; geometric patterns fill the graceful tracery. *Top right:* In the fourteenth-century north rose in Toledo Cathedral prophets and angels in quatrefoil circles surround the central crucifixion, which is distinguished by its brilliant red background. *Bottom left:* Unlike the central focus of most rose windows, curvilinear tracery forms a vertical double leaf in the fourteenth-century south rose at Lincoln Cathedral, called the "Bishop's Eye" because it looks out on the bishop's garden. *Center right:* In the fifteenth-century south rose at Angers Cathedral, twenty-four scenes radiate like the petals of a daisy from the central figure of Christ; the upper twelve contain the signs of the zodiac, the lower twelve seated figures. See color insert 9. *Bottom right:* In the Flamboyant tracery of "Paradise," the sixteenth-century north rose in Sens Cathedral, angels play musical instruments around the central figure of Christ.

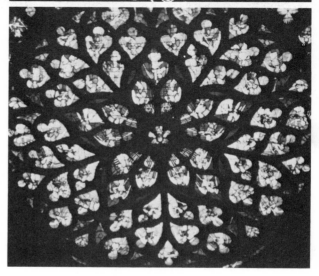

English medieval dress and artifacts are depicted in a thirteenth-century medallion (top right); French architecture in a thirteenth-century panel from Troyes (bottom right) in which a wing-footed, beak-nosed, hairy, viper-horned devil carries Christ to the Pinnacle of the Temple. *Above:* A sixteenth-century Flemish scene in which Abraham, Hagar, and Ismael, at front, and Sarah and Abraham, at rear, by a Flemish manor house, all wear period dress.

Photos top and bottom right courtesy Victoria and Albert Museum, Crown Copyright, London; photo above courtesy Sotheby & Co., London

Because the Church was so closely connected with the forms and conventions of stained glass, there was a certain universality in the art of different countries during the same periods. The same subjects were represented in the same symbolic language. Particularly in northern Europe the differences among countries were small, reflected mainly in the distinguishing dress or architectural details depicted in the glass, or in the representation of daily tasks that might differ from country to country and from one century to the next.

Of the European countries, only Italy and Spain had an independent air, born no doubt of the Mediterranean climate and its bright hot sun. Their rose windows—aptly called *occhio* or "eye" in Italy and *ojo de buey* or "bull's-eye" in Spain—were devoid of the stone spokes or webbing that create the wheel or flower effect in northern windows. And their glass was richly colored against the bright hot Mediterranean sun. Yet for all their superficial differences, Italian and Spanish windows shared essential characteristics with all stained glass art.

As an art form stained glass advanced at a slightly different pace in different countries. In Italy, it started late and ended early, and practically skipped the Gothic style altogether. Germany held on to its Romanesque forms until the fourteenth century, long after France and England were working in Gothic. Nevertheless, new advances in glassmaking and improved techniques and materials eventually spread to all glassmaking centers. And certainly, fundamental stylistic perceptions and changes were felt everywhere. So, despite imprecise definitions of styles and periods, medieval glass is distinguished more by its universality than by its national patterns.

The Twelfth and Thirteenth Centuries

The history of stained glass, at least as we know it, begins with the Abbey Church of Saint-Denis, at the edge of Paris, and its abbot, Suger. Because it was the royal abbey of France, Suger wanted to enlarge it in a grand manner. At his direction, the newly developed architectural innovations of the pointed arch, the ribbed vault, and the flying buttress were incorporated into the renovations, making possible the high clerestories and large windows of the Gothic style and, in the process, marking the royal abbey as the first essentially Gothic church.

Abbé Suger was as interested in stained glass as he was in architecture, and glazed windows were an integral part of his plans for the abbey. He is credited with developing the subjects for many of the windows, including the idea of a Tree of Jesse. In the abbey's Jesse window is a panel depicting Suger making a presentation of that same Jesse window, which makes Suger an early subject of a donor window as well. Most of Suger's twelfth-century windows were destroyed during the French Revolution, but many were restored in the middle of the nineteenth century by Viollet-le-Duc, the French architect and leader of the Gothic Revival. Suger also

Above: The two topmost panels in the twelfth-century Tree of Jesse show Christ surrounded by seven doves, symbolizing the gifts of the Holy Spirit, and the Virgin just below. This window in the Basilica of St.-Denis was the model for the Chartres Cathedral Jesse window. See color insert 1.

participated in the rebuilding of Chartres Cathedral after a disastrous fire in 1194. Of the four remaining twelfth-century windows there, three of them, including a Jesse window, were built with his advice and encouragement.

Fire was a serious hazard to all medieval buildings, and not least at Chartres, where five fires ravaged the churches that for centuries stood successively on the site of the present cathedral. Chartres was a center of learning and trade, a prosperous town, and a place of pilgrimage because of the sacred relic—the tunic of the Virgin, patroness of Chartres—enshrined in the church. When the tunic survived the last fire of 1194, the church was inundated with contributions from grateful donors in France and elsewhere, from kings and merchants to artisans and peasants. Reconstruction began almost immediately. In thirty years the main part of the church was ready, and the 176 superb windows were glazed in the twenty-five years between 1215 and 1240, a remarkable achievement of skill and craftsmanship.

Practically all of the 4,000 donors are honored as benefactors in the windows. Royal donors kneel at the bottom of panels, heraldic shields and banners decorate tracery lights, the gold fleurs-de-lis of Saint Louis dot the great north rose, known as the Rose of France, which was the gift of his mother, Blanche of Castile. But surely among the most interesting are the windows donated by the dozens of guilds of Chartres. At the bottom of each window in a small medallion is a scene of the donor guild at work—wonderful vignettes of winegrowers, goldsmiths, cobblers, tanners, money changers, shoemakers, bakers, butchers, furriers, masons, carpenters—all conducting their trades. If Reims Cathedral is

Above: Beneath scenes from the life of St. James the Greater in Chartres Cathedral, the two donor guilds show off their wares in their workrooms — the furriers, at the bottom left, and the drapers, at the bottom right.

Photo courtesy Caisse Nationale des Monuments Historiques et des Sites, Archives Photographiques, Paris

where kings were crowned and Saint-Denis where they were buried, surely the cathedral at Chartres is where the middle class worked.

Such scenes of medieval life, tucked away among the great religious scenes and figures, bring extraordinary richness to a cathedral which also has three great rose windows, monumental figures of Old Testament patriarchs and prophets high in the clerestories, and the beautiful "Notre Dame de la Belle Verrière," of all the many windows to the Virgin the only one before which adoring worshipers kneel and light candles.

Because its windows are still fully glazed, either original or restored, Chartres is one of the few places where a contemporary visitor can approach the transcendent experience of a medieval congregant. The almost mystical dimness of the vaulted interior, the ruby and blue glass mosaics that cast a blue-purple hush in the ambulatory, the strength of form and color of the Old Testament figures that dominate the transept, the flashing brilliance of the kaleidoscopic roses above them all evoke the spirituality and symbolism that Abbé Suger sensed in the illuminating quality of light as it passes through stained glass.

The stained glass at Chartres was the glory of the first half of the thirteenth century; the second half was illuminated by the incandescent windows of Sainte-Chapelle, an equally glorious but quite different achievement. The two churches are linked by Saint Louis (Louis

Above: Walls of glass surround three sides of Ste.-Chapelle, Paris.
Photo courtesy Gerald M. Philips

IX), who is often called the patron of stained glass.

The little Paris chapel, a Gothic wonder that seems constructed entirely of glass, was built by Louis to enshrine the Crown of Thorns he had bought on crusade from the Emperor of Constantinople. Impressed with the glass he knew in Chartres, Saint Louis had the walls of his royal chapel entirely filled with stained glass. There are fifteen lancets in the chapel, most of them glazed between 1243 and 1248, and they reach almost from the floor to the ceiling, separated only by thin mullions of stone. In 120 panels they illustrate 1,134 scenes from the Bible.

The windows display certain stylistic differences from earlier thirteenth-century glass. Plain glass mosaics replaced painted backgrounds in the individual scenes, simple red and white edging became borders; yellow, green, and violet were added to the primarily blue and red palette. Figures became much smaller to accommodate the smaller size of the medallion sections and the larger number of subjects illustrated. This miniaturization

Opposite: The central panels from "Notre Dame de la Belle Verrière," which show the wonderful faces of the Virgin and Child, survived the disastrous twelfth-century fire at Chartres. They are surrounded by thirteenth-century angels lighting candles and making offerings.
Photo courtesy Caisse Nationale des Monuments Historiques et des Sites, Archives Photographiques, Paris

sometimes makes it hard to identify subjects precisely, but the effect of the color and light produced by this jewellike style, called "Saint Louis" after its benefactor, is dazzling.

Paradoxically, at the same time that brilliant medallion and figure windows were being made with consummate skill and beauty, there was a growing trend toward fairly plain grisaille windows. Grisaille, from the French "to paint gray," describes glass that is lightly tinted and painted with foliage patterns or geometrics, then leaded into interesting patterns. It was often the only kind of window in country churches.

The origins of grisaille windows are often traced to the ascetic monk Bernard of Clairvaux, a founder of the Cistercian Order which in 1134 forbade narrative and colorful windows, permitting in its abbeys only white glass without figures or crosses. For the monks, grisaille that was leaded in interesting patterns provided decoration within the limits of the Cistercian ordinance, and the beautiful designs of Cistercian glaziers surely helped advance the popularity of grisaille. However, its widespread appearance suggests additional reasons for its continuing use: it was much cheaper than stained glass, and could be installed in a window with the hope of substituting a more elaborate stained glass panel when a donor materialized; it let much needed light into church interiors; and at different times and different places there may have been a shortage of stained glass artists to make the more demanding medallion and figure windows.

Opposite: Grisaille window painted with foliate patterns in Stodmarsh Church, Kent, England. Watercolor by Archibald Ward.
Photo courtesy Victoria and Albert Museum, Crown Copyright, London

Above: In Ste.-Chapelle, of the forty round medallions that tell the story of Judith, these three show the invasion by the army of Holofernes. See color insert 4.

The most spectacular grisaille windows are not in France at all, but in England, which made more use of the style. Five huge windows—each about 5 feet wide and over 50 feet tall—stand side by side in the York Minster, bathing the north transept in gray-green light. Known as the "Five Sisters," they form the largest expanse of grisaille glass in the world and are said to contain over 100,000 pieces of glass. Each of the windows, made around 1260, displays a different leaded medallion shape.

The great Gothic glass traditions flowered in France, but they crossed the English Channel and rooted easily in English soil. In both countries, the common arrangement was to place large figures in the high clerestory windows and small-section medallions in the lower windows, where the congregation could follow each scene closely.

Nor are there stylistic differences between Canterbury stained glass, for example, and the glass at Saint-Denis, Chartres, or Sens. Canterbury's similarity with Sens is no accident. After Archbishop Thomas à Becket was murdered in the cathedral, Canterbury became an important Christian shrine. When the choir was destroyed by fire a few years later, in 1174, the great French architect William of Sens was called to rebuild it. In honor of Becket, the Trinity Chapel was added to the choir, and there the body of the martyr lay enshrined until Henry VIII removed it in 1538. The chapel contains twelve windows—six on each side—called the "Miracle Windows" because they illustrate scenes and miracles from Becket's life. Part of the original glass was destroyed during the Reformation, but some thirteenth-century glass still remains, and is rich in details of daily life of the time.

French Gothic influence spread eastward to Germany as well as to England, and the

Above: The largest and earliest grisaille windows are the famous "Five Sisters" in York Minster, England.

The Trinity Chapel in Canterbury Cathedral contains a portrait of Thomas à Becket (top right) and scenes and miracles from his life. The scenes, bottom right and left, take place at Becket's tomb in the crypt.

first German cathedral to be built in a Gothic style was at Cologne in the mid-thirteenth century. It was a reconstruction, again following fire, that was intended to house in grand manner the church's relics, said to be the bones of the Magi. Not surprisingly, there are stained glass windows representing the Adoration of the Magi, as well as grisaille windows, brought to Germany by Cistercian monks.

General Characteristics of Twelfth- and Thirteenth- Century Glass

Medallion windows. Within each lancet a series of medallions—circles, diamonds, quatrefoils, or other regular shapes—were set vertically; each medallion was usually divided into four or five sections, with each small unit illustrating a scene from the subject of the entire window or the donor.

Some interesting examples:

AUSTRIA:
Graz. Joanneum Landesmuseum—a collection
Stifts Ardagger

ENGLAND:
Canterbury Cathedral—"Miracle Windows," "Theological Windows," also called the "Poor Man's Bible"
London. Victoria and Albert Museum—collection

FRANCE:
Angers Cathedral

Bourges Cathedral
Chartres Cathedral
Clermont-Ferrand Cathedral
Paris. Ste.-Chapelle
Paris. Cluny Museum
Rouen Cathedral
Sens Cathedral
Strasbourg Cathedral

GERMANY:
Cologne Cathedral—"Adoration of the Magi"
Cologne. Church of St. Kunibert—"Life of Saint Kunibert"
Freiburg Cathedral
Marburg. Church of St. Elisabeth
Soest. Church of St. Patroclus

SPAIN:
Leon Cathedral

UNITED STATES:
New York, N.Y. Metropolitan Museum of Art, The Cloisters—collection

Figure windows. Larger-than-life figures of saints, prophets, apostles, bishops, kings, patriarchs, and the like were set in single or double rows, high in the clerestory windows. Figures usually face front on a green mound to represent earth, or on labels inscribed with their names, and are framed in niches of architectural design.

Some interesting examples:

ENGLAND:
Canterbury Cathedral—"Ancestry of Christ," 38 of the original 84 figures remain.

FRANCE:
Bourges Cathedral—prophets, apostles, bishops

Chartres Cathedral—saints, Old Testament figures

Le Mans Cathedral—12th-century "Ascension" window

Poitiers Cathedral—12th-century "Crucifixion" window

Reims Cathedral—36 kings of France, each surmounting the archbishop who consecrated him

Sens Cathedral

Strasbourg Cathedral

GERMANY:

Cologne Cathedral

Cologne. Church of St. Kunibert

Marburg. Church of St. Elisabeth

UNITED STATES:

New York, N.Y. Metropolitan Museum of Art, The Cloisters—collection

Rose windows. Twelfth-century rose windows were like wheels, divided by thick spokes radiating from a central circle. Thirteenth-century roses had plate tracery—rosettes grouped around a central rosette, like a circle of petals—and later bar tracery—a network of thin tracery bars that integrate flower forms with wheel spokes. Rose windows were rare in England.

ENGLAND:

Lincoln Cathedral—north rose, called the "Dean's Eye," with plate tracery

FRANCE:

Chartres Cathedral—north and west roses, with plate tracery

Paris. Notre Dame de Paris—north rose with bar tracery

Reims Cathedral—west rose with bar tracery

Jesse windows. The family tree of Christ, from Jesse, father of David, to the Virgin.

Some interesting examples:

ENGLAND:

Canterbury Cathedral

FRANCE:

Chartres Cathedral—12th-century window

Paris. Abbey Church of St.-Denis

GERMANY:

Cologne Cathedral

Cologne. Church of St. Kunibert

Opposite: Two of the great "Ancestry of Christ" figures in Canterbury Cathedral: Methuselah (left) and Lamech (right).
Photos courtesy Victoria and Albert Museum, Crown Copyright, London

Right: The west rose window at Chartres Cathedral has plate tracery in which twelve minor prophets encircle a Last Judgment scene.

Above: In the great north rose of Notre Dame Cathedral, Paris, bar tracery radiates from the central figures of the Virgin and Child. See color insert 7. Photo courtesy Caisse Nationale des Monuments Historiques et des Sites, Archives Photographiques, Paris

Grisaille windows. Pearly, silvery tinted glass painted with leafy forms, thin stems with rosettes, or geometric forms like interlacing strapwork on a finely crosshatched background, occasionally interrupted with small motifs in bright colors for accents. Grisaille windows often included large areas of "quarries," diamond- or lozenge-shaped glass panes painted with a floral design. When quarries were leaded together, they formed a trellis pattern.

Some interesting examples:

ENGLAND:.
Lincoln Cathedral

Salisbury Cathedral
York Minster—"Five Sisters" windows

FRANCE:
Reims. Basilica of St.-Remi
Sens Cathedral

GERMANY:
Altenburg Abbey
Cologne Cathedral

Donors and heraldic devices. In the last half of the thirteenth century, the figure of the donor and/or his heraldic shield or symbol first appeared in stained glass. The figure was small, usually at the base of the window, so that the donor, with appropriate deference, was literally under the ecclesiastical message.

Above: Three golden leopards of England decorate the royal arms in a heraldic window in York Minster.

Above: Pictorial features were painted in, then details scratched out, as in the head of Resa in Canterbury Cathedral. See color insert 2 for full figure.

Some interesting examples:

ENGLAND:
> London. Westminster Abbey—apse
>> shields
> Salisbury Cathedral

FRANCE:
> Chartres Cathedral—guild windows;
>> north rose with the arms of Saint
>> Louis and his mother, Blanche of Cas-
>> tile

Paris. Ste.-Chapelle—fleur-de-lis of
France and the king, Saint Louis, and
the castles of Castile of his mother,
Blanche

Glazing style. Small simple shapes of glass joined together with thin leads in a mosaic jigsaw that sometimes used more than fifty pieces of glass in a square foot. Imperfections in the glass, and the multiplicity of pieces, created a flashing brilliance when light passed through.

Borders were very wide in early glass—often one-sixth of the total width of the window—and incorporated foliate and geometric forms like the circle and semicircle.

Later borders were narrower and simpler in form, often repeating a single leaf or alternating symbols like the fleur-de-lis and the castle of Castile.

Color. Early glass had rich, beautiful color—deep blue and ruby red that was left unpainted for background, and green, yellow, purple-pink, white.

Painting style. Opaque brown pigment was painted on the glass, then shading, background patterns, or pictorial details like facial features and drapery folds were scratched out with a pointed tool. A dense application of paint would completely block the light; a diluted application would diminish the amount of light passing through and reduce the strength of the color. Figures were stiffly posed.

The Fourteenth Century

In stained glass, the fourteenth century was characterized by diversity of style from country to country, often shaped by events and circumstances beyond the artistic experience. France, seat of the most extraordinary glass of the twelfth and thirteenth centuries, produced relatively little stained glass, her creative energies and funds sapped by the Hundred Years War with England and by the devastation of the Black Death, which killed one-third of the population of Europe. Al-

though the plague claimed almost half the British people, and a war—albeit fought on French soil—required funding, England was not as disrupted as France by these cataclysmic events. In fact, English stained glass flourished, animated by the changing forms of fourteenth-century English architecture that required artistic innovations and challenged glaziers to find new styles. In Germany, the late arrival of the Gothic style and the large number of new and splendid churches and cathedrals was an artistic invitation to German glaziers. In Italy, an altogether independent style of stained glass developed that reflected both the Italian climate and a unique aesthetic perspective.

Despite national differences, all stained glass work was influenced profoundly by the growing technology of glazing, and by two innovations in particular. The first was the accidental discovery that silver chloride or silver oxide, when floated on glass and fired, would penetrate the glass and stain it yellow. Depending on the strength of the silver solution, the composition of the glass, and the heat of the kiln, a range of tints from pale lemon to deep orange could be created on the glass.

The significance of this discovery was that for the first time two colors could appear within the same piece of glass. Yellow hair or a gold crown could be added to a face of white glass, for example, without the need for leading in a separate piece of yellow glass. In fact, the technique of staining was soon perfected so that more than one shade of yellow could be added to the same piece of glass, allowing the figure to have both blond hair and a gold crown. Yellow pot metal glass was still leaded in for large areas, but the use of silver stain was widespread for defining certain features,

Above: A trumpeting angel from Wells Cathedral Lady Chapel.
Photo courtesy Victoria and Albert Museum, Crown Copyright, London

for adding color around the face and to the folds of drapery, and for delineating architectural details in the often elaborate canopies under which so many fourteenth-century figures sat. Because staining appreciably reduced the amount of lead in a window, it had the serendipitous result of letting more light into the dark interiors of northern churches.

The second important technical discovery was that glass in a wide range of new colors could be made during the blowing process by dipping molten glass of one color into another

Above: The stonework in the tracery of the great west window in York Minster suggests a heart. The canopied figures below are apostles and archbishops.

to produce a layered, or flashed, glass. In this way, blue glass superimposed on red created purple glass, yellow on red produced orange, blue on yellow made green, and any color laid on clear glass gained in clarity and translucence.

In England, these glassmaking advances, as well as developments in domestic architecture, made fourteenth-century glass com-

pletely different in character from the glass that preceded it. The success with which glaziers met the challenge of changing architectural forms animated a great era of English glass, transcendent in its color, design, and luminosity, and best seen in the York Minster and Wells Cathedral.

As always, architectural forms shaped the glass, and in England the forms changed in the last quarter of the fourteenth century from the flowing graceful lines of what is called the Decorated Style to the austere linearity of Perpendicular Gothic.

In the wide windows of the Decorated Style, thin stone mullions divide the aperture into slender lights, then flow into graceful tracery forms above. At first, the tracery encompassed geometric forms like circles, or trefoiled, quatrefoiled, or cinquefoiled circles; later the tracery was more ornate and elaborate. At York Minster, for example, the graceful curvilinear tracery of the famous "West Window" forms what is affectionately called the "Heart of Yorkshire."

The tracery lights, with their variety of shapes and sizes formed by the curving stonework, often posed difficult design problems. Sometimes these small areas held grisaille in foliate patterns, and often heraldic devices; sometimes they held heads of saints, or animals, or diminutive angels, often playing musical instruments, contorted to fit an odd-shaped aperture. Perhaps in reaction to such exuberances, the rather austere lines of Perpendicular Gothic emerged in the last quarter of the century, and dominated English architecture for the next 150 years.

In Germany, as in England, the prevailing architectural forms shaped the stained glass, although here it took a somewhat different direction. The Gothic style came to Germany late, probably because the splendid German

Romanesque building had served so well. And when it did come, from neighboring France and distinctly French in character, the arrival was so sudden that buildings begun in the Romanesque style were abruptly finished in the Gothic. This is the case with the splendid Strasbourg Cathedral, a union of French and German styles in both its architecture and its glass.

As German Gothic moved east across the country, it developed a distinctive personality. Indulging a preference for interior height, the Germans evolved an architectural style in which the side aisles of a church were almost as tall as the nave, permitting windows of exceptional height. This available expanse of glass encouraged a revival of narrative windows, and in Erfurt Cathedral, for example, in what is now East Germany, there are 640 narrative panels. The glass also has a distinguishing warmth and radiance, derived from the generous use of greens, yellows, and reds. Regensburg Cathedral is a treasure of medieval German glass with superb examples from the fourteenth century. Grisaille, lacking the essential color that German glaziers loved, was used sparingly, and then usually in the upper half of a richly glazed lower window. This not only let light into the interior of the church, but had the added virtue of thrift, since so much glass was needed to fill the tall lights.

In Italy, the art of stained glass began later and ended earlier than in northern Europe,

The irregularly shaped tracery lights at Wells Cathedral contain the head of St. Leo in the trefoil (top) and the Crucifixion with a small figure of the donor (bottom). The narrow borders and heraldic devices—fleur-de-lis and heraldic lion—are typical. Both photos © Rev. C. Woodforde and courtesy Royal Commission on Historical Monuments, England

and while it flourished it had an altogether individual style. Grisaille was extremely rare, as were white or pale yellow canopies, both common ways in northern Europe for letting more light through glazed windows. In the brilliant Italian sun, the aim was not, in fact, to admit more light but to temper the blazing sun—and this was done with bright, rich pot

Above: A relatively simple canopy resting on side columns shelters St. Catherine in the Priory Church at Deerhurst, England. Her graceful S-shaped stance is characteristic of the early fourteenth century. See color insert 10.
Photo courtesy Royal Commission on Historical Monuments, England

metal colors. This is one reason why the Italians had at least as much interest in wall surfaces as in windows, and why mural and fresco painting flourished.

Moreover, unlike northern Europe, where windows were the joint efforts of the glazier and the glass artist, in Italy the art of stained glass was intimately associated with fine artists from the beginning. The upper and lower basilicas of St. Francis at Assisi, for example, contain frescoes by several early masters, among them Cimabue and Giotto, which greatly influenced the style of glass painting. The Giotto-like glass in the basilicas shows the beginnings of perspective, a hallmark of the coming Renaissance.

The glass at Assisi is early by Italian standards, although it was done—by German glaziers—almost two centuries after the same type of narrative, or medallion, windows were made in France and England. In these fourteenth-century Italian windows, the medallions which divide the lights and contain the separate scenes are more varied in form and more fanciful in shape than the geometric circles, squares, ovals, and diamonds of French and English mosaic glass. Italian medallion windows were made for about seventy-five years, until around 1370.

General Characteristics of Fourteenth-Century Glass

Canopy windows. A figure or group of figures surmounted by a peaked roof, called a canopy, was the most typical window of the fourteenth century. At first the canopies were simple arches standing on side shafts or columns. Then they grew taller, eventually dwarfing the figure beneath it and filling most of the upper part of the window. They also became more elaborate and richly decorated, with birds on peaks, tiny figures standing like statuary in the niches, angels peeking out of tiny windows. Sometimes rows of canopied figures in vertical tiers occupied an entire window. Occasionally a canopy surmounted a scene as well as a figure.

In northern Europe canopies were glazed in yellow or white glass, often stained with silver oxide, with architectural details scratched out of dark paint. These large areas of pale colored glass were an effective means of admitting light. In Italy, the canopies were made of richly colored glass.

Some interesting examples:

AUSTRIA:
    Strassengel

ENGLAND:
    Deerhurst Priory
    Gloucester Cathedral—"Battle of
        Crécy" in the east window
    Oxford. New College Chapel
    Tewkesbury Abbey
    Wells Cathedral

FRANCE:
    Evreux Cathedral
    Rouen. Church of St.-Ouen
    Strasbourg Cathedral

GERMANY:
    Cologne Cathedral—"All Saints'"
        Window
    Esslingen. Church of St. Dionysius
    Freiburg Cathedral
    Regensburg Cathedral
    Regensburg. Church of St. Thomas

Above: Elaborately decorated canopies with a forest of tiny gables, figures, even a crucifixion, tower over the pictorial scenes in this detail from the story of St.-Étienne in the Church of St.-Ouen, Rouen.
Photo courtesy Caisse Nationale des Monuments Historiques et des Sites, Archives Photographiques, Paris

Above: In Merton College Chapel, Oxford, a strip of canopied figures provides a band of color in the grisaille windows, which are set with decorative or heraldic medallions. The donor, Henry de Mamesfield, appears at least once in each of the windows he gave and is usually shown flanking a prophet, as in this detail.
Photo courtesy Royal Commission on Historical Monuments, England

SPAIN:
    Barcelona Cathedral

Figure windows in grisaille. In a variation of the canopied figure that filled the entire window, sometimes a band of canopied figures was set across a group of windows between two wide strips of grisaille, creating a sharp contrast in light and color. This was prevalent in England and France, and does not appear at all in southern Europe.

Some interesting examples:

ENGLAND:
    Oxford. Merton College Chapel

FRANCE:
    Evreux Cathedral
    Rouen. Church of St.-Ouen

Grisaille. The crosshatched background of thirteenth-century grisaille gave way to naturalistic foliate designs of recognizable leafs. These intertwined with other shapes and were often decorated in yellow stain. Sometimes the glass was divided into diamond-shaped quarries that formed a regular trellislike pattern, with each quarry repeating the same design. Sometimes decorative or heraldic medallions punctuated the grisaille with color.

Some interesting examples:

AUSTRIA:
    Heiligenkreuz Abbey Church

FRANCE:
    Evreux Cathedral
    Rouen. Church of St.-Ouen

GERMANY:
    Altenburg Abbey

Narrative windows. Mainly in the countries where the Gothic style arrived late, narrative windows were still popular.

Some interesting examples:

AUSTRIA:
St. Leonhard im Lavantal
Strassengel

ENGLAND:
Tewkesbury Abbey
York Minster, Chapter House

FRANCE:
Strasbourg Cathedral

GERMANY:
Erfurt Cathedral (East Germany)
Esslingen. Church of St. Dionysius
Esslingen. Church of St. Mary
Freiburg Cathedral
Regensburg Cathedral

ITALY:
Assisi. Church of St. Francis,
Lower Basilica

Donor windows. Except in Italy, where they are rare, donor windows were in great favor. The figures of donors may carry a model of the church or the window to signify their contribution, or they may be represented by their coats of arms.

Top: An Annunciation, believed to be from the Italian island of Torcello near Venice, displays multiple borders and the beginnings of architectural perspective in what is still a two-dimensional scene.
Photo courtesy Victoria and Albert Museum, Crown Copyright, London

Bottom: A German narrative panel with a saint preaching. The shape of the medallion is typically German.
Photo courtesy Victoria and Albert Museum, Crown Copyright, London

Above: Eleanor de Clare gave several windows in Tewkesbury Abbey and members of her family appear here in fourteenth-century armor.
Photo courtesy Council for Places of Worship, London

Some interesting examples:

ENGLAND:
Gloucester Cathedral—heraldic devices
Oxford. Merton College Chapel—the figure of Henry de Mamesfeld appears at least once in every window
Tewkesbury Abbey—the armored figures of the donor family
York Minster—"Heraldic Window"; "Bellfounder's Window"

Jesse windows. The tree of Jesse spread over all the lights in the window, ignoring the intervening mullions; the vine and its branches were more naturalistic.

Some interesting examples:

ENGLAND:
Bristol Cathedral
Ludlow. Church of St. Lawrence
Wells Cathedral—the "Golden Window"

Borders. An important element in the design, borders were narrower than in the thirteenth century. Blocks of alternating colors were common, as were floral designs and heraldic devices, among them the fleur-de-lis of France, the triple turrets of the castle of Castile, the heraldic lion of England.

Some interesting examples:

ENGLAND:
York Minster—monkey's funeral in "Pilgrimage Window"; monkeys playing musical instruments in "Bellfounder's Window"; workers at their trades in "Penitentiary Window"

Color. All shades of yellow—popularized by the new technique of staining—and green were used in backgrounds, replacing blue and red, which lost their richness and depth. A warm palette of greens, reds, and yellows distinguished German glass. White glass replaced pink for face areas, with silver stain applied for hair and crown.

Painting style. All forms were more naturalistic. Plants became identifiable, figures more graceful, loose clothing fell in easy folds. Perspective in canopies and modeling of figures began, with roundness and shading defined by a new technique called stippling, which laid a field of tiny dots on the glass by dabbing wet paint with a brush.

Above: In the fourteenth century, plants were drawn more realistically and became more identifiable; fleur-de-lis borders were common. Detail from Bristol Cathedral.
Photo © V. Turl, courtesy Royal Commission on Historical Monuments, England

The Fifteenth Century

In the story of stained glass, only in the most general way can the fifteenth century be called a transition between the Middle Ages and the Renaissance. Europe did not move in lockstep toward the Renaissance. The evolution and transformation from one style to another proceeded at different paces in different countries and, indeed, even in different areas of the same country. For example, French-style Gothic came to southern Netherlands sooner than it arrived in northern Netherlands and neighboring Germany. Then, when Gothic still flourished in Germany, the Renaissance was already under way in Italy. And while multiple-light pictorial Bible scenes were being glazed in Germany and England, and tall canopies still surmounted saints in France, master painters of the Italian Renaissance had furnished the Duomo in Florence with eleven extraordinary paintings on glass that gave an entirely new look to the art and had a great deal to do with its future course.

But despite the diversity of styles and the agreeable appearance of national and regional forms, the stained glass-producing countries of fifteenth-century Europe shared certain characteristics, and they were more important than their differences. First, there was an extraordinary vitality in the arts despite the turmoil, fighting, or factional disputes that disrupted the life of virtually every European country. Italy was plagued with internal rivalry among its cities. Not until the end of the century was Spain completely unified under a Catholic monarchy and finally able to expel the Moors. England prospered, despite the Hundred Years War and the Wars of the Roses. Even France, devastated by the war with England that ravaged so much of its countryside, managed to produce superb glass at Bourges and Angers.

This vitality was reflected in the inventiveness of various late Gothic styles. In England, the elongated lines of Perpendicular Gothic stretched right up into the tracery, dividing the window into a great expanse of tall, thin lights, then continued to the ceiling, where they spread into the delicate ribs of fan vaulting. In France, Gothic forms grew more

Above: The upper part of the great East Window in York Cathedral with perpendicular Gothic tracery.

elaborate and flowing, and the stone network in the tracery often took flamelike shapes that gave the style its descriptive name, Flamboyant. German Gothic took a different form—wide and high—and developed its own complex geometric style of vaulting.

General prosperity was another characteristic of the fifteenth century. After a century of war, famine, peasant revolts, and the Black Death, farmers as well as merchants were finding a measure of affluence. Trade among countries flourished. The wool trade in particular made merchants wealthy in many countries, from the wool producers in England to the manufacturers of cloth in Bruges, France, and Florence, Italy. Even the Medicis grew rich on wool.

Whenever people prospered, cities and towns got their churches—and their stained glass. In Germany, the great cathedrals of Nuremberg and Ulm particularly benefited from the prosperity of its citizens. In England, a wealthy middle class supported the construction of many new abbeys, priories, and parish churches. Many were truly built with wool money, and some, in such wool centers as the Cotswolds and Yorkshire, are even known as "wool churches." The new churches, and many of the existing ecclesiastical buildings, utilized the new Perpendicular style. At the very least windows were enlarged in order to accommodate as much colored glass as possible in a frenzy of glazing that reached a peak around 1485 and resulted in the most productive period of stained glass in English history.

The newly prosperous middle class was not often content to remain anonymous benefactors, and the most successful of them quickly joined that special class, heretofore restricted to the nobility and the Church, whose visible generosity signified wealth and power. Merchants, burghers, bankers, even guilds became patrons of the arts, commissioning writers, musicians, sculptors, artists, and stained glass artisans to create the artifacts of culture that would bear their names, their insignias, and, most desirable of all, their likenesses. The great French cathedral at Bourges, which, in addition to its superb thirteenth-century windows, has some of the best fifteenth-century glass, owes some of its fifteenth-century treasures to two wealthy and powerful benefactors—the Duc de Berry, who gave five windows representing figures of the apostles and prophets, and Jacques Coeur, merchant, banker, shipowner, and financier to King Charles VII of France.

Above: The famous "Pricke of Conscience" window in All Saints' Church, York, represents the last fifteen days of the world. Each daily catastrophe is depicted in a panel, and in this detail the donor family prays beneath the first six of the fifteen narrative panels. On the third day (middle row, right), the waters flood the land; on the fourth day (top row, left), sea monsters rise from the waters, and on the fifth day (top row, center), the trees and water are on fire. See color insert 11 (top).

Guilds were frequent donors of stained glass windows. In Flanders, where guilds were powerful, stained glass artisans were donors of windows. Even in Italy, where donors of any kind were unusual, guilds donated windows in the Milan Cathedral and dedicated them to the patron saints of the trade or profession. In the French Church of Notre Dame at Semur-en-Auxois, the donor guild—the clothmakers—is the only subject in the window. Such lack of restraint may be extreme, but fifteenth-century windows are full of figures of donors, usually kneeling at the bottom of the window, often accompanied by their family, the sons behind the father, the daughters behind the mother, or even entire generations crowding in eager for recognition.

There was also a secular spirit to stained glass now, born in part of the new humanism that was loosening the hold of ecclesiastical authority and in part of a middle class determined to enjoy the arts they had heretofore only supported in church. This spirit manifested itself in several ways. There were, for instance, secular subjects in ecclesiastical glass, among them the superb south rose window in the Angers Cathedral that contains the twelve signs of the zodiac, and the north rose facing it with the twelve labors of the months.

There was also more stained glass in private buildings that was both religious and secular in subject. At least since the middle of the thirteenth century stained glass was used in the principal rooms and apartments in castles and palaces, and windows in secular buildings were glazed with growing frequency in colored glass, but for the first time stained glass, always a costly medium, was within the reach of the affluent middle class.

Because homes required as much light as possible, stained glass styles were adapted to domestic use. Diamond-shaped quarry panels replaced richly colored glazing, with color provided by decorative inserts. Heraldic glass was the most popular, or some insignia of the owner. Jacques Coeur, for example, had one window of his sumptuous home in Bourges glazed with a replica of one of his trading ships under sail. Also popular were roundels that were sometimes of religious subjects, like the life of the Virgin or the

Below: A glass painting of one of the trading ships of the French merchant Jacques Coeur, installed in his home in Bourges.

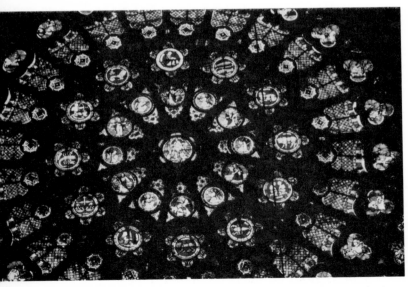

Above: The twelve signs of the zodiac encircle a ring of angels in this rose window from the Basilica of St.-Denis, outside Paris.

seven sacraments, and sometimes secular, like the twelve labors of the months or the Nine Worthy Conquerors—three pagans, three Jews, and three Christians.

Naturally, the increase in stained glass windows was good for the trade, and glass workshops flourished throughout Europe. In Italy, glass artisans in Bologna, Milan, and Florence produced marvelous glass for the great cathedrals of those cities. In Flanders, stained glass workers were important enough to organize themselves into guilds. In France, there were prolific regional schools of glaziers in Normandy, Champagne, and in other sections of the country. And in Germany, there were glaziers at work in Nuremberg, Cologne, Ulm, and other cathedral towns, with workshops throughout the country.

It was also a time when individual glass painters became prominent, losing the anonymity of the Middle Ages. One such artisan was Peter Hemmel von Andlau, whose work is often regarded as the best German glass of the last part of the century. With his sons, sons-in-law, and several workers, his atelier in Strasbourg developed a style and excellence that was in demand by cathedrals throughout Germany, in Salzburg, and even in Milan.

The spread of ideas across national boundaries was another hallmark of the fifteenth century. The general prosperity of Europe, trade among countries, and international financing all aided the cross-fertilization of artistic and cultural ideas. German architects and glaziers, for instance, were called for consultation on the Milan Cathedral. It is no reflection on the success of their mission to note that although Milan is the most Gothic of Italian cathedrals, it remained resolutely Italian in its white marble and the

Above: "November," a fifteenth-century English roundel in a series illustrating the twelve labors of the months.
Photo courtesy Victoria and Albert Museum, Crown Copyright, London

liveliness of its fanciful spires and pinnacles.

Nowhere was the influence of foreign cultures felt more strongly than in Spain. For centuries the Spaniards have naturalized alien styles. First the Moors, who migrated to Spain in the eighth century, brought splendid Oriental motifs. Then the Cluny monks introduced Romanesque forms on their eleventh-century pilgrimages. The austere Gothic lines came later with the Cistercians, and the more sophisticated cathedral Gothic of France and England arrived early in the thirteenth century. But this long history of foreign influence never prevented Spain from fashioning a

Above: The wide arch and the narrative scenes within a circle are typically Spanish in this window from Toledo Cathedral.

native style uniquely and recognizably Spanish.

Their first great Gothic cathedrals—León, Burgos, Toledo—are unmistakably French in architecture, especially inside, but they have characteristics that stamp them indelibly Spanish. The windows are smaller, in a typical Mediterranean effort to reduce the glare and heat of the sun. The roofs are less sloped than northern Gothic churches whose high roofs can easily shed rain and snow. And,

especially in Toledo, the windows have a distinctly Spanish cast—in the brilliant color, in the rather wide arches and rounded tops of many windows, and in the richly ornamental geometric designs of borders, backgrounds, and the eight "window eyes" of the ambulatory. Despite the fact that the architects and craftsmen of Spain's Gothic cathedrals were foreign—the glaziers were French, Flemish, German, and Italian—the architecture and the glass reflect the Spanish climate and character.

Italy shares with Spain a love for color and the Mediterranean climate with its bright sun. Not surprisingly, there are similarities in the stained glass of the two countries. The Duomo at Florence, perhaps the best of Italian glass, is richly glazed in resplendent colors. Its windows are small. In fact, aside from the eleven *occhi,* or window eyes, there are only thirty-eight stained glass windows in the mammoth cathedral, which is over 550 feet long and 340 feet wide. But here the similarity with Spanish glass ends.

Where the Spanish used foreign glaziers to fill their windows, the Italians turned to the best of their master artists, a decision that had far-reaching consequences for the art of stained glass. Half the glass in the Duomo was designed by Lorenzo Ghiberti, a painter, architect, sculptor, and the designer of the glorious bronze doors of the Baptistery that Michelangelo called the Gates of Paradise. In an astonishing group of stained glass paintings in the *occhi* that ring the famous dome, Andrea del Castagno designed one, two are by Paolo Uccello (a third has disappeared)—although neither painter had ever worked in stained glass before—the sculptor Donatello designed another, and Ghiberti the remaining three.

Paradoxically, these splendid circular paintings presaged the decline of stained glass art. Uccello used perspective skillfully in his "Resurrection," Del Castagno modeled his figures meticulously in the "Deposition," and Donatello's "Coronation of the Virgin" is heavily painted with thick enamel. Such painterly qualities may be estimable for easel art, but they are the antithesis of the qualities essential to good stained glass art—luminosity deriving from the dazzling brilliance inherent in the glass itself, and definition of line and form from skillful use of leading, rather than from shading. Perhaps this is the reason that the production of Italian stained glass, after a relatively short period, was finished by the end of the fifteenth century, earlier than in other countries. Indeed, when Pope Julius II wanted to glaze the Vatican windows in the early sixteenth century, he had to import glass artists from France.

If the classical style of the Italians gave stained glass an entirely different aspect, the realistic style of the Flemish painters taxed it almost beyond its capacities. The meticulously drawn, minute details of an interior or a landscape that make fifteenth-century Flemish easel art a joy simply cannot be rendered in traditional stained glass. As a consequence, the Flemish painters, particularly Jan van Eyck and Roger van der Weyden, simply designed pictures on glass, disregarding the leading that in good stained glass is an integral part of the composition.

The irony of fifteenth century stained glass is that when the medium attracted the master painters of the age, whose glasswork had far-reaching influence, stained glass gradually became a painter's rather than a glazier's art. It didn't start to recover its integrity and vigor for over 400 years.

General Characteristics of Fifteenth-Century Glass

Figure-canopy windows. The slender figures and the tall canopies that framed them nicely filled the tall narrow lancets, especially in English Perpendicular windows. The figures stood on bases, completing the architectural look of the canopy frame. English canopies used a lot of white glass, with elaborate details—turrets, angels, canopy ornaments of all kinds—stained in yellow. German canopies were glazed with strong yellow stain, French Flamboyant canopies used yellow stain to simulate gold, and Italian canopies were richly colored with pot metal glass.

Some interesting windows:

ENGLAND:
    Coventry. Guildhall
    Oxford. All Souls College Chapel
    Warwick. Church of St. Mary—Saint
        Thomas à Becket and Saint Albans in
        jeweled robes
    York Minster—kings and archbishops in
        "East Window"

GERMANY:
    Lüneburg Rathaus
    Nuremberg. St. Lawrence Church
    Soest. Wiesenkirche
    Tübingen. St. George's Church

ITALY:
    Florence. Duomo—Ghiberti prophets and
        saints

Opposite: Three saints atop architectural pedestals stand under fancifully decorated Gothic canopies. Formerly in the chapel of Winchester College, the window portrays, from left to right, St. John the Evangelist, the Prophet Zephaniah, and St. James the Greater.
Photo courtesy Victoria and Albert Museum, Crown Copyright, London

    Florence. Santa Maria Novella—
        Domenico Ghirlandaio saints

SPAIN:
    León Cathedral
    Seville Cathedral
    Toledo Cathedral

UNITED STATES:
    New York, N.Y. The Metropolitan Museum of Art, The Cloisters—canopied figures from a Rhine convent

Narrative windows. A single scene, heretofore confined to a single panel, now spread out over two or more lights of a window, or even the whole window; visually, the common background—landscape, architecture—that carried over from one panel to the next unified the multiple lights. The Crucifixion, for example, always spread over three lights, with Christ in the center light flanked by Mary and Saint John in the outer lights.

    Some interesting narrative windows:
AUSTRIA:
    Graz. Joanneum Landesmuseum—collection
    Leoben. Church of Maria-Waasen

Right: Two delightful scenes from the narrative window "Acts of Mercy," in All Saints' Church, York—"Giving Drink to the Thirsty," top, and "Visiting the Sick," bottom. See color insert 11 (bottom).
Photo courtesy Royal Commission on Historical Monuments, England.

Salzberg. Nonnberg Abbey—Peter Hemmel von Andlau scenes

Saint Leonhard im Lavantal

Tamsweg. Church of Saint Leonard

ENGLAND:

Great Malvern Priory Church

Margaretting. Church of St. Margaret—Jesse window

York Minster—"Life of Saint William"; Saint Cuthbert window; Old Testament scenes in the "East Window"

York. All Saints' Church—"Acts of Mercy" and "Pricke of Conscience" windows

GERMANY:

Munich. Frauenkirche—Bible scenes and Jesse window by Peter Hemmel von Andlau

Nuremberg. Church of St. Lawrence—Jesse window by Peter Hemmel von Andlau; Old Testament scenes

Tübingen. St. George's Church—Jesse window by Peter Hemmel von Andlau

Ulm Cathedral—Bible scenes by Hans Acker in the Besserer Chapel; "Life of Christ" in the Jesse window and "Ratfenster" by Peter Hemmel von Andlau

SPAIN:

Barcelona Cathedral

León Cathedral

Seville Cathedral

Toledo Cathedral

ITALY:

Florence. Duomo—*occhi* by Ghiberti, Uccello, Del Castagno, Donatello

Florence. Santo Spirito—*occhio* by Perugino

Donor windows. Donor figures were important, and often appeared prominently in the donated window, sometimes at the bottom of the panel with the entire family or even several generations. The donor wore the contemporary dress, which reflected his class and occupation, and if he were particularly prominent, he might be shown at a desk. Heraldic shields and insignia borne by angels in the tracery lights also identified donors.

Some interesting donor windows:

ENGLAND:

Great Malvern Priory Church

York Minster—Saint William and Saint Cuthbert windows

York, All Saints' Church—"Acts of Mercy" and Blackburn windows

FRANCE:

Le Mans Cathedral—Louis II and family

Rose windows. The stone tracery of rose windows continued to develop from geometric to flowing forms, and took many different shapes. The south rose at Angers Cathedral, with radiating spokes, looks more like a daisy than a rose; the west rose at Toledo Cathedral, with its concentric rings of tracery, resembles a chrysanthemum.

Tracery. Tracery took different forms in each country. In England, the Perpendicular style dictated vertical tracery with upright lines. Since the shape of the Perpendicular tracery was very much like the tall, narrow

Opposite: The donor, with his wife, of the "Acts of Mercy" window in All Saints' Church, York. Above them is one of the six acts of mercy depicted—"Visiting Those in Prison." See color insert 11 (bottom).

Above: The tracery of the west rose window of Toledo Cathedral forms a series of rings around an ecclesiastical insignia.

window lights below it, into which the tracery was often incorporated, the tracery was usually filled with smaller versions of the same subject—predictably canopied saints or prophets—and with heraldic devices or angels.

The Flamboyant tracery of French windows formed undulating flamelike openings, which were best filled with floating angels, sometimes carrying scrolls or emblems, that could be manipulated to fill the odd-shaped areas. Spanish tracery, reflecting the late arrival of Gothic in Spain, was geometric and often had the three- and four-sided foiled circles that characterized fourteenth-century tracery in England.

Quarry windows. Quarry windows grew out of, and replaced, grisaille windows, and were popular for the same reasons—they admitted light and they were economical. Quarries were diamond- or lozenge-shaped, with a design that was sometimes stained centered in each quarry. The interlacing foliate patterns of the fourteenth century were replaced by separate motifs centered in each quarry, among them birds, flowers, insects, leaves, heraldic devices. A quarried window might be decorated with roundels or heraldic devices, and be framed by borders of alternating heraldic motifs or colored rectangles.

Above: The Flamboyant tracery of the fifteenth-century rose window at Ste.-Chapelle, Paris, which represents the Revelations of St. Jean, is filled with men on horseback, angels, fleurs-de-lis in odd-shaped sections.

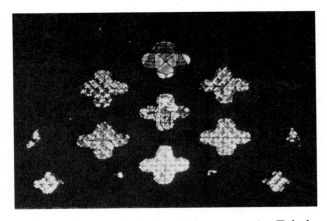

Above: Characteristic Spanish tracery in Toledo Cathedral uses tilelike geometric patterns in quatrefoil openings.

Glazing style. Leading lost its importance as a design element. Since it was still needed as a structural support, the leading was placed where it interfered least with the designs, which were being made with larger and larger pieces of glass. Yet even while the traditional techniques of glazing were losing favor, the practice of leading individual glass

jewels to decorate robes and heraldic shields was flourishing in a large area of central England; a particularly sumptuous jeweled window is in the Beauchamp Chapel of Saint Mary's Church in Warwick.

Above: Typical heraldic-type insignias frame a quarried window in All Saints' Church, York. Each quarry contains a delicate rosette.

Color. While the color of English glass was getting softer and more disperse, partly the result of thinner sheets of glass, French glass had stronger, richer, and more varied colors than before, and its glass was often imported by other countries. Italian and Spanish glass was also richly colored. Silver stain was used extensively for halos, flowers, border designs, architectural details on canopies, and to produce shades of yellow on white glass. It was also used to create green on the lighter blue glass that was being made.

The principal technical innovation was

the discovery that by a process of abrasion, the thin colored layer of a flashed glass could be scraped or abraded to expose the underlying glass, thus displaying two colors on the same glass. And if the underlying glass were stained, a third color could be added.

Painting style. Sophisticated drawing techniques—among them stippling a matt-painted area—were used for shading and modeling figures, defining facial details, and establishing perspective in backgrounds and in architectural features. Figures were large, naturally posed, and wore loose robes in heavy folds.

Below: Manna from heaven falling on the Israel camp in the Wilderness. The golden tents and the Sinai landscape are drawn in perspective, the figures are naturalistic, and the placement of leading has little to do with the design. Church of St.-Étienne du Mont, Paris.

The Sixteenth Century

For most of Europe, the fifteenth century saw the end of great stained glass. In the sixteenth century, glassmaking in its traditional forms came to an end—precipitously in the northern countries, more slowly in the Catholic south, and everywhere for similar reasons.

From its beginnings, stained glass was an art of the Catholic Church. It flourished under Church patronage, it glorified the imagery and symbols and stories of the Bible, it educated and delighted the faithful. And when the Catholic Church came under attack by the

powerful forces of the Reformation, the fortunes of stained glass art and artists were profoundly affected. In the north, where the voices of Protestantism were loudest and most vigorous, the story of stained glass and its decline is tied most dramatically to the Reformation. But even in those countries remaining predominantly Catholic, stained glass eventually fell into decline, a victim not of religious persecution, but of two circumstances that converged artistically.

The first was the increasing use of enamel paints in a wide range of colors, with which a glass could be painted and then fired, thus creating a colorful design without having to lead together different pieces of colored glass. As leading became not merely less important but virtually unnecessary—and indeed, a visual distraction—the skills of the glazier became superfluous. And as enamel covered the glass to furnish all necessary color, the essential translucency of the medium was lost.

The second circumstance was the growing influence of Renaissance forms, introduced

Two English heraldic panels. *Left:* The arms of Henry VIII on the left and those of his queen, Jane Seymour, on the right, within a wreath of green foliage and white roses and beneath a royal crown. The golden fleur-de-lis and "H" is for Henry, the white unicorn and "I" for Jane (1536–37). *Below:* The arms of the Duke of Suffolk contain a lion rampant and a variety of geometric heraldic motifs in white, red, blue (1515). Both panels are 19 inches high overall.
Photos courtesy Sotheby & Co., London

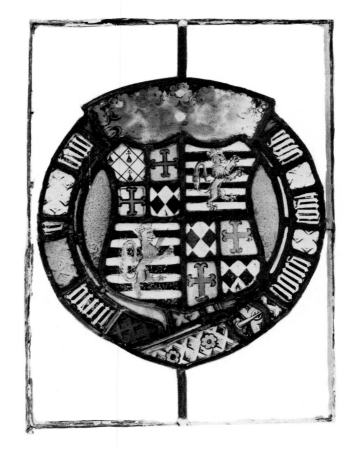

by both Italian and Flemish painters. These stressed naturalism, perspective, detailed architectural features, realistic landscape backgrounds, and humanized figures—all of which were difficult to translate into glass. This Renaissance style, coupled with the spreading use of enamel paints, eventually bankrupted the traditions of stained glass and transformed it into glass painting.

Enamel paints and the naturalistic style of the Renaissance changed the look of sixteenth-century glass art, but it was the spirit of the Reformation that changed the subject matter. The Protestant distrust of religious images, regarded as idolatrous, turned glaziers from the production of ecclesiastical windows—except for some religious roundels for worship at home—to secular glass for churches, civic buildings, and private residences.

The most prevalent type of secular glass was heraldic. Because the forms and colors of heraldry were prescribed, heraldic glass was the only type to retain its former vigor, a crispness of geometric form, and a vividness of color that was lost in the pictorialization of most other contemporary glass. But even here the rich identifying colors of heraldry were eventually painted on clear glass with the newly developed enamels, rather than derived from translucent glass meticulously leaded together.

Historical scenes were also popular since they, too, came within the limits of antireligious art. In the Netherlands, the windows were populated with the tangled royal families of Netherlands and Spain; in a library in Troyes the visit of Henry IV to that French city is recorded by a prominent glass painter, Linard Gontier; in Champigny-sur-Veude a series of beautiful windows in the chapel of the privately owned French château

records events in the life of Louis IX (Saint Louis) of France.

The preference for secular glass coincided with the rise of wealthy merchants, who were building private chapels and town houses that offered a ready market for stained glass.

Above: One of thirty-two small French panels by Linard Gontier in the old library at Troyes shows Henri IV—designated Le Roy—in front of the cathedral—designated St.-Pierre—during Henri's visit to the town in 1595. The chicken wire is protecting the old glass.

Here the nobility and burghers could memorialize themselves in glass—in portraits, in their heraldic devices, even associate themselves with Greek and Roman myths which the classical revival made popular. And if more themes were needed, the glass painters could turn to Dutch and German woodcuts, manuscripts, drawings, and engravings based on the paintings of Italian Renaissance artists, particularly Raphael—all widely

disseminated after the invention of the printing press in the fifteenth century. Sometimes this secular glass was installed in homes, and sometimes it took the form of small individual panels which, through the sixteenth and seventeenth centuries, were much in vogue as gifts to commemorate special family occasions.

All of these strands in sixteenth-century glass were present in Germany, where they were particularly influenced by Martin Luther and Albrecht Dürer. Luther, of course, focused attention on the excesses of the Catholic Church when in 1517 he tacked his manifesto, *Ninety-Five Theses*, on the door of a Wittenberg church and energized the pro-

Above: The dedication of Ste.-Chapelle in Paris, a thirteenth-century event, is portrayed in sixteenth-century French glass in Ste.-Chapelle at Champigny-sur-Veude. The Bourbon donors kneel below.
Photo by Jean-Marc Cailleau, courtesy Mrs. Bryan Wallace
Right: In a scene after a Lucas van Leyden engraving, Joseph, standing in front of his brothers, interprets his dreams to Jacob. The small individual octagonal panel, with a hook for hanging, is 7¾ inches high.
Photo courtesy Sotheby & Co., London

test movement that came to be called the Reformation. At about the same time, the aesthetics of the Italian Renaissance, fostered in large part by Albrecht Dürer, affected the style of glass artists in such glass centers as Nuremberg and Cologne. Dürer's woodcuts, engravings, and drawings furnished designs for European glaziers in other countries, and carried the Renaissance ideals across Europe.

The same twin strands of Renaissance and Reformation colored the stained glass of the Netherlands as well. The landscapes in perspective, the minutely detailed realism, the human figures with individualized characteristics that mark the style of the great Flemish Renaissance painters all influenced the sister art of stained glass and increased the distance from its traditional beginnings. But even more destructive was the effect of the Reformation, and the extensive devastation of church art in the middle of the century. The religious struggle was particularly virulent in the Netherlands. Eventually Flanders in the south stayed Catholic, and the north became the Protestant Dutch Republic.

Of the stained glass that was produced in the Netherlands in the sixteenth century, the most interesting by far are the windows in the Church of Saint John in Gouda, which contains both Catholic and Protestant glass. The twenty-two Catholic windows were done between 1555 and 1571 in the Renaissance style, most of them by the brothers Wouter and Dirck Crabeth. All glassmaking stopped when the town rebelled against Philip II of Spain and the Inquisition, and during the establishment of the Protestant Dutch Republic in 1581. When the glazing of the church was finally resumed, it was by Protestants whose windows embraced heraldic shields and historical scenes of the religious liberation.

Above: Job sits on a pile of corn sheaves while his wife pours water over his sores. Behind them is a scene of sixteenth-century Flemish farm life (28 by 18 inches, 1540).
Photo courtesy Sotheby & Co., London

The increased commerce between the Netherlands and England in the last part of the fifteenth century had encouraged an influx of Flemish and German glass artists to England, who brought with them the style of the continental Renaissance. The new English glass was now produced either by English glassmakers following foreign designs or by foreign artists under the patronage of the English nobility.

Fairford Church in Gloucestershire was probably the first English church to be glazed by Flemish artisans. It marked the end of Gothic glass in England and the transition to English Renaissance. The full flowering of Renaissance glass in England, however, is at King's College Chapel, Cambridge, a triumph of Gothic architecture and fan vaulting. Under the patronage of Henry VII, who enjoyed Flemish art, most of the chapel's twenty-six huge windows were glazed between 1526 and 1531 by Flemish or German artisans in their continental style—more natural figures, no canopies, landscapes and architectural details delineated in perspective and realistically.

Three years after the glazing of King's College Chapel was completed, Henry VIII split with Rome and a century of devastation of church artifacts began. The first stained glass to be destroyed was in the monasteries. Thirteen years later the Royal Articles of King Edward VI ordered the destruction of all religious images— "monuments of feigned miracles, pilgrimages, idolatry, and superstition," they were called.   The wasting

Above: In St. Mary's Church, Fairford, the Transfiguration in the central light is flanked on the left by a double-light scene of St. Mary, and on the right by a double-light scene of the Holy Women. The Perpendicular Style tracery above is filled with canopied saints.

Right: "The Betrayal," in King's College Chapel, Cambridge (ca. 1516).
Photo courtesy Council for Places of Worship, London

of ecclesiastical artifacts in cathedrals, churches, and chapels proceeded slowly only because of the expense of substituting clear glass. Eventually, in 1559, the royal order was amended to elevate stained glass to "monuments of antiquity," primarily because unglazed windows made the churches uninhabitable in bad weather.

The savaging of ecclesiastical art continued with greater virulence in the seventeenth century under the Commonwealth and Oliver Cromwell. In 1643, by authority of the House of Commons, the Roundheads embarked on a campaign that stripped and vandalized stained glass and other ecclesiastical art, sometimes smashing just the heads, sometimes just the bodies, sometimes just whitewashing the glass. By the seventeenth century, the bitter consequences of the Reformation had taken a heavy toll on great English glass, and the acceptable contemporary glass, robbed of its ecclesiastical themes and richness, overpainted with opaque enamels, and overdrawn in the naturalism of the Renaissance style, fell victim to the decline of the stained glass art.

In the Catholic countries of France and Spain stained glass fared better for a longer period, but eventually was bankrupted by the same artistic sterility. Italy had no native stained glass at all in the sixteenth century—the little of note was done by the French glass painter William de Marcillat—primarily because the forms and proportions of Italian Renaissance buildings were not hospitable to stained glass windows.

In France, stained glass flourished in the Flemish–Italian Renaissance style that was common to all European glass. French interest in Italianate forms began with the forays of Charles VIII and Louis XII into Italy at the end of the fifteenth century, and the later visits by Francis I, who incorporated some of the features of the Italian Renaissance into his châteaux on the Loire. Gradually, the motifs of classical architecture infiltrated French Flamboyant Gothic of the fifteenth century; in glass, for example, classical shell-shaped niches replaced Gothic canopies. The Flemish strain came with the stained glass artist Arnoult de Nimègue, who worked in Rouen and other towns of Normandy, and from the influential glass workshop of Engrand le Prince and his three brothers in northern France.

The most interesting French glass had been made by the middle of the century. Typical are the forty-four panels in monochrome and yellow stain exhibited in the Château of Chantilly, outside Paris, that tell the story of Cupid and Psyche in a typically Italianate style. The drawings are technically excellent, the panels pale paintings on glass, crossed at random by leads wherever support is required. They are emblematic of the state of glass art in sixteenth-century France.

Spain fared somewhat better in the sixteenth century. Despite the wars with France, internal fighting, the Spanish Inquisition, and the mortifying defeat of the Armada at the hands of the English, literature, scholarship, and painting flourished, and with them the art of stained glass. Again, many of the glass artists were Flemish or Dutch, and they too worked in the Renaissance style of Flanders and Italy, particularly in the glass centers of Seville, Segovia, Salamanca, Granada, and Toledo. They provided glass for the new Gothic cathedrals in Segovia and Salamanca and the Renaissance cathedral at Granada, and for the older cathedrals of Seville, Toledo, and Ávila. Seville became the showcase for two talented brothers, Arnao de

Vergara and Arnao de Flandes, who worked in the high Renaissance style of classical motifs and architectural details wedded to the rich color that the Spanish love.

General Characteristics of Sixteenth-Century Glass

Pictorial windows. Large pictorial windows were the most common type of glass, and after the Reformation frequently depicted historical scenes. The subjects often spilled over into more than one light, and sometimes occupied the entire window, ignoring any intervening mullions.

Some interesting windows:

BELGIUM:
Brussels Cathedral
Hoogstraten. Church of St. Catherine

ENGLAND:
Cambridge. King's College Chapel
Fairford. Church of St. Mary
Great Malvern Priory Church—Magnificat window
London. St. Margaret's Church at West-minster Abbey

FRANCE:
Auch. Church of Ste.-Marie—"Creation of the World"
Beauvais. Church of St.-Étienne—choir glass
Bourg-en-Bresse. Church of Brou—"Crowning of Virgin" and "Assumption," after Dürer
Champigny-sur-Veude. La Ste.-Chapelle—"Life of Saint Louis"
Chantilly. Château de Chantilly—Cupid and Psyche
Conches. Church of Ste.-Foy
Les Andelys. Church of Notre Dame
Paris. Church of St.-Gervais—windows by Jean Cousin and Robert Pinaigrier
Paris. Château de Vincennes—windows by Jean Cousin
Pont-Audemer. Church of St.-Ouen—Bible scenes
Rouen Cathedral—"Virtues" by Jean Cousin
Rouen. Church of St.-Patrice—Jean Cousin windows in Lady Chapel
Sens Cathedral—windows by Jean Cousin
Troyes Cathedral—windows by Linard Gontier
Troyes Library—visit of Henry IV by Linard Gontier

GERMANY:
Cologne Cathedral

HOLLAND:
Gouda. Church of St. John—Bible scenes by Dirck and Wouter Crabeth; liberation scenes

ITALY:
Arezzo Cathedral—"Life of Christ" by William de Marcillat
Arezzo. Church of San Francesco—William de Marcillat
Arezzo. S.S. Annunziata—William de Marcillat
Siena Cathedral—*occhio*

SPAIN:
Granada Cathedral
Segovia Cathedral
Seville Cathedral—work of Arnao de

Vergara and Arnao de Flandes
Toledo Cathedral

Figure windows. Historical figures and
royalty were common subjects for figure windows. Canopies often became an architectural
background rather than a frame, and were
sometimes decorated with classical motifs
like cupids, scallop shells.

Some interesting windows:

ENGLAND:
Fairford. Church of St. Mary

HOLLAND:
Gouda. Church of St. John—royal portraits

SPAIN:
Ávila Cathedral
Granada Cathedral
Seville Cathedral—saints by Arnao de
Flandes and Arnao de Vergara
Toledo Cathedral

Donor windows. Portraits of donors were
an important part of sixteenth-century glass.
Donors were included alone or, more often in
this century, with their families, their patron
saints, their forebears and their followers,
and often overshadowed the subject of the
window. Nobility, church fathers, guilds—all
kinds of donors were honored in the windows they presented. After the start of the
Reformation, heraldic windows were commonplace.

Some interesting windows:

ENGLAND:
London. Henry VII chapel at Westminster
Abbey—heraldry

Left: Detail from the Miracle of Theophilus, who
sells his soul to the devil and is delivered by the
Virgin (1540). Church of Notre Dame, Les Andelys, France.

Right: A beautiful window from the chapel at
Champigny-sur-Veude combines the coronation
of St.-Louis (Louis IX) at Reims with the kneeling
figures of the Bourbon donors below.

Photo by Jean-Marc Cailleau, courtesy Mrs. Bryan
Wallace

FRANCE:
Bourg-en-Bresse. Church of Brou—
Philibert and Margaret of Austria
Champigny-sur-Veude. La Ste.-
Chapelle—Bourbon portraits
Montmorency. Church of St.-Martin—
House of Montmorency

Above: The donor of the ''Legend of St.-Patrice'' in the Church of St.-Patrice, Rouen, included his entire family. The presence of the desk indicates his importance.

Right: The large Jesse window by the Flemish glass artist Arnoult de Nimègue, in the Church of St.-Godard in Rouen, is populated with large figures of lavishly robed saints and prophets, some of whom stand in Renaissance-style niches with classical ornamentation.

GERMANY:
Nuremberg. St. Sebald's Church

HOLLAND:
Gouda. Church of St. John—heraldry

Jesse windows. The tree of Jesse was still a traditional theme, although the figures and foliage were drawn more realistically, following sixteenth-century style.

Some interesting examples:

FRANCE:
Beauvais. Church of St.-Étienne—by Engrand le Prince, including his self-portrait
Rouen. Church of St.-Godard—by Arnoult de Nimègue
Troyes Cathedral

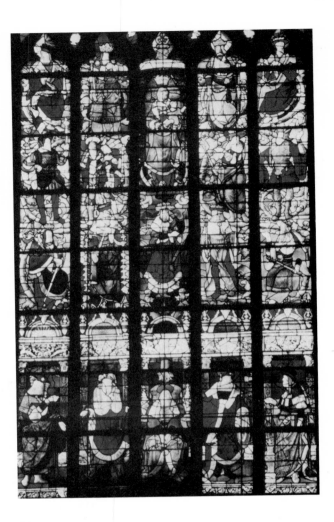

GERMANY:
Cologne Cathedral

Quarry windows. Always popular, quarry windows came into extensive use during the Reformation, when they were painted with heraldic devices, insignias of all kinds, and floral designs. In England particularly quarries were painted with animals and especially birds.

Glazing style. Leading was used primarily to support the glass where needed, not as an integral part of the design.

Color. Silver stain and a wide range of colored enamels were used extensively. Spanish windows used richly colored pot metal glass and less painted-on enamel.

Painting style. Figures were drawn naturalistically and features strongly defined by light and shade. Landscapes or interiors formed backgrounds, which were drawn in perspective and included structures in a landscape or walls and floors.

The Gothic Revival

After two dismal centuries of the destruction and neglect of existing windows and the production of banal new painting on glass, there was renewed interest in the traditions of stained glass in the nineteenth century. It was born primarily of the Gothic Revival, that enthusiasm for the Middle Ages, and especially its architecture, that flourished in the middle of the century, chiefly in England and the United States.

Actually, it had its beginnings in the last half of the eighteenth century, when Horace Walpole, the English writer, planned an imitation Gothic abbey with stained glass windows at his country estate near London. By the nineteenth century, the passion for Gothic detail had spread from the homes of the wealthy to ecclesiastical buildings. The decorative style had a fanatical devotee in A. W. N. Pugin, a young architect who in 1841 wrote the textbook on Gothic Revivalism, *The True Principles of Pointed or Christian Architecture.* Pugin, who shunned the pagan classical architecture with the same fervor he espoused the Christian Gothic, built and restored many churches and public buildings in England, designed stained glass for some of them, and was co-architect of the Perpendicular Gothic Houses of Parliament.

Pugin's followers inherited his mania for, but not his understanding of, medievalism. With the enthusiastic support of the Church of England, they embarked on a vigorous program of church restoration, under which hundreds of buildings were restored. As the Industrial Revolution created an affluent middle class yearning for emblems of their rising status, secular glass became more commonplace in private as well as public buildings. Coats of arms proclaimed the prestige of homeowners; floral panels blocked out their undesirable views.

In France, Eugène Viollet-le-Duc, an architect and writer, became internationally known for his work in restoring Gothic structures and their windows, as well as for his treatise on stained glass, called *Vitrail.* In the United States, which had no Gothic heritage, the Gothic Revival was an opportunity for new building rather than restoration. In the nineteenth century, it was used primarily in residences without distinction. In the beginning of the twentieth century, American Gothic produced some distinguished architecture when Ralph Adams Cram and Bertram G. Goodhue were designing ecclesiastical and institutional buildings, among them the Cathedral Church of St. John the Divine in New York, and the chapels at Princeton University and the U.S. Military Academy at West Point.

Above: "Second-Floor Landing and Hall, 1884," a representative late-nineteenth-century interior in which Victorian-style windows were often used in halls and bathrooms.
Photo courtesy National Gallery of Art, Washington, D.C., Index of American Design

Not surprisingly, the enthusiasm for the Gothic style renewed interest in stained glass. Not since the fifteenth century had the opportunity for stained glass art been so great,

nor, unhappily, the pool of gifted glass designers and glaziers so small. Predictably, many medieval windows were poorly restored, and many of the new designs were pedestrian.

Despite the relatively low level of design and technical skill, the nineteenth century focused needed attention on stained glass. The first aspect to profit from this interest was the quality of the glass itself, which over the years had lost much of its dazzling luminosity. There were several successful efforts to produce a luminous colored glass that more closely matched the early glass of medieval windows, and, in fact, by 1863 "antique" glass of quality was being made commercially.

The principal figure in decorative arts in the last decades of the nineteenth century was William Morris, who, with a group of colleagues, produced a wide array of furnishings from wallpapers, tapestries, and carpets to architectural carvings and stained glass. Morris and his associates had a profound influence on stained glass, as they had on so many aspects of the style and taste of the time.

For Morris stained glass was a natural interest. As a medievalist, he was understandably drawn to the art, one of the glories of the Middle Ages. As a leader of the Arts and Crafts Movement that rejected the technology of the Industrial Revolution he appreciated the skill and craftsmanship required of the glazier, a skill that could never be duplicated by machine. Indeed, glazing was an art that Morris learned and mastered.

Curiously, although Morris turned to the Middle Ages for his artistic inspiration, he did not espouse a Gothic Revival. In fact, he abhorred restorations and often refused to make windows for restored buildings. He

Right: Two of thirteen panels designed by Edward Burne-Jones, now in the William Morris Room of the Victoria and Albert Museum. The flowing robes and garden scenes are characteristic.
Photo courtesy Victoria and Albert Museum, Crown Copyright, London

preferred, instead of recreating a Gothic past, to integrate his artistic expression in contemporary thought, and this he found most sympathetically expressed by the Pre-Raphaelite principle to study nature and record it truthfully.

The windows that the Morris firm produced were distinguished by their high technical standards. In the early years of the firm, which was formed in 1861, many members, among them Ford Madox Brown and Dante Gabriel Rossetti, designed windows. In the later years, Morris's lifelong friend and colleague Sir Edward Coley Burne-Jones designed all the stained glass and Morris did all the glazing, or at least supervised it. The division of labor was productive. Burne-Jones was an artist of some reputation, and Morris, the colorist and technician, chose the glass and leaded it. It was a collaboration that revi-

talized stained glass and produced the best glass of its time.

General Characteristics of Gothic Revival Glass

Subjects. Biblical scenes were popular, with Annunciations, Nativities prominently displayed in large window formats. Commemorative windows and memorials were in favor, as were heraldic devices.

Painting style. Figures were usually large and clothed in medieval dress, often flowing robes; occasionally men appeared as warriors. Figures were sometimes surmounted by Gothic canopies. At best the figures have a

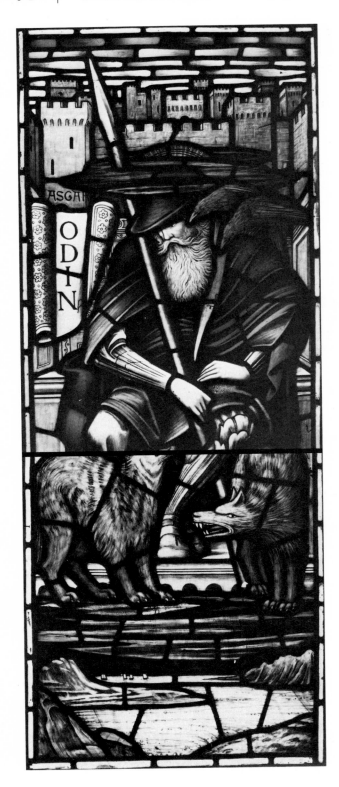

romantic air, at worst, a cloying sentimentality. Naturalistic flowers and foliage appeared in borders, backgrounds, and were important design elements.

Glazing style. By the end of the century, with the work of William Morris, the use of leading again became an integral part of the stained glass design, with the leads defining as well as supporting the glass.

Above: One of several windows in Christ Church Cathedral, Oxford, by Edward Burne-Jones and William Morris, this one depicts, from left to right, Hope, Charity, and Faith, each figure in flowing robes and a garden setting.

Left: "Odin," designed by Edward Burne-Jones and made by Morris & Co. for a Newport, R.I., mansion, is part of a set of windows depicting Norse gods. Odin holds a magic spear while two ravens rest on his shoulder and two wolves snarl at his feet. Made in two panels, 20 by 52½ inches overall, 1883.
Photos courtesy Christie's, London

Some interesting windows:

ENGLAND:
    Birmingham Cathedral—Burne-Jones and
       Morris
    Oxford. Christ Church Cathedral—Burne-
       Jones and Morris
    Salisbury Cathedral—Burne-Jones and
       Morris

UNITED STATES:
    Baltimore, Md., Cathedral
    Boston. Trinity Church
    New York, N.Y. Cathedral Church of St.
       John the Divine
    Princeton, N.J. University Chapel
    San Francisco, Calif. Grace Cathedral
    Washington, D.C., Cathedral
    West Point, N.Y. U.S. Military Academy
       Chapel
    Wilmington, Del., Cathedral Church of
       St. John

Art Nouveau and Louis Comfort Tiffany

The natural forms that William Morris utilized were typical of the Art Nouveau style that began about 1883—toward the end of Morris's great stained glass work—and flourished for the next twenty years. Characterized by curving, sinuous lines that defined its designs—by undulating plant forms and tendrils, by a profusion of flowers, and by languid women with flowing hair—Art Nouveau left its influence on all the decorative and applied arts, and not least on stained glass.

From Scotland to Spain, architects throughout Europe were beguiled by the possibilities of stained glass, and they began to incorporate it in their contemporary structures. When the style belatedly arrived in France, it came to be called Art Nouveau after the name of a shop that carried stained glass, including the works of Louis Comfort Tiffany and John La Farge. In the world of stained glass, the brief flowering of Art Nouveau was the link between William Morris and Louis C. Tiffany, between Europe, where stained glass had flourished for centuries, and the United States, where it acquired an entirely different character.

The contributions of Louis Comfort Tiffany to the world of glass were stunning. He developed a radically different type of glass, he used it in new ways, and he introduced the technique of joining glass sections with copper foil. With these new tools he bent an ancient art to his own creative needs. And as if that weren't enough, through his genius for publicity and his flamboyant life-style, he publicized himself, his artistic principles, and his projects, and in the process excited great interest in glass.

Although Tiffany is most prominently associated with glass, he came to it after a successful career in the fine and decorative arts. Expected to enter the well-known family jewelry business, Tiffany chose instead to be a painter, and apprenticed himself in the studio of George Inness. After a decade of serious painting, he was drawn to the applied arts, and in 1881 he formed a company for interior decorating and architecture. The firm designed or decorated many fashionable places, among them Madison Square Theatre, the houses of Mark Twain, the Vanderbilts, Hamilton Fish, the Havemeyers, and even the White House under Chester Arthur, a commission that crowned Tiffany's career as a fashionable decorator.

During this period Tiffany was intrigued by the possibilities he saw in glass—its refractive qualities, its shine, its use in chandeliers, skylights, colored windows. Dissatisfied with the quality of the glass he could buy or import, he became interested in manufacturing his own glass. Like John La Farge, a fellow artist and rival glass designer, he studied chemistry and worked in a glass shop, intent on producing iridescent glass with a metallic lustrous patina similar to the kind he had seen on Roman vases buried underground for centuries. He finally devised the chemical formula for such an iridescent glass, and in 1881 received a patent for the application of a metallic luster to one surface of glass.

The efforts of Tiffany produced an array of marvelous glass—new kinds of opalescents, swirling color mixes, fractured glass incorporating flakes or splinters of different colored glass, glass with various textures on one or both sides, even transparent and opaque glass jewels, molded in many sizes, shapes, textures, and colors. Quite different from the purity and radiance of Gothic glass, Tiffany's glass is no less splendid.

But for stained glass the monumental contribution was the creation of multicolored glass that incorporated many colors and tones within a single sheet. Produced by the Tiffany method of melting and annealing the glass, his workshop became so proficient in the new technique that it made thousands of different color combinations, and supplied many other glass designers in addition to the Tiffany artisans.

This polychromatic glass—very few sheets are single color, and even those have variations in tone—became the palette for the artist turned glass designer. With this new glass, Tiffany could represent a purple-gray mountain, a multihued sunset, a pool of water with all its blue-green subtleties, a delicately shaded flower petal—each from a single sheet of glass and without further painting on the glass. So descriptive were the colors, tones, and markings in individual sheets of glass that Tiffany applied for and received a patent listing "Favrile sunset glass," "Favrile horizon glass," "Favrile twig glass," "Favrile lace glass," and "Favrile fabric glass."

The trademark Favrile, incidentally, comes from the word "fabrile," meaning belonging to an artisan. In a patent issued in 1894, Favrile covers all polychromatic glass produced by Tiffany, but it has come to designate only the blown glass vases and bowls, and the few blown lamp shades, probably because those were signed "Favrile," whereas leaded Favrile pieces were signed "Tiffany Studios," one of several firm names.

Working with the American architects of the 1880s and 1890s, Tiffany Glass Company made windows from that glorious mul-

Opposite: Louis Comfort Tiffany's "Autumn Landscape at Sunset" uses polychromatic glass to depict the variegated colors of clouds, tree trunks, and purple hills reflected in the lake. The autumnal scene spans the three panels and the vertical tracery of the Gothic-style wooden frame (11 feet high and 8½ feet wide, 1923).
Photo courtesy The Metropolitan Museum of Art. Gift of Robert W. de Forest, 1925

ticolored glass for churches, museums, theaters, homes. One of the best known was "Four Seasons," an opulent hosanna to each season that was meant to outshine the windows of his rival, La Farge, then having a vogue in Europe. The "Four Seasons" was exhibited in Paris in 1892 and attracted so much admiration that Tiffany's European dealer asked ten contemporary French painters—among them Vuillard, Bonnard, and Toulouse-Lautrec—to make cartoons for stained glass windows. These were executed by Tiffany in his glass and shown at an exhibition in Paris three years later, in 1895. The triumphant "Four Seasons" was later divided into four panels and installed in Tiffany's opulent mansion on Long Island.

In the 1890s lamp shades were more fashionable, and as electrification spread around the turn of the century lighting became an important industry. Many craftsmen made lamps and lamp shades, but none equaled the inventiveness of design and skill of execution of the leaded lamp shades produced by Tiffany Studios.

The leaded and foiled shades made superb use of the Tiffany polychromatic glass. With it the Tiffany Studios turned out a gardenful of floral patterns in which leaves and petals were shaped like their real-life prototypes and cut out of the multicolored or tonal glass most closely resembling the subject. From apple blossoms to wisteria and water lilies, the Tiffany Studios planted a profusion of garden blooms on a variety of cone-, globe-, and circular-shaped lamp shades in which the integrity of each floral form was sustained by the glass piece that represented it. Not content with the dazzling luminosity of the glass, the Tiffany artisans often joined leaf- or petal-shaped pieces of glass with copper to replace the heavier look of the lead lines. Several of the blown glass lamp shades were actually designed by Tiffany himself, but the leaded and foiled shades were the work of the studio assistants.

As the vogue for Art Nouveau passed, and with it the appeal of opalescent peacock feathers and lamp shades festooned with gourds and mushrooms, Tiffany's reputation declined. In a poignant visit to the Armory

Left: Tiffany's wisteria lamp shade, with blue-gray glass and trailing branches, sits atop a bronze stand formed like a tree trunk. The lamp is 27 inches high, the shade 18½ inches in diameter. It sold for $21,000 at auction in 1975. See color insert 12.

Show of 1913 that introduced Fauvism, Cubism, and Post-Impressionism to the American public, Tiffany recognized that his aesthetics, his special truth and beauty, were no longer accepted by others. His time had passed. And not until half a century later did Tiffany's great contributions to glass come to be appreciated again. Meanwhile, the wellsprings of stained glass again bubbled in Europe, where the most creative work in the medium was taking place.

Top and Center Right: Petals and leaves are individually cut from multicolored glass in Tiffany shades. Flowering peony lamp (top right) is 22 inches in diameter; red oriental poppy (center right) 26½ inches in diameter. The former sold for $16,000, the latter for $38,000 at auction in 1975. See color insert 12.

Bottom Left and Right: In Tiffany's dragonfly table lamp, round and oval jewels dot the golden glass, which is foiled in a membranelike pattern; the wing grillwork is laid-on filigree (see detail). The lamp is 28½ inches high, the shade 21¾ inches in diameter. The lamp sold at auction in 1975 for $12,000. See color insert 12.

Above: An early window by John La Farge, called "Peonies Blown in the Wind," comes from the Henry G. Marquand house in Newport, R.I. The white and red flowers and their green leaves are defined by the shapes of the opaline, translucent, and iridescent glass and by the leading; the borders are studded with glass jewels (75 inches high and about 50 inches wide, 1878–79).
Photo courtesy The Metropolitan Museum of Art. Gift of Susan Dwight Bliss, 1930

General Characteristics of Art Nouveau Glass

Subjects. Female figures, usually with long hair and wearing flowing gowns, and landscapes that incorporated flowers, birds, trees, natural forms were common subjects, as were abstract designs that suggested foliate forms. Lamp designs were primarily floral and geometric.

Painting style. Designs were executed in curving, fluid lines that gave movement to the composition.

Glazing style. There was very little painting on glass, the color in the glass being used to define the design. Multitone glass created sophisticated pictorial effects.

The new technique of assembling pieces of glass with copper rather than lead allowed small jewels or intricately cut pieces of glass to be joined with a light delicate look. The lead or copper foils were completely integral to the design and underscored the lines and rhythm of the composition.

Some interesting Art Nouveau glass:

UNITED STATES:
> Boston, Mass. Boston Museum of Fine Arts—Tiffany and La Farge
> New Haven, Conn. Yale University Library—Tiffany
> New York, N.Y. Metropolitan Museum of Art—Tiffany, La Farge
> Winter Park, Florida. The Morse Gallery of Art—Tiffany

The Twentieth Century

Stained glass, still the handmaiden of architecture, flourishes in the twentieth century for several reasons. First, contemporary architecture that utilizes steel and concrete can support large areas of glass. Not since the tall, narrow lancets of the Gothic cathedral replaced the small arched openings in Romanesque churches and abbeys has the opportunity for glass art been so inviting or interest in the medium so great.

Coupled with the possibilities that contemporary architecture offers is the increase in construction. In Europe, this was the result of two world wars. New buildings rise to replace old, abandoned, or destroyed structures; derelict buildings are refurbished. Both kinds contain many windows to be glazed. In the United States, population shifts to the suburbs create the need for new religious and secular centers where people can worship, play, assemble—just the types of large public structures most hospitable to stained glass art.

Historically, ecclesiastical buildings have been the primary employer of stained glass artisans, and this is still true. After the first world war, most new church windows looked backward, repeating familiar ecclesiastical themes, memorializing the war dead. But following World War II, windows became as innovative and nontraditional as the buildings that contained them. One important reason was the change in the function of church windows. For centuries, stained glass was the way congregants were instructed in the history and traditions of their religion and inculcated with a sense of reverence and awe as they worshiped. In the twentieth century, however, as books, weekly sermons on radio and television, even comic books performed the same instructive role, ecclesiastical glass lost its narrative imperative. Stained glass could, and did, become primarily an artistic medium—color plus light—to be explored and transformed by the genius of the artist. Understandably, the liberation of stained glass from its traditional themes excited the imagination of a number of contemporary artists. Architects, sculptors, and primarily painters—among them Matisse, Rouault, Chagall, Léger, Braque, Josef Albers—turned to glass, bringing with them the artistic idioms in which they customarily worked. And so we have in glass not only the uniquely personal signatures of gifted artists, but also a welcome vitality born of new ideas and new forms applied to old traditions.

France

The entry of fine artists into the world of glass was particularly noteworthy in France, where, at the invitation of the Church, painters turned their talents to this new medium. One influential group in the postwar revival of liturgical arts was the Dominicans—and especially Father M. A. Couturier—who in 1937 invited a number of artists to contribute to a church in Assy. By the time Notre Dame de Toute Grâce was consecrated in 1950, Georges Rouault had designed stained glass windows, Marc Chagall had designed two grisaille angels in profile, tile murals, and low marble reliefs, Henri Matisse had painted and glazed a tile drawing of Saint Dominic, Henri Bonnard had painted an altarpiece, Fernand Léger had worked on the façade mosaics, Jean Lurcat on a large tapestry for the apse, and Georges Braque and Jacques Lipchitz had made sculptures.

The astonishing constellation of artists who contributed to the small provincial church in the Haute Savoie represented an ecumenical sample of artistic styles—abstract, cubist, and expressionist. Of these twentieth-century masters, only Rouault had serious training as a craftsman: as a youth he had been an apprentice in a stained glass workshop. Instead of continuing to work in glass, he had borrowed the visual aesthetic of the lead line and translated it into the heavy dark lines that are characteristic of his prints and paintings.

If the church at Assy presents an artistic chorus, the Dominican Chapel of the Rosary at Vence sings with the clear solo voice of Matisse. Working on this chapel during the last four years of his life, from 1947 to 1950, Matisse designed the entire ecclesiastical environment—the painted and glazed tile murals and floors, the crucifix, candlesticks, even the chasubles worn by the priests, as well as the stained glass windows.

The windows are tree-of-life designs, stark and clear and simple—gold and blue leaves against a grass-green background, in some windows reaching toward a brilliant sun at the top. To make the design, the bed-ridden Matisse mixed his colors in gouache, painted them on paper, then cut out his shapes with scissors. They were pinned on the wall opposite his bed, where he could

Above: Using bold colors and abstract shapes, Fernand Léger combines thick and thin lead lines, opaque and transparent glass in the same composition.
Photo courtesy French Embassy Press and Information Division

study them to determine the final arrangement. The simple shapes and clear colors wash the stark black and white interior with a dazzling radiance. As Matisse himself described it, "In the chapel my chief aim was to balance a surface of light and color against a

solid white wall covered with black drawings.'' Despite Matisse's late entry into the world of stained glass, tile murals, and liturgical artifacts, he considered the chapel at Vence his masterpiece, the culmination of his life's work.

Like Matisse, Fernand Léger worked in a style that was superbly suited to stained glass—bold shapes in pure flat color. One splendid example is the abstract mural that circles three sides of the Church of the Sacred Heart in Audincourt. Léger used inch-thick sections of slab glass set in concrete, and the installation started the vogue for the technique called *dalle de verre* glass art.

Prompted by the splendid glass at Vence and Audincourt, a number of churches sought to enrich their buildings with glass art of quality. Alfred Manessier, a religious painter interested in investigating how light

Left: "Scenes from the Life of Christ" by Marc Chagall in Reims Cathedral include "Christ on the Cross," "Descent from the Cross," and "The Resurrection."

Right: Multitone glass in blues, golds, beige, mauve, rose create evocative patterns of color in this contemporary abstract window in the Church of St.-Séverin, Paris.

permeates color, designed abstract windows in slab glass and conventionally leaded glass for a number of churches in France and Germany. Braque created stained glass windows for the Chapel of St.-Dominique in Varangeville, near the coast at Dieppe, and Jean Bazaine made several for St.-Séverin in Paris. Le Corbusier designed a series of extraordinary windows for his church of Notre Dame du Haut at Ronchamp in the Vosges. They are all small, some just inches square, and they punctuate one wall of the church where they are carefully placed to admit shafts of light at directed angles through the thick concrete walls.

One of the most popular painters turned glass artist is Marc Chagall, whose best-known glass is the twelve Jerusalem windows that form the lantern of the synagogue at the Hadassah-Hebrew University Medical Center in Jerusalem. The windows represent the twelve sons of Jacob and the twelve tribes of Israel from whom they descended, and are placed in sets of three around the square lantern in the same formation in which the tribes grouped themselves to protect the Holy Ark as they journeyed to the Promised Land. The iconography of the windows, like their placement, is based on Bible texts; then the windows take on the marvelous color, sense of fantasy, and folkloric references that distinguish the best of Chagall's art. Because Hebraic tradition forbids the representation of humans, the windows are crowded with other living things—animals, birds, fish, flowers.

Unlike many artists who design for glass, Chagall learned how to work in the medium. He studied the techniques, painted the final design on the glass with grisaille, and participated at every step with the Reims atelier of Charles Marq that actually cut, fired, and leaded the windows. The glass itself was specially made for Chagall, and incorporates the subtle luminosity and tonalities of color that he specified. Doubled glass was fused to blend different colors, glass surfaces etched with acid to becloud, lighten, reduce the thickness, or create bubbles in the glass.

The Jerusalem windows were profoundly important to Chagall. He was 75 when they were installed in 1962, and at the dedication he said, "How is it that the air and earth of Vitebsk, my birthplace, and of thou-

Above: Two of the twelve windows by Marc Chagall at Hadassah-Hebrew University Medical Center, Jerusalem. *Left:* The window of the agricultural and scholarly tribe of Issachar is predominantly green-colored glass and populated with creatures of nature: a donkey with a blue head rests in a field, a bird perched on his back and a sheep grazing behind him; various birds circle the two hands which hold the tent, on which is Issachar's blessing in Hebrew. The only window with a border, it is encircled with intertwining snakes, symbol of fertility and wisdom.

sands of years of exile find themselves mingled in the air and earth of Jerusalem? . . . The tragic and heroic resistance movements and the War of Independence in Israel are blended in my flowers and beasts and fiery colors.''

Although Chagall's identification with

Above: The Tablet of the Law, surrounded by Sabbath candles, in the lower half of this window, carries the blessing of Moses to the tribe of Levi. At the top of the golden window a dove wearing a crown and a bird with two horns of wisdom flank a red, white, and blue star of David. Below them two fanciful animals present a basket of fruit and flowers.
Photos courtesy Hadassah. © Hadassah Medical Relief Association, Inc., 1961

Israel is palpable in the Jerusalem windows, his glass art transcends the synagogue traditions. He drew from New Testament texts in windows in the Union Church of Pocantico Hills in North Tarrytown, N.Y., and in the extraordinary windows at Reims Cathedral that coexist in complete harmony with the medieval stained glass surrounding them.

England

In England, contemporary church windows have their most moving expression at Coventry, where a new cathedral rises at the side of the ruins of the fourteenth-century church that was destroyed in 1940 in the longest air raid on Britain during World War II. Linked by a porch to the ruins of the earlier cathedral in a stirring gesture of resurrection and continuity of faith, the new cathedral is illuminated at its entrance by the towering bowed baptistery window designed by John Piper, and by the beautiful wall of clear incised glass panels that looks out on the porch and the medieval ruins. Tall nave windows, an immense tapestry by Graham Sutherland, sculpture by Sir Jacob Epstein and Sir Basil Spence, gifts of art and religious artifacts from many artists and many countries make Coventry an extraordinary symbol of survival and goodwill.

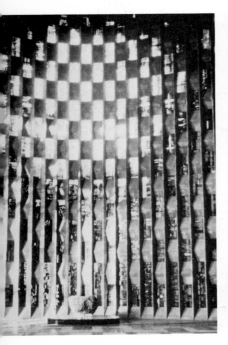

Germany

Although the best-known war-related windows are probably those at Coventry Cathedral, ironically the most innovative work in contemporary institutional glass was being done in Germany, where glass artists and architects have a particularly intimate association. The fountainhead of architectural glass was Jan Thorn Prikker, who worked in the first decades of the century. His early Cubist designs, which bridged the abstract geometrics of Mondrian and the severe functionalism of the Bauhaus, were so revolutionary that some of them couldn't be installed until after World War I. At the Bauhaus, where one would expect to find great interest in the architectural possibilities of stained glass, only the painter Josef Albers had a serious interest. For a few years, he headed a department of stained glass, designed a few leaded windows in geometric shapes, then focused his attention on opaque glass compositions, using the square as a module, and investigated opacity, shape, and color.

The opportunity for new forms of stained glass burgeoned after World War II when Germany needed to rebuild so many public

Far left: The huge, bowed baptistery window of Coventry Cathedral, designed by John Piper and fabricated by Patrick Reyntiens. The bright central panels in yellow and white glass represent the Holy Spirit and are encircled by darker panels of green, blue, gold, ochre, amber, sienna, grays, browns. At the base of the window rests the Bethlehem Font, a three-ton sandstone boulder from the Holy Land.
Photo courtesy Council for Places of Worship, London
Left: Several of the 198 separate panels of stained glass, set between deep stone mullions, that make up the baptistery window at Coventry Cathedral.

Above: The superbly balanced and delicately leaded design in Ludwig Schaffrath's "Labyrinth" window, set in a Gothic arch in St. Joseph Roman Catholic Parish Church in Aachen, Germany, leads to and from the cross above. The limited range of color—shades of stone gray and blues—intensifies the almost mystical centering focus of the design.
Photo by Inge Bartholome, from *Ludwig Schaffrath, Stained Glass and Mosaic,* © C. & R. Loo, Inc., Emeryville, Calif.

Above: The parallel leading in this stained glass window wall by Ludwig Schaffrath bears a close relationship to the banded ceiling of St. Martinus Roman Catholic Parish Church in Hagen, Germany.
Photo by Inge Bartholome, from *Ludwig Schaffrath, Stained Glass and Mosaic,* © C. & R. Loo, Inc., Emeryville, Calif.

buildings that had been leveled during the war. What resulted was a flowering of stained glass art that had been unparalleled in its vigor and originality since the thirteenth century, although quite different, of course, in style and content. It was aided by the cooper-ation between stained glass artists and those architects who were hospitable to glass art and understood its close relationship to architecture. This mutually dependent relationship has produced glass art that is an integral design and structural element, completely appropriate in scale and feeling to the architectural environment that contains it.

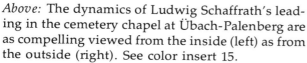

Above: The dynamics of Ludwig Schaffrath's leading in the cemetery chapel at Übach-Palenberg are as compelling viewed from the inside (left) as from the outside (right). See color insert 15.
Photos by Inge Bartholome, from *Ludwig Schaffrath, Stained Glass and Mosaic,* © C. & R. Loo, Inc., Emeryville, Calif.

Contemporary German glass has other distinctive characteristics. Lead lines, tolerated for so many centuries for their necessary support, now became as important as glass to the design. Parallel bands, straight or curvilinear, the undulating lines of spirals and snails, concentric and half circles, abstract shapes and geometrics—whatever the configuration of lead lines, they seem to have a rhythm, a calligraphy that is essential to the design and quite separate from their structural responsibilities. The composition of the lead lines is often so stunning that many stained glass windows become elegant linear sculptures when viewed from outside.

Accompanying the linearity of the leading, perhaps even the result of it, is a spareness of color. German glass has not so much a limited as a restrained palette. There is little contrast, little painting on glass, large areas of muted tones—blue, green, gray, tan monotones or related colors that seem to produce an interior light similar to medieval grisaille as they transmit the outside gray or blue sky and green grass. From inside, the neutral tones of the glass change with the seasons, and with the exterior scene, becoming brown, white, green, bright, as the seasons change, the sun shines. Most of the well-known contemporary German glass artists—Ludwig Schaffrath, Wilhelm Buschulte, Johannes Schreiter—work in this spare palette. Others, among them Dominikus Böhm and Heinz Bienefeld, reduce it still further, creating church windows out of rolled mechanical glass.

The superb matching of natural glass and lead in an architectural environment of appropriate scale has produced a body of glass art that seems to speak in a contemporary idiom. One senses in the elegant leading patterns a suggestion of traffic and movement, roads and routes, machinery and levers, pipes and productivity, the strata of the earth, albeit in the colors of the sky, serenity and quest—a curious amalgam of seemingly conflicting yet harmonious symbolism. "A mystical computer," as Narcissus Quagliata, a stained glass artist, said of Ludwig Schaffrath.

United States

After the dazzling triumphs of Tiffany glass in the secular world of decorative art, the best of American stained glass in the early twentieth century was found in Gothic-style cathedrals like St. John the Divine in New York City and in the Washington, D.C., Cathedral. They contain, for the most part, windows on familiar ecclesiastical themes by respected glass artists like Charles J. Connick, Henry Lee Willet, and Nicola D'Ascenzo, who worked in traditional techniques.

Since the middle of the century, however, American glass has flourished with astonishing vigor in new and inventive directions. One is in architectural-related slab glass construction, primarily in public buildings. Another is in the personal artistic expression of new young artists and their adventurous explorations in glass as an art form. Both directions are expanding the present boundaries of glasswork.

Slab glass—also called *dalle de verre,* which means "flagstones of glass"—utilizes cast glass almost an inch thick, which is cut in sections, sometimes chipped or faceted around its edges to increase the light refraction, then embedded in concrete, plaster, or epoxy. Its solidity and denseness make it an architectural element.

Although *dalle de verre* originated in Europe, one early building to use it in an original way was the First Presbyterian Church in Stamford, Conn. The structure forms the shape of a fish, an early Christian symbol, and its high gabled walls of precast concrete are studded with 20,000 pieces of faceted slab glass in a design by the respected French stained glass designer, Gabriel Loire, that represents the Resurrection and the Cru-

cifixion. Since the church was built, in 1958, many buildings—both religious and secular—have used this technique of setting thick slabs of glass in concrete or epoxy.

At the same time that slab glass is following an architectural mode, a more personal kind of stained glass is being revived. All across the country artists are doing interesting work in glass, and in northern California a group of artists, exuberantly reexamining traditional techniques, are creating what almost might be called an American school of stained glass. Although they are allied only in their support for each other and their com-

Below: The high gabled walls of the First Presbyterian Church in Stamford, Conn., constructed without piers or lintels in the symbolic shape of a fish, utilize inch-thick slab glass designed by Gabriel Loire as an essential construction element. Photo courtesy First Presbyterian Church, Stamford, Conn.

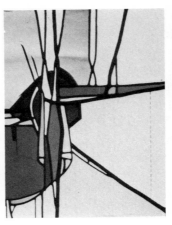

Above: "Fugue in Flow" (detail) by Beverly Reiser uses repeated configurations of fish and curvilinear leading to suggest motion and flow. The golden fish seem to swim in a blue-green sea, an illusion enhanced by the movement and color in the sky and trees beyond. The entire window is 3 by 9 feet.
Photo courtesy of the artist

Above left: In "Window for Buck Rogers," Elizabeth Quantock combines large flat areas of color with narrow bands of glass and a mix of wide and narrow leading (19 by 25 inches, 1974).
Photo courtesy of the artist

Above right: "Altarpiece," by Kathie Bunnell, is in a starkly modern idiom. The flames are double-glazed and sandblasted (23 by 39½ inches, 1977).
Photo courtesy of the artist

Left: Kathie Bunnell describes "Tears," a composition using opal grays of all tints and minimal color: "Like a folded paper with tears forming along the creases; the endless destruction of one thing giving way to another" (19 by 30 inches, 1975).
Photo courtesy of the artist

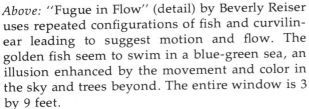

mon work, the glass art they produce shares certain characteristics. By and large, the glass is private rather than public (although stained glass commissions for public buildings are increasing); it is more likely to be autonomous panels—translucent artwork, so to speak—than architectural elements; and it is usually made by the artist rather than fabricated by a glass workshop.

The physical contact between artist and glass is a crucial element in this contemporary genre. When stained glass has an architectural or structural function, ordinarily there is a natural division of labor between the artist-designer and the artisan-fabricator. But when most of the work—or at least most of the experimental work—is not architectural, the stained glass is more likely to be produced by the artist himself, or at least under his close supervision. In fact, the physical handling of the glass and the understanding of its nature are, for many glass artists, such an important part of the artistic experience and the creative process that many of them construct all their work themselves—even those for architectural installation.

Close association with his materials inevitably leads a curious artist to new perceptions and fresh approaches to his subjects, and just this kind of searching characterizes West Coast glass. Optics, illusion, depth, light, reality, and the illusion of reality are all being explored, as well as new materials. Paul Marioni, one of the more daring and unorthodox artists, introduced automobile headlights, two-way mirrors that transmit outside light during the day but reflect inside light at night, photographic negatives, and a variety of other optical tricks. His glass portrait of Salvador Dali has a removable eye, a small working doorway in the throat, and Fresnel lenses for hair, which create the illusion of motion. In "Sink," blue-white glass represents the water stopped in a sink, but a plastic tube filled with real water forms the plumbing pipe below. Narcissus Quagliata laminates X rays between two thin sheets of clear glass in an artistic effort to reveal the inner structure of his subject.

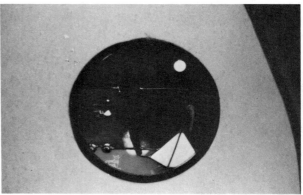

Top right: In "Howling at the Moon," Paul Marioni's personal iconography includes a pair of fake eyes-in-glasses, an egg, and a dog baying at the moon. The disembodied arm at the right can rotate and point to moon or pyramid, the circle at left holds a transparency of the whole surrealistic stained glass composition (see detail, center right), echoing itself through time and space. To expand spatial planes still further, a three-dimensional glass model of the pyramid (not shown) sits on a table in front of the stained glass window. From the collection of Sy and Theo Portnoy. See color insert 17.

Bottom right: "Farmer's Dream," Paul Marioni's composition in opaque glass, is mounted in a light box in the corner of a picture window. From the collection of Mr. and Mrs. Joseph S. Blank.

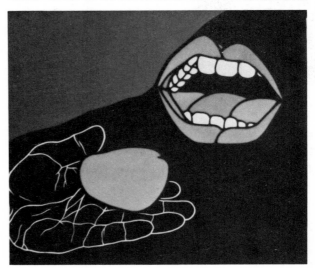

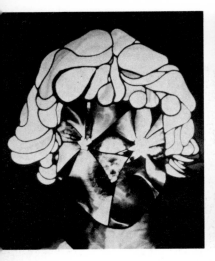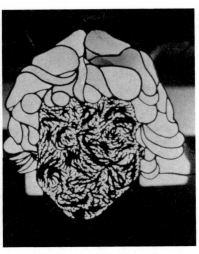

Above: Inspired by the writings of Carlos Castaneda and modeled on a portrait of a friend, Narcissus Quagliata explores materials and techniques in a series of portraits using almost identical cartoons. "Neil as Don Juan, A Portrait With Bones" (left) incorporates medical X rays; "Neil as Don Juan, A Portrait Without a Face" (right).
Photos courtesy of the artist, © Narcissus Quagliata, 1977

Depth as a dimension intrigues some artists. Judy Jansen, incorporating dimensional blown glass in flat leaded panels, adds the sense of touch to sight. Robert Kehlmann elevates wires and glass an inch or two above a flat panel, creating a relief that defines different levels. Peter Wickman incorporates slumped glass that he forms by firing glass sheets over clay shapes. Kristin Newton adds motion to dimension in a series of stained glass louvered windows designed to replace functional louvers; as the windows open and close, the colored layers overlap, creating a kinetic composition.

Almost alone among his contemporaries, Peter Mollica uses lead lines as graphic elements in nonrepresentational designs, following the German traditions of Thorn Prikker as well as Ludwig Schaffrath, with whom he studied. One of the few glass artists who learned his craft as an apprentice in a glass workshop, Mollica collaborates with architects and fabricators to realize his compositions, rather than making them himself. Ed Carpenter, another Schaffrath student, is primarily an architectural glass artist, and works closely with landscape designers as well as architects. His linear, abstract designs, like those of Schaffrath that they evoke, are as handsome viewed from outside as they are from inside. Casey Lewis, also influenced by the graphic possibilities of leading in contemporary glass, introduces enameled lead lines, colored on both sides of the glass assembly, that become compelling visual components whether the glass is seen from inside or outside.

No matter how far these artists stretch the horizons of their craft, they all share a basic respect for the integrity of the materials and for their physical properties. For Kathie Bunnell, glass, "the super-cooled liquid," has movement, change. Her compositions, fashioned with exacting care from often small and intricate shapes, coax the glass to reveal its own structure, as well as the changing scene beyond them. Combining glass of varied textures, juxtaposing opaque, translucent, and transparent glass, she heightens the sense of lyrical unfolding, of the mysteries of nature that seem to be an organic part of her compositions.

There are many possible reasons that this exuberant explosion of creativity is taking place on the West Coast. It may be because experimental environments flourish in that soil, or because of the keen interest in crafts, or because there is an easiness in abandoning old forms and trying out new ones.

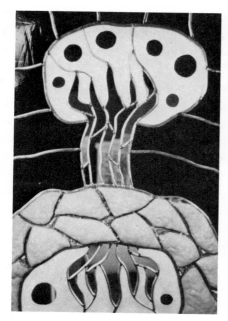  

Above left: "Ching/Tree-well" is an opaque wall piece utilizing stoneware relief and leaded black glass and mirror with sandblasted details to suggest that the roots of the tree in the earth are also the reflection of the branches in the well. By Beverly Reiser in collaboration with Anna de León, a ceramic sculptress; in the collection of William Henderson.
Photo courtesy of the artist

Above center: A detail of "Envisioning a Marriage" by Kathie Bunnell reveals the precision with which she works. The details on the fingers are etched, the nail sandblasted pink over clear glass, and the net foiled with narrow strips of opalescent glass, even to their knotted intersections. See color insert 16.
Photo courtesy of the artist

Above right: "Tassajara Creek" is Kathie Bunnell's impression of a creekbed in midsummer with stones, sycamore roots, small plants, and flowing water, using antique, opal, opalescent, and clear glass (22 by 27 inches, 1973).
Photo by Dan Fenton, courtesy of the artist

Perhaps it is the quality of the light, or simply that a few enterprising artists and craftsmen turned to this medium, saw in it a great potential for artistic expression, and attracted colleagues who shared their enthusiasm.

One who came to stained glass early was Narcissus Quagliata, at a time—the late 1960s—when only a small group of artists were working in glass, among them Kathie Bunnell, Paul Marioni, and Peter Mollica. In many ways Quagliata seems prototypical of the varied, sometimes conflicting characteristics of contemporary glass artists and the new directions the art is taking. Like most of his colleagues, he came to stained glass accidentally. Quagliata learned the rudimentary techniques at a stained glass hobby course, others picked it up in books, from friends, several were artisans in the apprentice tradition, but no one learned formally in art or architecture classes.

For Quagliata, glass has both liquidity and brittleness, seemingly contradictory properties that he incorporates in his designs. He loves to represent the human body with large sheets of glass and often with erotic

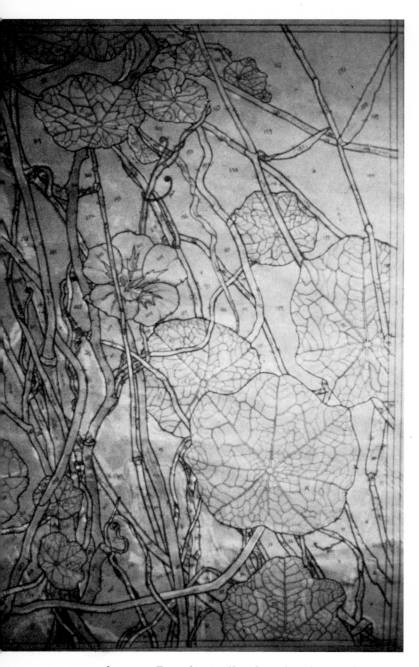

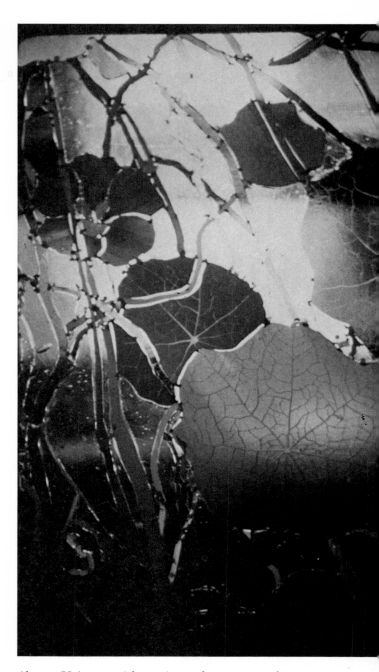

shapes. Paradoxically, he also loves the way glass breaks and uses the shatter lines to add tension and interest to a design. Sometimes he breaks glass randomly, using the accidentally formed shards in a composition in which

Above: Using a wide variety of opaque and transparent glass, Kathie Bunnell interprets a caterpillar's view of nasturtiums. The working drawing is at left, a detail of the work in progress at right. Details on leaves and petals were sandblasted (1977). Photos courtesy of the artist

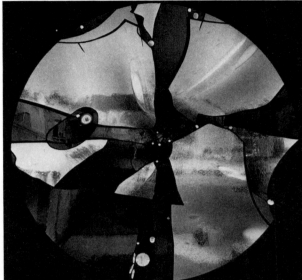

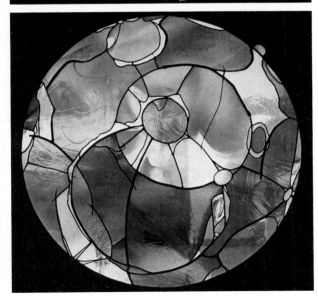

Left: Like portholes to outer space to delight young students, three stained glass windows in the Commodore Sloat Elementary School Media Center by Narcissus Quagliata represent, from left to right, "A Galaxy," "Jupiter," and "Moon" (top). The artist chose the glass, then designed "A Galaxy" for the imagery he saw in it (center). Well-designed leading gives dimension to "Moon," and well-chosen glass suggests the texture of a moonscape (bottom). See color insert 18. Photo (top) © Narcissus Quagliata (center and bottom) by Bill Kane, all courtesy of the artist

the glass dictates the design rather than the artist imposing the design on the material. Embodying both types of contemporary American glass art, at times he functions as a studio artist, creating large figure panels, transparent artwork that disregards any particular setting or space; at other times he works as a glass muralist, creating architectural walls of light for public and private environments.

These two paths surely presage the future. For the stained glass artist, the medium is slowly evolving into a serious art form. Art galleries and museums are starting to mount contemporary stained glass shows. Great museums already have collections of medieval glass, and occasionally a museum will buy the glasswork of a contemporary artist who has earned his reputation in another medium. Soon, perhaps, museums will start to collect contemporary glass seriously.

At the same time, stained glass is gaining acceptance by architects and planners as an integral element of construction, as a window treatment worthy of commission. Architects are beginning to understand the contribution stained glass can make to public and private environments, bringing color and greater visual pleasure to living and working spaces. For the American Airlines Terminal at John F.

Above: The stained glass images of breaking water, by Narcissus Quagliata for the entry in a Mill Valley, Calif., residence, sweep from a horizontal to a vertical panel, so a visitor enters the house as if under a wave. The reflection of light through leaves enhances the sea foam associations. The artist explains that the design is meant to suggest both the liquidity and brittleness of the material, glass under stress, "as if I made a window, then broke it and used the shatter lines in the design" (6 by 11 feet, 1976–77).
Photo courtesy of the artist

Opposite: A large stained glass window, about 15 feet wide and 12 feet high, by Marc Chagall for the United Nations building in New York depicts themes of peace and man in all shades of blue. It honors Dag Hammarskjöld and the fifteen who died with him in a plane crash in 1961.
Photo courtesy United Nations/Nagata

Kennedy Airport in New York, for example, Robert Sowers created a vast wall of glass—317 feet wide and 23 feet high—of two-way coated glass that can be viewed from both sides, an abstract design in strong color suggesting the power and motion of a jet-age transportation terminal. For the KLM Royal Dutch Airlines office in New York City, Gyorgy Kepes designed a slab glass mosaic that recalls the far-off lights of a night flight when lit from behind.

Glass art is an invigorating medium now. There is no nostalgia for the past as those who work with glass are testing its limits and investigating the qualities of translucency, transparency, and opacity. Stretching its boundaries, in the center of an age of technical exploration, they are examining refinements in etching on glass; sandblasting; laminating foreign objects between clear or translucent sheets of glass; combining glass with mosaics, with mirrors; painting on both sides of glass; gluing glass compositions to plate glass, eliminating the need for a metal structure entirely.

For hobbyists no less than for professionals, stained glass offers an excitement in its discovery. For the neophyte, it also offers the beguiling inspiration that many of the most vigorous glass artists of our time also started out untutored and lacking in technical skills and knowledge of the medium. The next section, "Working in Stained Glass," is one way to begin.

Above: Almost one thousand separate lights make up this massive wall of glass at John F. Kennedy International Airport, held in a welded steel frame cushioned against sonic booms. The abstract design by Robert Sowers is made of two-way coated glass for interior and exterior viewing.
Photo courtesy American Airlines

Some interesting twentieth-century glass:

ENGLAND:
    Coventry Cathedral

FRANCE:
    Assy. Notre Dame de Toute Grâce—
        Chagall, Rouault
    Audincourt. Church of the Sacred Heart—
        Léger
    Metz Cathedral—Chagall, Villon
    Paris. Musée des Arts Decoratifs
    Paris. Church of St.-Séverin—Jean Ba-
        zaine
    Reims Cathedral—Chagall, Charles Marq
    Ronchamp. Church of Notre Dame du
        Haut—Le Corbusier

Varangeville. Chapel of St.-Dominique—
Braque

Vence. Chapel of the Holy Rosary—Matisse

GERMANY:

Aachen Cathedral—Schaffrath, Wendling

Aachen. Maria-Rast Priest House—
Schaffrath

Aachen. St. Joseph—Schaffrath

Bad Zwischenahn. St. Marien—Schaffrath

Bonn. St. Winfried—Schaffrath

Cologne Cathedral—Thorn Prikker

Cologne. St. Christoph—Meistermann

Cologne. St. Clemens—Buschulte

Cologne. Church of St. Maria-Königen—
mechanical glass by Böhm in baptistery; Böhm and Bienefeld in nave

Cologne. St. Marien—Meistermann

Cologne. St. Ursula—Buschulte

Essen Minster—Buschulte, Manessier,
Schaffrath, Schreiter

Hagen. Karl Ernst Osthausen Museum—
Thorn Prikker

Hagen. Railway Station—Thorn Prikker

Hagen. St. Antonius—Schaffrath

Leutesdorf-am-Rhein. Cloister Chapel,
Order of St. John—Schreiter

Merkstein. St. Thekla—Schaffrath

Neuss. Christ Church—Thorn Prikker

Schweinfurt. St. Kilian—Meistermann

Schweinfurt. St. Michael—Schaffrath

Wegberg. St. Peter and Paul—Buschulte

Würzburg Cathedral—Meistermann,
Schaffrath

Übach-Palenberg. Cemetery Chapel—
Schaffrath

Übach-Palenberg. Public pool—
Schaffrath

ISRAEL:

Jerusalem. Hadassah-Hebrew Medical
Center—Chagall

UNITED STATES:

Bridgeport, Calif. Mono County Court-
house—Ed Carpenter

Carmel, Calif. All Saints Episcopal
Church—Mark Adams

Columbia, Mo. Stephens College—Paul
Marioni, Robert Sowers

Greenwich, Conn. Temple Shalom—
Robert Sowers

Lake Oswego, Oregon. Christ Episcopal
Church—Ed Carpenter

Muir Beach, Calif. Zen Center—Kathie
Bunnell

New York, N.Y. Kennedy International
Airport. American Airlines Terminal—Robert Sowers

New York, N.Y. United Nations Secretar-
iat building—Chagall

North Tarrytown, N.Y. Union Church of
Pocantico Hills—Chagall, Matisse

San Francisco, Calif. Salvation Army
Chapel—Judy Raffael

Stamford, Conn. First Presbyterian
Church—Gabriel Loire

PART 2

WORKING IN STAINED GLASS

The Glass-Working Techniques

The two principal glass-working techniques—lead and copper foil—each have their special ways of holding pieces of glass together. These are explained in detail in subsequent chapters. But before you turn to the special techniques involved in each process, it is helpful to have a general understanding of the differences between them, of the kinds of projects and designs each is best suited to, and of the various skills each demands. The two techniques offer quite different opportunities, and a thoughtful glass artisan will match the strengths of each technique to the requirements of the design and the project.

For centuries, leading has been the traditional way to assemble pieces of glass. The relatively thick lead strips hold the flat glass sections in channels, their heavy dark lines boldly punctuating areas within the composition. The leads are an integral part of the design, providing linearity and visual strength, as well as an essential part of the structure. Since even the narrowest of lead strips is still fairly wide, tending to overwhelm small pieces of glass with its bulk, leading is scaled for larger pieces of glass and is more effective with and appropriate to strong simple designs.

At the beginning of the twentieth century, copper foil was introduced to do the same structural job with greater delicacy of line.

The snugly nesting pieces of foil-wrapped glass, the narrow margins of copper along the glass edges, and the flexibility of the foil, which can follow faithfully any angle or curve of glass, make copper foil superbly suited to designs of great delicacy and intricacy. And because small irregular nuggets of glass are so easily utilized, color and texture in dazzling juxtaposition can be easily incorporated into a composition.

In addition to stylistic considerations, the demands of the project itself often dictate your choice of technique. For example, exterior window panels are leaded because the putty that cushions the glass in its lead frame also creates the necessary weatherproof seal. A similar waterproofing compound is not commonly applied to foiled projects because it may undermine the bond between foil and glass, exposing the copper-foiled seams to penetration by weather.

Lead, however, melts at a much lower temperature than copper foil, making lead unsuitable for a fire screen. Moreover, despite its visual bulk, lead is not as strong as soldered foil and has a tendency to stretch if not handled carefully. This makes lead less desirable in some three-dimensional projects—certain styles of lamp shades, for instance—where the weight of many pieces of glass might cause the leaded piece eventually to sag and release its grip on the glass.

Copper foil, on the other hand, is superbly suited to multiglass constructions, especially the domed shapes characteristic of Tiffany-type shades, where the light weight and delicate lines of the foil skeleton belie the strength of its soldered seams. (Actually, it is the solder rather than the foil that holds the pieces of glass together, the foil merely providing the route for the solder to follow.)

If the project or your design does not immediately suggest the preferred use of lead or copper foil, you may be influenced by one or more of the following considerations.

For beginners a piece of glass is easier to wrap in copper foil than in lead came, but each glass section must be cut and trimmed precisely to its pattern in order for the contiguous foiled pieces to fit tightly together. In a leaded project, the jagged or unevenly cut edges of a novice glass cutter can be hidden under the flanges of the lead channels.

A foiled project is more expensive than a leaded one of the same design. Although the foil itself is cheaper than the lead came, all the foiled surfaces must be covered with solder—actually, they are covered twice—and the solder is expensive. Lead came is soldered once and only at its joints.

Foiled projects require more soldering skill than do leaded ones—first, because they require soldering along the entire length of the foiled seams, whereas the leading only requires spot soldering at the intersections; and second, because the continuous soldered line must form a neatly rounded ridge of unbroken beading. However, the foil, which melts at a high temperature, is never in danger of being burned by an overheated soldering iron as is lead, which has a much lower melting point.

Finally, if you are confident of your glass-cutting and soldering skills, you may find it more congenial to work with copper foil because you can move back and forth from one stage of work to another, a luxury rarely possible with leaded projects. For instance, in a leaded piece you should cut all your glass pieces before assembling them in a particular and logical order. With a foiled project, you can cut some glass sections, wrap them in foil, even solder small segments together and then go back and cut glass for an entirely different area, thus providing a choice of tasks to suit your mood.

As you read the following chapters on working with lead, with copper foil, and with solder, you will quickly become familiar with both techniques, with their limitations and their possibilities, and with the circumstances in which you may want to use one or the other. But basic to them both is an understanding of how to work with glass, and this starts with designing for stained glass.

Designing for Stained Glass

As with all creative efforts, designing for stained glass rests on a thorough understanding of the medium—the characteristics of different kinds of glass, of the metals that hold them together, and of what is—and what is not—possible within the boundaries of the raw materials. Sharing with other art forms the considerations of line, form, texture, color, and perspective, stained glass design in addition involves light in a palpable way. Beyond the nature of the materials that form it and how they are put together, stained glass responds to its setting in a unique way. Because it transmits light, it exists not only by itself but in relation to its environment. The same stained glass panel can glow incandescently as the diffused light of late afternoon illumines the glass encased in its dark metal skeleton, it can glare with brilliance in the direct light of morning, or it can wash out into flat pieces of colored glass held by grayish metal bars at night when artificial light falls on its interior surface, robbing it of all mystery.

Many elements interact with each other in a glass composition. Glass involves light and opacity, texture as well as color. Lead or soldered foil involves weight, linearity, and the dynamics of line and density. And when all these relationships have been resolved, the design for a stained glass composition rests finally on the question: Can it be executed—or, at least, can it be done easily enough for your skills?

Light

The quality of the light is an important element in the finished stained glass, and it derives from the kind of light transmitted, from the areas of glass, their size and placement. This light originates from a source behind the glass and can be artificial or natural. Artificial light is constant, always illuminating and projecting the same image; natural light is never constant, always changing and alive, continually altering the visual quality of the glass through which it passes as it catches different textures and relationships at different moments.

Other considerations influence the design: How much light do you want to pass through the glass? How much of the outside scene do you want to see? Do you prefer clear visibility or a muted image? These are some of the questions that dictate the opacity, translucence, or transparency of the glass you will use, where you will place it, and the intensity of the colors.

Color

Hand in hand with light goes color, which transmits its visual impact not only through hue, but also through saturation (the vividness or intensity of the color) and brilliance (the lightness or darkness of a color, sometimes called value). Moreover, the area of a color and each color's relationship to all the others are important factors in the design equation. As you test glass colors in juxtaposition with each other, you will find that the eye more easily tolerates larger expanses of some colors than others—that a small amount of red, for example, has a visual impact far exceeding its size, that certain colors next to each other actually seem to form a third color optically, that certain colors appear more soothing to the eye than others. Even though color in glass introduces the additional element of light, an understanding of the relationships among colors is critical to designing, and ready access to a color wheel is helpful (see Figure 1, next page).

As you work out your design ideas, you can fill in areas of color with crayons or watercolor, or cut shapes out of colored paper. These methods are helpful in seeing the relationships among shapes, colors, and areas, but they cannot, of course, help you gauge the ultimate luminosity of the stained glass. For this you must move to glass samples, once you have a general idea of your colors.

You will find it most productive to work with samples of the actual glass you are considering. Try out different combinations on a

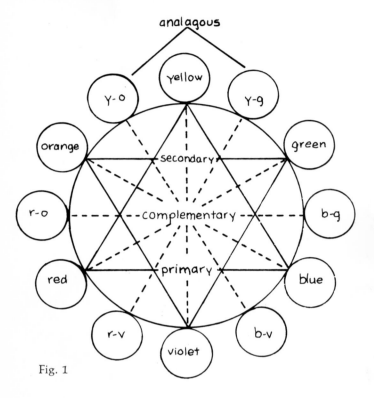

Fig. 1

light box or on a glass easel held against a window, testing contiguous areas of color and then putting together larger units of colored glass for cumulative effects. Move the glass samples around, experimenting with all sorts of relationships, testing colors not only side by side but overlapping them to create new colors (you can assemble glass in two layers). Make your color choices carefully. This is, of course, one of the most essential elements on which the success of your design rests.

Line

While light and color derive from the glass components, line as a design element is formed by the metal skeleton—be it lead or copper foil—which holds the glass in place.

Not merely an essential support, it is an important component to be considered as much for its design as for its structural contribution.

By your choice of the width and placement of the metal strips, you can define shapes, suggest moods, create dynamic tensions. Take a tree trunk, for example. You can plan it as one piece of glass (see Figure 2); you can divide the trunk vertically to suggest height and elevation (see Figure 3); you can separate the trunk into horizontal sections, into the rings of an aging tree, as it were, to suggest permanence and longevity or to designate a particular type of tree (see Figure 4).

As you plan the structure of the design components, then combine them into a unified whole, you will see that a well-conceived metal structure will lead the eye from one area to another in the composition, visually supporting the design without competing for attention.

Tips and Reminders for Designing Stained Glass

• Design your projects according to your ability as a glass cutter. Start with designs that incorporate fairly straight cuts, then add more complex shapes—inside curves, points—as you become more proficient.

• When planning your first projects, limit the number of glass pieces to ten to twenty, then work up to about fifty pieces per project. Any project requiring more than 100 pieces of glass is a long-term commitment.

• Design each color area—that is, each piece of glass—with no more than five cuts

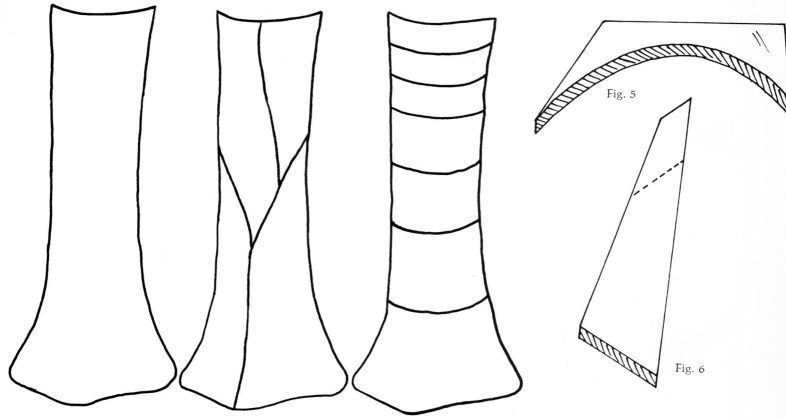

Fig. 2　　　　　　Fig. 3　　　　　　Fig. 4

Fig. 5

Fig. 6

per piece. Any more cuts in one piece will create stress and weaken the glass.

• Plan for relatively small pieces of glass— but no smaller than 1 by 1½ inches. Small pieces are easier to cut than large ones; the cuts are shorter, giving you more control and placing less stress on the glass. Moreover, if you make a mistake, you can replace a small piece of glass more easily.

• Be adventurous about incorporating all kinds of different glass in your designs, especially if you are a novice. In this way you can become familiar with the many beautiful types of glass that are available and at the same time focus your design on the color and texture of the glass rather than on the intricacy of the shapes, even allowing the char-

acter of the glass to suggest the design.

• Avoid shapes with sharp angles or deep curves cut out of them (see Figure 5). Angles will probably snap and must be strengthened across the weak point; curves are hard to cut, as you will see in the chapter "Working with Glass."

• As a beginner, try to avoid narrow points in your composition. Not only are they hard to cut—they often splinter around the tip—but they are difficult to lead or foil without losing most of the point under the solder. If long, narrow pieces are an important part of your design, plan a reinforcing lead or copper foil strip across the weak area which will carry out the thrust of the design (see Figure 6).

• Plan the lead or copper foil skeleton in

proportion to the areas of glass. In general, large pieces of glass call for wider lead cames or foil strips, small pieces of glass call for narrower metal supports.

• Within the bounds of appropriate scale combine wide and narrow leads or copper strips for visual interest and variety.

• As you carefully design a metal skeleton to unify the composition, don't be tempted to converge too many lines at one point. Since each joint must be soldered, rather than simplifying the design, you may be creating a mass of solder that obscures the clarity of individual lines (see Figure 7a). If your composition requires the joining of several lines, move some of them slightly away from the central point; you will find that your eye will usually make the visual connection even when the actual metal does not (see Figure 7b).

• If your glass design is spare—for example, clear glass panes of identical shape—consider using beaded or ornamental leads. In such panels, a decorative metal façade would enhance the essential simplicity of the design. In more complex designs, however, an ornamental metal face would unintentionally divert attention from the glass.

• When drawing up a design, plan for exactly the type of construction you will use. For example, if you include reinforced lead strips in any part of the design, remember that it has a much thicker core than other leads and that it will not bend as easily. If you brace a project with reinforcing bars, note their placement as you work out the initial design and try to locate them where they will be relatively unnoticed.

• Sketch your design ideas with charcoal, rubbing out the lines and forms you have discarded and spraying with a fixative those

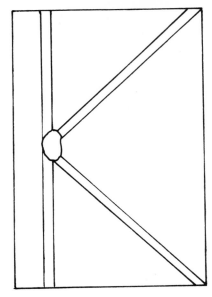

Fig. 7a

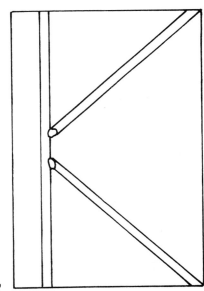

Fig. 7b

areas you want to retain. When you finally arrive at a pleasing design, you will see how to turn it into working drawings in the next chapter.

A feeling for the design of stained glass grows naturally with experience. Each project you work on, each piece you view helps sharpen and train your eye and your sense of color, and makes you more certain of what makes a good composition and how to blend the different elements together. Meanwhile, to help you gain this familiarity, work with the designs and components in Part III, "Stained Glass Designs."

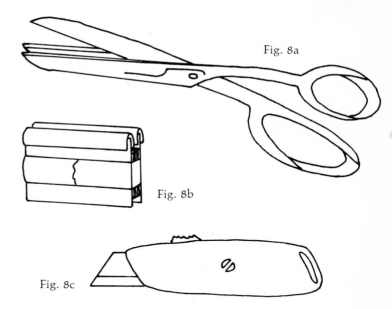

Fig. 8a

Fig. 8b

Fig. 8c

From Design to Working Drawings

Tools and Supplies

Medium-weight white paper for the cartoon, the project-size design.

Oak tag for the cutting pattern. You can substitute another material, such as a manila file folder, as long as it is thin enough to slip under the housing of the glass cutter, sturdy enough to guide the cutting wheel without bending or crumpling as the wheel rides against its edges, and a little larger than the project. Professionals use 90-pound Kraft paper.

Brown wrapping paper on which to trace the assembly diagram. Professionals use 30-pound Kraft paper.

Carbon paper, preferably as large as your project.

Masking tape or *push pins* with which to secure the sandwich of oak tag, brown

wrapping paper, carbon paper, and cartoon as the design is being traced.

Pattern shears to cut out the glass patterns when you are making a leaded project. Its double blades remove a strip of paper $1/16$ inch wide to allow for the heart of the lead strip that will hold the glass (see Figure 8a). You can improvise your own double-bladed cutter by taping two single-edged razor blades on either side of a $1/16$-inch-thick cardboard spacer (see Figure 8b).

Scissors or *mat knife* (see Figure 8c) to cut out the patterns when the glass pieces will be held by copper foil, which is so thin you need not compensate for it in the assembly diagram.

Straightedge, T square, or *right angle* to help you line up the outside dimensions.

The Cartoon

Whether you use a design from Part III or create one of your own, all stained glass work starts with a project-size design called a cartoon. The cartoon is the master blueprint that designates all necessary information for making the stained glass project: the shape and color of each piece of glass, the lines for the lead strips or copper foil. It is the guide for tracing both the cutting pattern and assembly diagram. The cartoon itself is kept for future reference or for making duplicate projects.

To transform your design into a cartoon, it must, first of all, be the same size as your contemplated project. If it is not already project size, scale it up by the box method or by photostating. Both techniques are described in "Enlarging the Design," page 179.

Now number each area of glass. This is good housekeeping with any project, since it will help you keep track of the individual components, and a necessity if your design includes a great many pieces or if they are similar in shape or size. You can number these areas in any sequence, but it will be more helpful if you can number them in the general order in which the glass pieces will be assembled. If your project is rectangular, start numbering in the lower left-hand corner and then fan out to the right and up; if you are making a free-form project, start the numbering at a central piece and then branch out around it. Follow this procedure whether you are planning to lead up your design or use copper foil.

In addition to numbering each area on the cartoon, you should also indicate the type of glass that will fill it. One easy way is to devise a color code that denotes the hue, tint, and opacity of each piece of glass. For example, you can use a letter to note the color, as R for red, G for green; a numbered scale from 1 to 5 designating light to dark; and perhaps Roman numerals to distinguish among opaque, translucent, and transparent glass. You can

devise even more specific codes if you wish, but for basic reference you need no more than the color, tint, and type of glass.

If you are working with copper foil, your cartoon as marked carries all the necessary information for assembling the project. Because copper foil is so thin, the same lines on the cartoon designate both the cut lines for each piece of glass and the assembly lines after each piece of glass has been wrapped in foil—that is, each piece of cut glass will fit its designated area on the cartoon both before and after it has been wrapped in foil.

This is not the case if you will be using lead strips to assemble your project. Each lead strip has, by its nature, a heart or core of specific thickness which separates one piece of glass from another, as well as a flange or lip which covers a narrow edge of the glass it holds. Thus, the "sight" line, or the edge of the glass that is visible, is smaller than the "cut" line, the actual size of the glass, and these are both smaller than the "full-size" line showing the overall dimensions of the project (see Figure 9). The exact placement of these lines depends on the particular lead strips you will use: the sight line on the width of the flange; the cut line on the thickness of the heart of the lead; and the full-size line on the

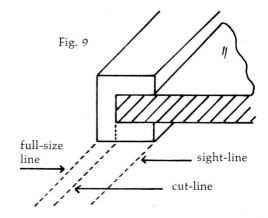

Fig. 9

full-size line

sight-line

cut-line

dimensions of the face of the lead (see Figure 10). These three perimeter lines—the sight line, the cut line, and the full-size line—are essential guides during the leading up of rectangular panels and must be designated on the cartoon; however, they are not needed for leading up free-form designs. (The leading-up process is fully explained in the chapter "Working with Lead.")

Tracing the Cutting Pattern and Assembly Diagram

All the information on the cartoon—including, of course, the design itself—must now be transferred to a cutting pattern from which you will cut each piece of glass and to an assembly diagram on which you will assemble your project. To do this, make a "sandwich" for tracing, as follows.

Lay the oak tag for the cutting pattern on your worktable, or on any flat surface.

Cover the oak tag with a sheet of carbon paper, carbon side down. If one sheet of car-

bon paper doesn't cover the design, tape several sheets together as needed.

Over the carbon paper lay a sheet of brown wrapping paper, which will become the assembly diagram.

Cover the brown wrapping paper with a second layer of carbon paper, carbon side down, piecing several sheets together if necessary.

Over this layer of carbon paper lay the cartoon, design side up, and tape or pin the sandwich to your work surface so none of the components shifts (see Figure 11).

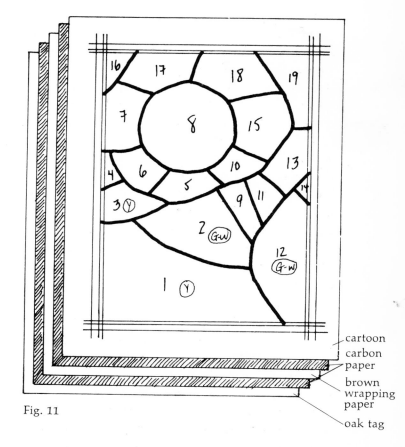

Fig. 11

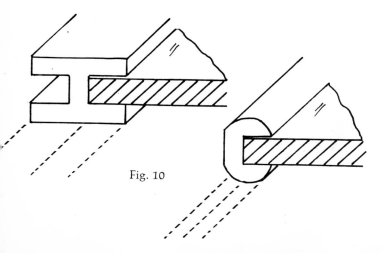

Fig. 10

With a pen or sharp pencil go over all the lines on the cartoon, pressing hard enough to transfer the impression to the brown paper assembly diagram and on down to the oak tag cutting pattern. Be sure to trace the three perimeter lines around the border and the number and color code for each area of glass. Use a straightedge, T square, or right angle to draw the border guidelines accurately.

Disassemble the tracing sandwich. Lay the cartoon on a board or in a tray and set aside the assembly diagram while you divide the cutting pattern into its component parts.

The Cutting Pattern

Using a pair of regular scissors, carefully cut the design on the border cut line, the middle of the three parallel perimeter lines. If the design is a square or rectangle, you may want to make these cuts using a single-edged razor or mat knife against a straightedge rather than with scissors (see Figure 12); if you use a knife or razor, cushion the cutting pattern on several sheets of newsprint or corrugated board. You will note that the outside perimeter line—the full-size line—will fall away as you cut; it is not needed for this process, nor is the remaining inside perimeter line—the sight line—which you can ignore (see Figure 12).

If you are working with copper foil, continue to use the regular scissors to cut out all the individual pieces of the pattern. You can use a mat knife if you prefer, cutting the oak tag on a bed of newsprint.

If you plan to assemble your project with lead strips, cut the component paper patterns apart with pattern shears, which will automatically remove a thin strip of paper that

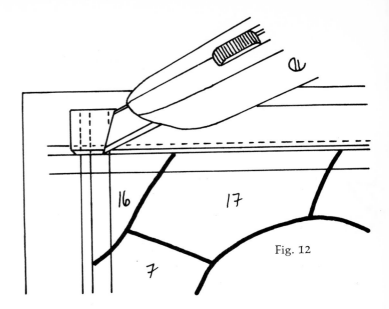

Fig. 12

allows for the heart of the lead. Hold the oak tag near the joint of the blades and make short cutting motions rather than long cuts with the length of the blades; center the shears over each line (see Figure 13).

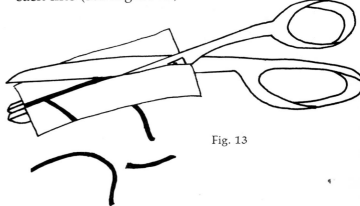

Fig. 13

You can remove the same strip of paper from the cutting pattern with the razor blades taped together around the 1/16-inch-wide cardboard spacer. Lay the cutting pattern on several thicknesses of newsprint or corrugated board, center the double blades over the cut line, and hold the tool at an angle as you bite into the oak tag (see Figure 14).

If you have a steady hand, you can even

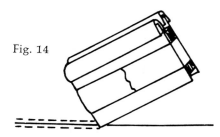

Fig. 14

cut the paper strips with regular scissors, making two parallel cuts ¹/₁₆ inch apart on either side of the cut lines, and letting the thin strips between them fall away (see Figure 15). This is a time-consuming and less accurate method of preparing the paper patterns, but it can be done. In fact, in the project-size components and designs in Part III the heavy lines that define all glass areas are exactly ¹/₁₆ inch wide for this purpose.

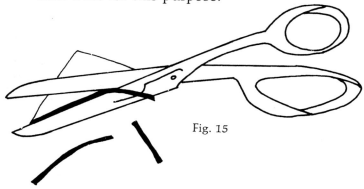

Fig. 15

As you cut out each paper pattern, lay it in place on the cartoon, matching its identifying number to the master number on the cartoon. The paper patterns for a foiled project will fit together snugly like a jigsaw puzzle, but each pattern for a leaded project will be surrounded by a thin gap—in fact, you should see the original cut lines marked between each paper pattern—representing the heart of the lead strips that will hold the glass pieces together (see Figure 16).

When all the paper patterns are cut and laid over the cartoon, check each piece carefully to see that it is the proper shape and

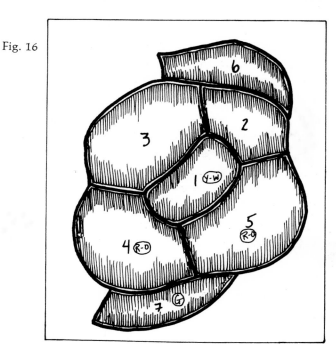

Fig. 16

size. For foiled projects, the pieces must nest tightly together, for leaded projects contiguous patterns must have enough room between them to allow for the lead strips. If any pattern is improperly cut, now is the time to replace it. Since each piece of glass will be cut from and exactly match its pattern, any mistakes in the pattern will be passed along to the corresponding piece of glass.

Working with Glass

Glass, of course, is the primary ingredient, so familiarity with the kinds available is essential, as is an understanding of the ways in which it can be used and the effects it can achieve. When you select glass, you should consider many things. Will it be seen through bright light or in a shady area? Do you want to blunt the bright rays of the sun or capture all available light? Do you want to view a handsome scene through the glass? Hide an unattractive view outside? Preserve your privacy inside? If you are a beginner, do you want to limit yourself to easily cut glass? An understanding of the different types of glass will help you choose materials that will solve your design problems and contribute to the success of your project.

Types of Glass

The two kinds of glass most generally used in stained glass work are hand-blown, or "antique," glass, and machine-made, or rolled, glass. Hand-blown glass is usually imported, the sheets of glass are smaller and more expensive than machine-made glass, and their irregularities in texture and thickness provide greater richness and aesthetic interest. Hand-blown glass has a softer surface than machine-made glass, which makes it easier to cut. Either type can be used with lead or copper foil. Both are available in a dazzling variety of textures, patterns, and colors.

Whether blown by hand or rolled by machine, the glass is colored during its manufacture by the addition of varying amounts and proportions of metal oxides such as cobalt, copper, chromium, manganese, selenium, and even gold. In no sense is the glass "stained" after it is produced. Most glass is one color, with the color spread throughout the glass. In machine-made glass, the color is uniform. In hand-blown glass, despite the uniform density of color through the glass, the same sheet will appear to have darker and lighter areas if the thickness of the sheet varies.

Antique Glass

Named not for its age but for its process of manufacture, antique glass was first introduced in the nineteenth century. It is made by what is believed to be the same method used to produce glass for medieval stained glass windows. The glass is blown into a large cylindrical bubble with a blow pipe, the cylinder is cut off at both ends, then slit down one side. The resulting tube—or muff, as it is called—is subjected to slow, gentle heat in an annealing oven, which causes it to flatten into a sheet of glass after several hours. The glass produced by this method is extremely beautiful, with crystal clarity, brilliance, translucence, and rich vivid colors. Its characteristic bubbles, striations, and imperfections catch and reflect light, providing richness and dimension.

Most antique glass is made in Germany, France, and England. German and French sheets are not uniform in thickness within each sheet; English glass is usually thicker than both and more expensive. The only American antique glass is made by Blenko and has even greater variations within a sheet. If you are using lead strips to assemble the project, you may not be able to use the same size lead for the thicker and thinner sheets of glass, which may vary from less than $\frac{1}{8}$ inch to over $\frac{1}{4}$ inch.

Pot glass refers to glass that is one color throughout (although all glass is colored in the pot and could legitimately be called pot glass).

Streaky glass combines two or more colors in the sheet in wonderful patterns and swirls.

Flashed glass is a double layer of hand-blown glass comprising a thicker base that is usually clear or lightly colored glass and a thinner veneer of a brighter color. Light passing through the double layer mixes the two colors visually. Red is the most commonly flashed color, appearing on a base of clear, yellow, blue, rose, light green, or deep blue; blue and green are also flashed occasionally. Opaline glass is flashed with opal, but this is not the same as opalescent glass (although both use the same mineral—opal—to achieve an iridescent effect). The flashed layer can be etched, engraved, or even sandblasted to produce interesting designs, or to incise a legend or dedication, a name or date.

Seedy glass is punctuated by tiny bubbles that catch and scatter light. It is made by blowing the molten glass before the silica sand, borax, and pot color have become completely refined.

Reamy glass, primarily made in England and in Germany, where it is called Danziger Glas, has a swirling surface and usually comes in light colors.

Sanded glass is sprinkled with small indentations formed by cooling the glass sheets on iron tables that have been sanded.

Striated glass is formed during the blowing process by twisting the molten ball of glass in a special bowl lined with spikes.

Crackle glass has a webbed pattern created by dipping the hot glass briefly into water.

Machine-made Glass

There are two general types of machine-made glass—transparent glass, which is called "cathedral," and a translucent mar-

bleized glass called "opalescent." Both types are of fairly uniform texture and thickness, usually about 1/8 inch thick, and are available in much larger sheets than antique glass.

Cathedral glass has a medium hard cutting surface. One side (the cutting side) of the glass is smooth, the other is usually textured with one of various patterns that diffuse and scatter the light passing through. These patterns, impressed on the glass while it is hot by metal rollers, often have descriptive names: *hammered* has a pebbly pattern; *granite* a dense texture; *seedy,* also called *seedy marine antique,* incorporates air bubbles; *double rolled* has two smooth sides. Other textures are called *oceanic, ripple, moss, figure C, antique, Florentine,* and *Flemish.*

Although not every texture is available in every color, you will find machine-made glass commonly made in semibrilliant hues—blue, green, amber, red, yellow, purple; in tints of green, amber, purple, and blue; and in black, white, gray, brown, orange, flesh pink, and crystal clear.

Opalescent glass is the hardest of the machine-made glasses, and this makes it the most difficult to cut. Most opalescents are smooth on both sides, but some are available with a light-diffusing pattern on one side that is called *granite.* Don't confuse these machine-rolled opalescents with the glorious hand-made opalescent glass that Tiffany made famous, nor with hand-blown opal-flashed glass.

Machine-made opalescents usually mix white with one or more colors such as amber, greens, blues, blue/green, purple, pink, yellow, red/orange, as well as making tones of milk white, bone beige, honey, brown, green/amber, and red/orange. Some opalescents are virtually opaque. The colors in imported opalescent glass are often softer and more glowing than those in domestic opalescents.

Miscellaneous Kinds of Glass

Rondels are circles of glass made by spinning glass bubbles on a rod until the centrifugal force opens them into flat disks. The surface of a machine-made rondel is smoother than that of a hand-blown rondel, which has a center mark where the rod has been broken off. These disks come in various colors and sizes.

Jewels are small decorative forms used singly or in combinations, particularly in lamp shades and jewelry. They are hand-pressed or machine-made in a variety of colors and shapes—square, diamond, oval, rectangular, circular, even fanciful shapes that simulate apples and pears—and are often impressed with a design. They can be translucent or opaque, faceted or unfaceted.

Globs are smooth nuggets of colored glass, varying in size from about ⅜ inch to 1⅛ inches and in shape from round to oval. They are used to represent berries, flower centers, or any other circular object in a design. They are sold by the piece or by the pound, with a pound containing about 400 of the smallest or about twenty-five of the largest-size globs.

Mirrored glass, often used in boxes and panels as well as in mirrors, is commonly available in green, bronze, and deep gray as well as silver, and in single thickness (¹⁄₁₆ inch) and double thickness (⅛ inch).

Window glass, the most common type of glass, is ¹⁄₁₆ inch thick (single-strength glass) or ⅛ inch thick (double-strength glass) and

graded A or B. For stained glass work use the thicker glass for its additional strength and because it will fit the channels of the lead strips better.

Plate glass is a smooth glass of uniform thickness, ground and polished on both sides, that is used for large areas of glass in home and commercial installations because it is essentially free of distortion. It is made in thicknesses ranging from ⅛ inch to over 1 inch. Although the ⅛-inch plate glass can be used in stained glass projects, it is much more expensive than window glass, and is valuable primarily as a base for epoxied stained glass compositions.

Buying Glass

Glass is sold by the sheet in various sizes. Stock sheets of both domestic cathedral and opalescent glass, for example, are commonly 32 by 84 inches; half sheets are 32 by 42 inches; sheets may also be cut to 16 by 21 inches and 10 by 16 inches. Imported cathedral glass may be 36 by 72 inches. Antique glass is sold in sheets of about 23 by 34 inches for French and German glass, and about 15 by 24 inches for English glass. To add to the confusion, some suppliers may offer their glass in one size only—sometimes it is 8 by 12 inches or 12 by 16 inches, or 8 by 10 inches. No matter what their size, the sheets are usually sold by the square foot.

You can also buy glass remnants by the pound, in scraps up to 3 inches square, or as irregularly shaped "cutoffs" of up to 4 by 8 inches or even 6 by 8 inches. A pound or two of remnants may yield an interesting assortment of different types and colors of glass, and will obviously be less costly than sheet glass. A pound of cathedral or opalescent remnants ⅛ inch thick will equal about ⅔ square foot; a pound of antique glass will cover a little less area.

You can buy all types of glass by mail order (see "Sources of Supplies," page 253). Many suppliers offer sets of sample glass for a few dollars, which may include anywhere from a dozen to seventy samples of colors and/or textures. Most mail order suppliers require a minimum order.

Of course, if a glass dealer is conveniently located, it is easier and cheaper to buy glass where you can see and handle it. And as stained glass work grows in popularity, more glaziers are starting to carry glass for stained glass artisans in addition to their commercial stock. Art glass from a glazier may be less expensive than from hobby shops and stained glass supply stores.

Note: It is possible to salvage old glass from wrecking companies, but beginners should be wary of this source. Old glass is frequently priced at more than its value, it must be cleaned of all weatherproofing cement before being used, and it may be colored with enameled paint that will crack off and peel. If you do find satisfactory old glass from leaded windows at a good price, discard the lead, which is not reusable. In fact, salvage companies who want just the lead may give you the glass for nothing.

Storing Glass

Storing glass requires special care because of the fragile nature of the material and the risks inherent in mishandling it. The most efficient and safest way to store glass is to stand the sheets vertically in wooden racks that are deep enough so the glass doesn't protrude from the rack but not so deep that you can't get to small pieces wedged in the back. If you buy sheets of widely varying dimensions, you may have to provide racks of different sizes. However, don't set smaller racks on top of larger racks—all racks holding sheets of glass should be at floor level. But you can safely set bins or boxes for scrap glass on top of racks.

All racks, no matter their size, should have wooden bases and vertical divisions every 6 or 8 inches to prevent jamming too many sheets of glass into one slot. In some glass workshops, these vertical divisions are made of wood slats so you can reach into one slot from the neighboring space.

As soon as you get new sheets of glass, check them for any imperfections, especially at the edges. If you find any cracks, either cut off and discard the damaged section, or divide the sheet along the crack.

Before putting new glass away in its rack, get in the habit of cutting a sample from each different sheet. You can keep these small pieces—1 by 2 inches is big enough—in a box or mount them with Plasticine on a sheet of plate glass. The collection will provide a neat inventory of all the kinds and colors of glass you have on hand. After you have used up the glass, remember to retire the sample, or send it to the supplier for reordering if you want more of the same glass.

Tips and Reminders for Selecting Glass

• When choosing glass for a project, try to select all the colors and glass at the same time so you can see the relationships among them. And try to view the glass against the same type of light against which the stained glass project will ultimately be viewed.

• Choose glass for its texture as well as its color. Warps, bubbles, ridges, and other seeming imperfections can be an asset—they catch light and heighten visual interest, and can even simulate pictorial effects—as long as these imperfections are not structural defects in the glass. Even the pressed mechanical glass that is used for office partitions and shower doors can provide interesting patterns and new concepts of glass design.

• Give texture in glass more weight if the project is to be viewed close at hand; at long distances, textured glass becomes less important visually, except as it diffuses the light.

• For clarity and transparency, consider antique glass. For translucency, consider glass rolled or pressed with an allover pattern that diffuses transmitted light more than antique glass does.

• If you are a beginner, select antique glass, which is easier to cut and use than machine-made glass. But avoid yellows, reds, and oranges in early projects because the selenium that provides those colors creates a brittle glass that makes cutting difficult.

• Opalescent glass of all kinds is harder to cut than transparent glass.

• Textured glass is more difficult to cut than smooth surfaces, so use it in patterns that don't require difficult cuts.

• Choose machine-made glass when you want a uniform visual effect throughout the glass pieces, and if your glass budget is low.

• For brightly lit and sunny environments, consider deep dense colors.

• For areas of little light, consider lightly tinted, textured glass. The pale color increases

visibility; the texture helps to diffuse the light.

• Use opalescent glass—or any other translucent glass—in lamps and wherever you want to mask the source of artificial light.

• Don't use flashed glass in any project where it will come in contact with high heat, as the flashed layer may pull back from the base.

• Test glass by tapping it with a finger. If you hear a dull thud, reject the glass. It may be badly tempered—that is, poorly annealed during its manufacture—which may cause it to crack easily or not break properly on the score lines.

• If you are stuck with a piece of glass you feel is defective, don't use it for large design areas. Score the glass in the direction it tends to break.

• Avoid glass with widely varying thicknesses.

• Larger pieces of glass are more unstable than smaller ones. Cut large sheets in half or quarters before storing them.

Tools and Supplies

The tools needed for working with glass are fairly specialized and not likely to be part of an all-purpose tool chest. Buy high-quality tools; you'll find that they will make working in glass easier and improve the quality of your work.

Glass cutters, or cutting wheels, as they are commonly called, have a small rotating wheel at the tip of the cutting head that scores the glass in straight or curved lines so it can be snapped apart. Most cutters also have three notches of varying widths in the head with which to break off the scored glass. The most popular cutters have metal handles which have either a straight end (see Figure 17a), which is used as fulcrum for breaking scored glass, or a ball end (see Figure 17b), which is used to tap a score line in order to break it.

Many different types of cutters are available, including some with replaceable wheels, and they differ mainly in the material the wheel is made of and its cutting angle. Wheels for stained glass work are made of harder steel than the cutters used for window panes, so buy your cutters from a supplier of stained glass equipment (see "Sources of Supplies," page 251) rather than the local hardware store. Carbide wheels are also available, which last much longer and cost more than steel wheels. Diamond-tip cutters, favored mainly by professionals for cutting extra hard or plate glass, are expensive and difficult to use.

Keep several cutting wheels on hand since they wear out and sometimes become damaged. You can sharpen a dull wheel on an oil-stone, but it is difficult to recapture the original angle of the cutting edge; replacement is a wiser course since all successful glasswork depends on a sharp and properly honed cutting wheel.

Circle cutters are used to score perfect circles on glass. They are available in different styles. One type (see Figure 18a) has a steel wheel that rotates around a central point and cuts circles from ½ inch to 5 inches in diameter; another type (see Figure 18b) functions with an extension rod and cuts circles from 3 to 23 inches. With a steady hand you can score an acceptable circle with a cutting wheel, but when you want a perfectly formed disk, use a circle cutter.

Glass pliers, sometimes called plate pliers, have wide flat jaws that are used for snapping

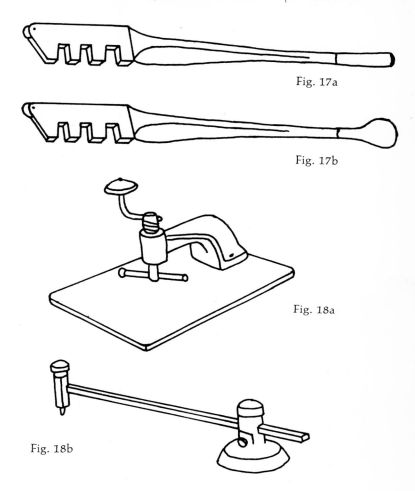

Fig. 17a

Fig. 17b

Fig. 18a

Fig. 18b

off small pieces or narrow strips of glass after they have been scored (see Figure 19). They are available in different sizes, with and without grooved jaws.

Fig. 19

Grozing pliers (see Figure 20, next page) nibble away, or groze, jagged edges of glass. The narrow, grooved jaws of the pliers have been softened, or detempered, so they can shape the glass without crushing it. Grozing pliers are available in several sizes and styles.

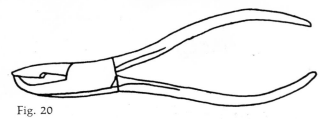

Fig. 20

Round-nose pliers (see Figure 21) are also used for grozing. The shape of the jaws makes them useful for trimming small pieces of glass and cleaning out narrow areas.

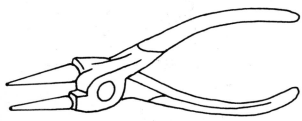

Fig. 21

Needle-nose pliers (see Figure 22) have long narrow jaws that are primarily used for tight work with copper wire and lead strips, but because they are already detempered they can be used for grozing, if necessary.

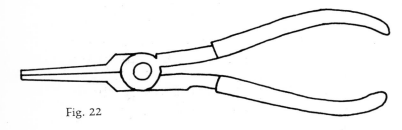

Fig. 22

Running pliers (see Figure 23) are used to separate straight cuts, particularly on opalescents, so you don't have to tap the brittle glass. When you place a sheet of glass be-

Fig. 23

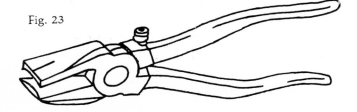

tween the curved jaws of the running pliers, the lower, convex jaw becomes a fulcrum as it presses the glass against the upper, concave jaw. A set screw can keep the pressure on the glass minimal so the glass will snap rather than shatter.

A *straightedge* of metal or wood is helpful in making long straight glass cuts. It guides the cutter along a straight line, then can be used as a fulcrum in breaking the scored glass.

Plasticine is an artificial substitute for wax and is used to affix samples of glass to a window or a glass easel for viewing against natural light. It is easily applied and removed, and holds the glass safely in a vertical position.

A *glass easel* is a sheet of clear plate glass on which you can affix samples of glass for viewing. It can also be used to see the relationships among different colors and kinds of glass in an entire design after the glass shapes have been cut but before they have been assembled. The glass easel need only be as large as your designs; a sheet 2 by 3 feet is adequate for most small projects.

A *light box* supplements natural daylight when you are making a selection or working out the relationships among several glass samples. Portable light boxes (see Figure 24) are available at art supply shops.

You can also make your own light box by installing fluorescent lights in a wooden box about 8 inches deep. A useful size is 2 by 4 feet, but you can alter the dimensions to suit the size of projects you normally work on. Make the two long sides ¼ inch higher than the two ends that will support the glass (see Figure 25). Drill holes for ventilation in the two end pieces and paint the inside of the box white. Lay a piece of frosted glass ¼ inch thick on the two ends, between the side sec-

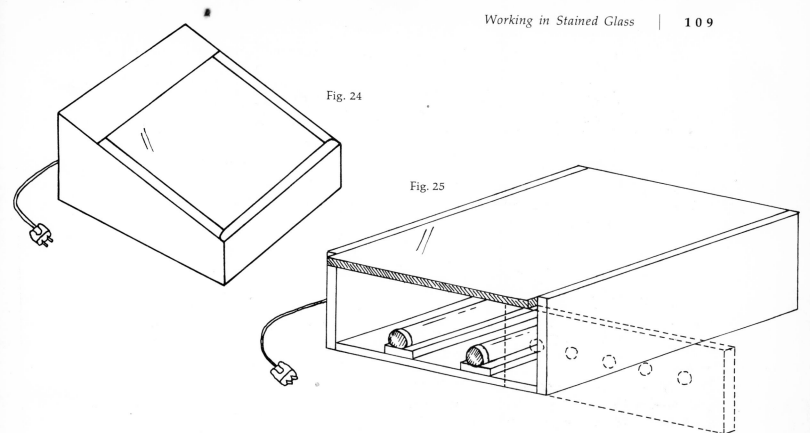

Fig. 24

Fig. 25

tions, shiny side up (see Figure 25).

A *spring clamp* is useful for securing a straightedge against a large sheet of glass when you are scoring a long line.

Homasote, a lightweight composition board, is a good cutting surface when scoring glass because it cushions the glass somewhat. Other good cutting surfaces are short pile carpet, pressed cork sheet, or several thicknesses of newsprint.

A *bench brush* keeps your worktable free of glass chips.

A *glass tray* is a good way to store and keep track of the glass pieces while they are being cut and before the composition is actually assembled. You can use any tray that is larger than the design, or you can make your own, using ⅛-inch masonite or ¼-inch plywood for the base and 1-by-1-inch wood strips for the four sides.

How Glass Is Cut

In theory, cutting glass is simple: score the surface of the glass with a sharp instrument, then apply pressure along the score to complete the break. In practice, it's somewhat harder, for the glass has a tendency to misbehave if you hold the glass cutter at a tilt, if you put too much or too little pressure on the cutter or on the glass itself when attempting the break, and even if you wait too long between scoring and breaking the glass. Moreover, some glass is easier to cut than others, requiring differing amounts of pressure during the scoring. Glass cutting is a skill that is mastered with a little practice and experience, but it may come easier if you understand its principles.

Glass is not cut in one motion; the cutting wheel does not—cannot—shear through the sheet of glass. The wheel scores the surface of the glass, fracturing it and creating a fissure just under the score line that encourages the glass molecules to part and separates the glass to a shallow depth (see Figure 26). The glass

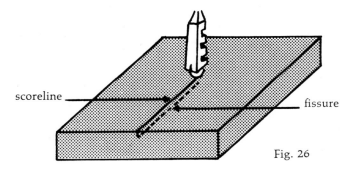

scoreline _____   _____ fissure

Fig. 26

must be snapped, or broken, as soon as possible after it has been scored in order to get a clean break. If you wait too long and the score "cools off," allowing the stress patterns to dissipate, the break may be jagged and not even follow the score line at all.

Whether you are cutting straight lines, curves, circles, or irregular-shaped patterns, the actual technique for cutting glass is the same.

Holding the Cutter

Grip the glass cutter between your first and second fingers and support it with your thumb (see Figure 27). If you prefer, you can hold the cutter in the palm of your hand, wrapping all four fingers around the shaft and bracing the cutter with your thumb on top of the shaft (see Figure 28). However, do not hold the cutter between the first finger and thumb, as you would a pencil. Whatever grip you use, hold the cutting wheel perpendic-

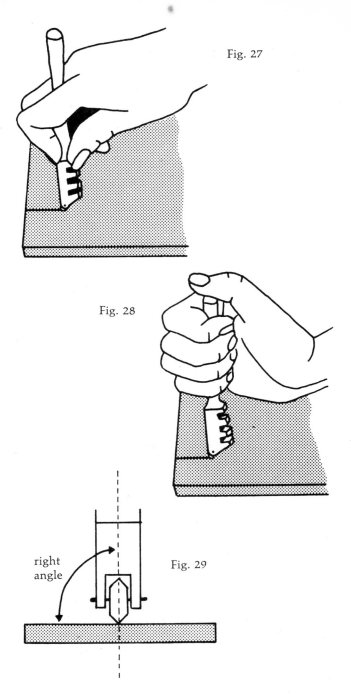

Fig. 27

Fig. 28

right angle   Fig. 29

ular to the surface of the glass (see Figure 29). If the cutter tilts to one side, the wheel may skid and interrupt the score.

Although the wheel itself must be at right angles to the glass, the cutter need not be upright. In fact, you will have good control if the cutter—not the wheel—is at a slight angle to the surface of the glass (see Figure 30), leaning toward the direction of the cut. Usually you will draw the cutter toward you, but you may push it away from you if that seems easier in certain situations. You may

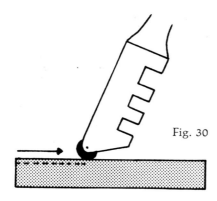

Fig. 30

find it most comfortable to stand while scoring the glass so you can lean the weight of your body into the cut instead of generating all the pressure from your wrist and hand alone.

When not in use and between cuts, immerse the cutter head in a solution of kerosene or light oil, alone or in a mixture of equal parts. This will lubricate the wheel bearing and keep the cutting wheel cool by reducing the friction as the wheel traverses the glass. Or you can store the cutter in a capped jar with a wad of kerosene- and/or oil-soaked cotton at the bottom that will cushion as well as lubricate the wheel bearing during storage.

Preparing the Glass

Clean the sheet of glass well with a liquid cleaner, or with warm water and a detergent. Dirt or film lying on the surface will interrupt

the smooth passage of the cutting wheel, which is necessary to develop a continuous fissure and insure a clean break.

Lay the glass on your cutting table with its smoother side up. The cutting surface should be nonrigid and pliant to accommodate any irregularities or differences in thickness in the glass. A magazine or sheets of newsprint make a good work surface for cutting small pieces of glass; a sheet of Homasote, a lightweight composition board, or a piece of cork, or even discarded carpeting are excellent surfaces on which to score large pieces of glass. Avoid an unyielding wood or metal surface that may cause the glass to crack under pressure.

Scoring the Glass

Remove the cutter from its lubricant, and wipe any excess kerosene or oil on a paper towel.

Hold the cutting wheel firmly and place it just inside the top edge of the glass sheet. Press down on the glass with the same amount of pressure you would use in making a carbon copy, and score the glass in one continuous motion, letting up on your pressure as the cutting wheel runs off the opposite edge of the glass. Once you have started the cut, don't stop. Once you have finished the cut, don't go back over the score line. An interrupted cut or a second pass will destroy the fissure and gouge out a furrow.

When scoring glass, try to maintain a relatively fast and constant speed—about a foot or more a second—to create a good fissure. Slow cuts often result in shallow fissures, uneven speeds in fissures of irregular depths. If you have difficulty maintaining the recommended speed at first, make your score at a slower pace but be sure it is steady, continuous, and well controlled.

The amount of pressure required to score glass properly depends on the type of glass and the condition of the cutting wheel. Some glass is harder than others. Brightly colored glass—yellow, red, orange, for example—is more difficult to cut because of the metals in the glass that color it; antique glass and glass with little texture or color is more easily cut. And as cutters dull, they require more pressure. Since circumstances vary with each sheet of glass and with each cut, there are no fast rules for the right amount of pressure to use in scoring glass. That is a judgment that comes with practice and experience.

There are guidelines, however. If you are holding the cutter properly, so that all the pressure is exerted vertically on the back of your hand, a new cutting wheel requires about 10 pounds of pressure to score cathedral glass. (Holding the cutter at a slant will dissipate some of this pressure.) If you want to get the feel of 10 pounds of pressure, one supplier of stained glass equipment suggests you lay a 10-pound weight—two 5-pound bags of sugar, for instance—on the back of your hand as you hold the cutter.

If you are using too little pressure, the cutter will not score the glass at all. If you are using too much force, the wheel will plow a furrow in the glass, throwing glass dust along the score line and causing multiple internal fissures (see Figure 31a). If you are using the right amount of pressure, you will hear the glass "sing" or "hiss" and see a clean, neat score (see Figure 31b).

When scoring straight lines, you may want to use a straightedge for accuracy. Hold it firmly on the glass surface with one hand

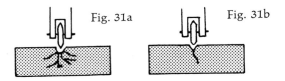

Fig. 31a   Fig. 31b

and use its edge to guide your cutting wheel. Be sure the cutting wheel housing clears the straightedge so the wheel can ride at a right angle to the glass.

When scoring shapes, lay your cutting pattern over the glass and guide the cutting wheel around its edges (see Figure 32). If you

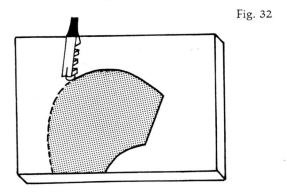

Fig. 32

find it difficult to cut around a paper pattern, you can lay the pattern under the glass and follow it freehand with the cutter (see Figure 33). This technique requires a steady hand

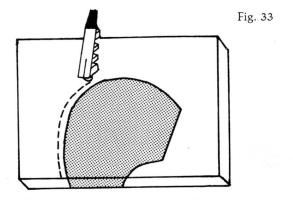

Fig. 33

and good control of the cutter as well as good visibility; it works best with light-colored translucent glass and is not possible with opaque glass.

Some common scoring problems. Occasionally a cutting wheel will skip while scoring the glass. This may happen for various reasons: the wheel has a nicked edge; it doesn't rotate smoothly because it is out of alignment or the bearing is not well lubricated; there was dirt on the glass; there was uneven pressure during scoring. First check the wheel and the cutter for any irregularities, and discard a damaged wheel before trying to correct the scoring problem. Then check the glass.

If there are tiny regular breaks in the score line (see Figure 34), indicating a small nick in

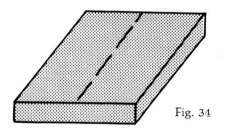

Fig. 34

the cutting wheel, try to snap the score nevertheless. If there is a longer interruption in the score line (see Figure 35a), try to bridge the gap. Start the intervening score next to—but not connected with—one side of the already scored line and stop it just short of the other side (see Figure 35b). Never retrace the entire original score, hoping to fill in the skipped portion.

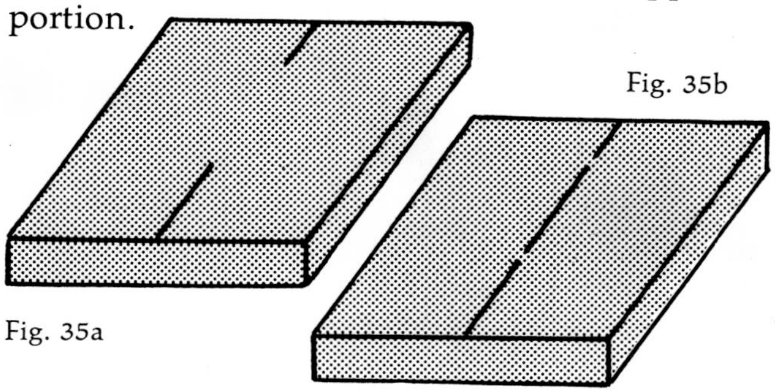

Fig. 35b

Fig. 35a

Breaking the Cut

As soon as the glass is scored it must be broken. The glass will not break properly if too much time elapses between making the cut and breaking, or snapping, the score.

There are several ways to break the cut. Your choice will depend on the shape of the cut—whether it is a straight line, a curve, a circle—as well as on the size of the sheet of glass you are working with, and how near the score is to the edge of the sheet. But all the methods depend on exerting pressure upward from the underside of the glass just below the score while simultaneously pushing down on each side of the score from above (see Figure 36). To get a clean, straight-

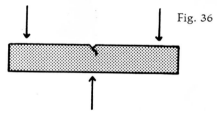

Fig. 36

sided break, be sure that the point of pressure from below is just under the score line and not slightly to one side of it.

To snap the score with your hands, make two fists and place them on either side of the score, with the thumbs on top of the glass (see Figure 37). Hold the glass with the score line

Fig. 37

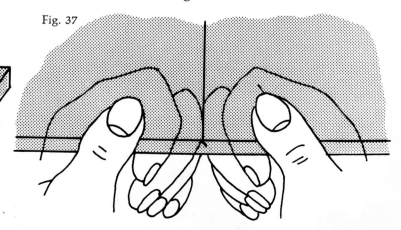

perpendicular to your body—and to your thumbs and fists as well—and at a slight downward angle. To make the actual break, roll your wrists outward while you push your clenched fingers up against your thumbs. To minimize any danger from flying glass slivers, keep the glass tilted away from you.

Another way to start the break is by tapping the glass under the score with the ball end of the glass cutter. Make the tap precisely under the score line and about an inch inside the edge of glass where the score ended (see Figure 38). Never start the break at the edge

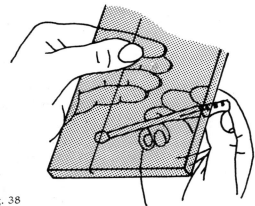

Fig. 38

where you began the score; never tap down on top of the score line; always apply breaking pressure from the under side—the non-scored side—of the glass.

As soon as the break starts at the edge of the glass, grip the edges with your hands as described above to complete the separation. If you have difficulty making the break, continue to tap along the length of the score line from underneath, holding the glass on both sides of the score with your free hand (see Figure 38), so one side of the glass can't fall and break when the glass separates.

You can also start the break by laying the tip of a nail under the end of the score and

lightly but firmly pressing down with your hands on either side of the score (see Figure 39). Some artisans use the end of the cutting wheel in this manner.

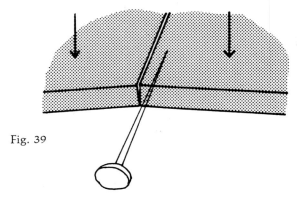

Fig. 39

When breaking narrow strips of glass, use glass pliers with wide flat jaws. Place the jaws of the pliers on the narrower strip of glass at one end, close to the score line (see Figure 40).

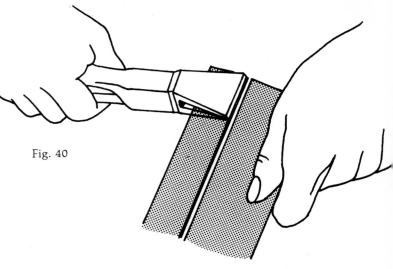

Fig. 40

Hold the other side of the glass with your free hand and exert upward pressure with the pliers to snap the score. If the strip is long and cannot be snapped off in one bite, start the snap at one end of the cut, then move the pliers along the score line until the glass separates.

You can also break narrow strips of glass with the breaker notches in the head of the glass cutter. Choose the notch whose opening most closely matches the thickness of the glass while still allowing a little leeway. Place the notch over the glass edge about half an inch in from the side where the score ended (see Figure 41) and exert the same upward pressure described above.

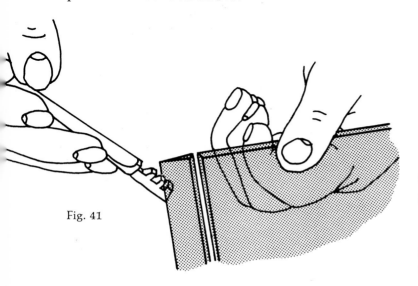

Fig. 41

Cutting Special Pieces and Difficult Shapes

Straight line cuts on large sheets. Occasionally you will have to cut large sheets of glass, perhaps to divide a sheet for easier storage or even to use in a project, and you may find that the conventional methods of cutting glass are awkward with these unwieldy sizes.

To score a long straight line accurately you will need a straightedge as a guide. If it tends to slip, even slightly, press pieces of nonskid rubber backing along one side so that it will

remain absolutely stationary throughout the scoring.

To snap the score, carefully lift the sheet of glass and slide the straightedge under it, placing one of its edges just under the score line (see Figure 42). With your fingers close

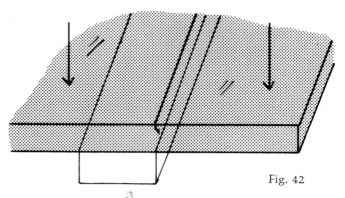

Fig. 42

together, place one hand on each side of the glass. Press down sharply with both hands simultaneously to snap the glass.

To break the cut another way, move the glass so that the score line is just over the edge of your worktable (see Figure 43). Using

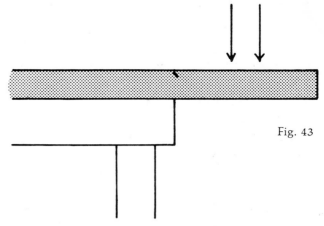

Fig. 43

gloves, hold one hand flat against the side of the glass on the tabletop, and with the other hand grab the side that extends over the edge. Lift the extended side of the glass so it is at a slight angle and, holding it tightly, snap it smartly downward toward the floor.

A third method of running a long straight score is with a running pliers. Insert the glass between the two curved jaws with the score line on the glass directly under the line on the upper jaw of the pliers. Tighten the screw gauge only until the jaws bite gently into the glass, then press the jaws together to start the break.

Circles. You can score a circle by following a circular pattern and making the pass in one continuous motion of the cutting wheel. Or you can use a circle cutter to score a perfect circle. But in order to free the glass circle from the sheet of glass, you cannot simply tap the scored line and expect the circle to fall out.

To break a circle out of a glass sheet, score a number of lines at a tangent—not perpendicular—to the circle and going out to the edge of the glass (see Figure 44). Make at least

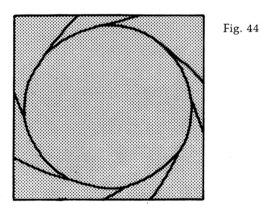

Fig. 44

four such tangential cuts; more would be preferable. Break the waste pieces of glass off by the hand method, or tap the tangential scores and use a glass pliers to free the glass. Score, then break, each of the tangential cuts until you have freed the entire circle.

If you don't want to use a circle cutter or follow a circular pattern by hand, you can ap-

proximate a rounded shape by making a number of short curved cuts (see Figure 45). After you have scored and broken these lines, you will have to groze the projections for a smooth curved edge, as shown by the dotted lines in Figure 45.

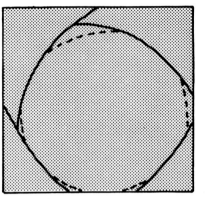

Fig. 45

Curves. There are two general kinds of curves—outside curves and inside curves (see Figure 46). A shallow curve of either type is

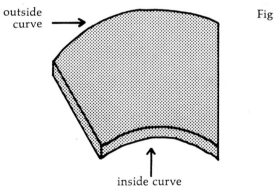

outside curve

inside curve

Fig. 46

easy to score and relatively simple to break. Handle them like straight line cuts: score in one continuous motion from one edge of glass to another, then complete the break with your hands. To start the break, you may want to tap under the score an inch in from one end with the ball of your cutting wheel.

Deep outside curves should be treated as if they were segments of a circle. If the curve represents no more than a quarter of a circle (see Figure 47a), tap the underside of the score and break it out with your hands. However, if the curve is larger than a quarter circle, score one or two lines at a tangent to the curve (see Figure 47b). Then break each of the tangential cuts until you have liberated the curve.

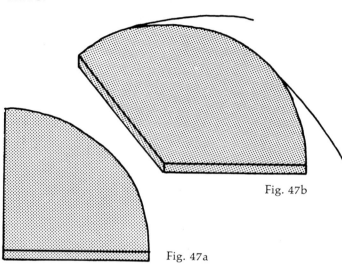

Fig. 47b

Fig. 47a

Deep inside curves are the most difficult of all cuts to break. Because the glass tends to break in fairly straight lines, putting excessive strain on the two thin ends of a deep curve, you have to take a series of shallow bites out of the glass until you reach the inside, or primary, curve you want. If you tried to break out a deep curve in one break, the glass would probably shatter.

The general procedure for breaking out a deep inside curve is to make a series of cuts between the primary curve and the edge of the glass, then to break them out one by one, using glass pliers. If your inside curve is not too sharp, you can make these intervening cuts parallel to the primary cut (see Figure 48). If the inside curve is quite deep—like a C, for instance—you must make a number of shal-

low scores that eat their way into the curve (see Figure 49). Work your way carefully from the outermost cut into the heart of the curve. As you approach the primary cut, you may want to nibble the waste glass away with grozing pliers rather than risk a fracture.

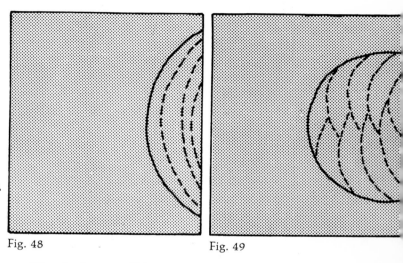

Fig. 48

Fig. 49

Nearly impossible cuts. There are certain shapes that simply cannot be cut out of a sheet of glass, or are so difficult that the effort is not worth the trouble.

A deep curve with an undercut, like a keyhole (see Figure 50), exacerbates the already formidable problems of a deep curve.

Fig. 50

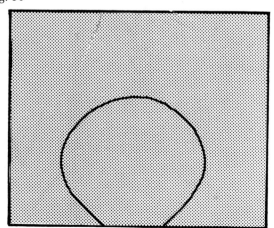

Any sharp-angled shape, like a square or a triangle, cannot be cut out of a sheet of glass because such cuts require more than one score, and every score must travel from one edge of glass to another. To cut out either of these shapes, you must make one cut from one edge to the opposite edge of the glass, then make the second cut from the newly cut piece (see Figure 51).

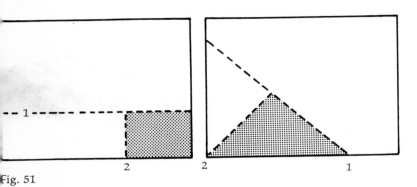

Fig. 51

Finishing Rough Edges

Even the cleanest cut often leaves some jagged edges, and these must be removed with grozing pliers. Hold one handle of the pliers stationary with your thumb and first finger, and use your other fingers to work the other handle of the pliers. Loosely close the jaws of the pliers on a protruding piece of glass, then roll your wrist to the side and at the same time tighten your grip on the pliers. The jaws will grind away a little glass at a time.

Grozing will not produce a smooth, polished edge, but it will remove gross protrusions so that the glass pieces can fit together neatly in the assembly. The smoother you can make these edges, the

tighter the fit in the finished assembly. This is especially important when you are using copper foil and the glass pieces actually nest next to each other; it is less critical if you are using lead strips to hold the glass and small imperfections will be hidden by the flange of the lead.

After grozing—or after breaking the cut if you didn't have to groze—scrape or sand newly cut edges to remove any sharp slivers of glass. The easiest way to do this is to scrape the edge against another edge of glass (see Figure 52). You can use a Carborundum stone if you prefer.

Fig. 52

Tips and Reminders for Cutting Glass

• Clean all sheets of glass before cutting. Any dirt or film on the surface may cause the cutting wheel to skip and ruin the score.

• Keep the cutting head lubricated with kerosene and/or light oil when not in use. Periodically check the wheel to be sure it is free of nicks.

• Practice cutting techniques and hard cuts on window glass, which is relatively inexpensive.

• Never retrace a score with your cutting wheel. You will gouge an irregular furrow that will not yield a clean break, and you may damage the cutting wheel if the first fissure forces the wheel to ride at an angle.

• Whenever possible, snap a newly made score before making another score.

• Score all glass on its smoother side. If you can't identify it, make test scores on each side of the glass, then snap them to see which score breaks more easily.

• Score flashed glass on its unflashed side. To determine which side is the unflashed, thicker layer, move the glass around in the light, look at its profile, or chip off a corner, if necessary.

• For the most economical use of glass, select a sheet that is fairly close in size to the shape you want to cut, but be sure it is large enough to handle comfortably. If the glass is much larger than your pattern, cut off and save the area not needed so you won't shatter more glass than necessary in case your break is faulty.

• Don't be slavish to glass economy at the expense of an interesting use of glass. Take advantage of all the striations and varied tones and textures to enhance your design wherever they may occur in the sheet of glass, even if that causes some waste. You may want to use a particular streaky portion that falls in the center of the sheet, or directional patterns or textures that will give depth to your design (see Figure 53).

• Try to place each pattern on the glass in such a way as to utilize at least one edge of the glass (see Figure 54). The pattern may be laid on the glass in any direction since glass, unlike fabric, does not have a grain.

• Generally, start the first score on the side of the pattern nearest the cut edge of

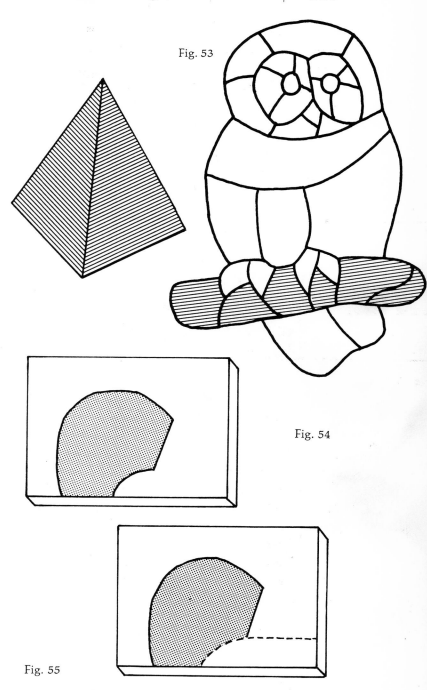

Fig. 53

Fig. 54

Fig. 55

glass and cut along the side of the pattern in one continuous motion, cutting past the pattern and off the edge of the glass (see Figure 55). If you make a poor cut, you can simply move the pattern over a little, thus wasting very little glass.

• Always make the hardest cut first (see Figure 56). There is no point in making all the other cuts in the piece only to find that the last and hardest one will shatter and ruin the entire piece.

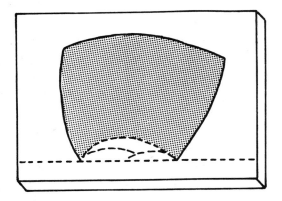

Fig. 56

• Try to reduce the number of cuts you have to make by combining pattern pieces. This is sometimes possible in geometric designs where pieces of the same width can be sliced off one long strip (see Figure 57). This practice not only reduces the number of pieces that must be cut and broken individually, but it also ensures uniform measurements in certain dimensions.

Fig. 57

• As soon as you have cut each piece of glass, mark it with its pattern number, using a marking crayon or a self-adhesive label, both of which can be easily removed. This will help you keep track of glass pieces, especially if many of them are similar in shape or color.

• Grozing is useful for taking off sharp edges and for shaping pieces that are essentially cut correctly. However, if a piece requires so much grozing that you are really shaping it with your pliers, you will find it easier simply to recut the pattern.

• Confine all your glass cutting and grozing to one area of your worktable. If possible, groze over a garbage can or box.

• Keep your work area brushed free of glass dust and shards at every stage of your work. This is not only a good safety precaution but it is good glass-working practice. Bits of glass that lodge on your cutting surface, for example, can act as a fulcrum and cause glass to break if you lean even lightly on it; glass dust on the surface of the glass may interrupt the smooth pass of the cutting wheel.

• Save all your glass scraps in a box or bin. Even the smallest remnants are likely to enhance some future design.

Safety Precautions

There are some obvious safety measures to take when working with glass—and not only during the cutting procedures.

• Before moving large sheets of glass, check them for cracks by tapping them gently.

• Handle glass lightly but carefully, and with both hands. Avoid having an edge rest against the web of a hand between thumb and first finger, an area particularly vulnerable to a nasty gash.

• Carry glass sheets and assembled panels vertically, and never carry them over your—or anyone else's—head.

• Store glass sheets vertically, with sharp and pointed edges facing the rear or bottom of the storage cabinets.

• Take particular care when retrieving small pieces of glass from a bin or when selecting glass buried under a few other pieces.

• When cutting glass wear glasses or sunglasses, especially if you are a novice. Don't wear sandals or shorts when working with glass.

• Scrape a newly cut glass edge against another piece of glass to remove sharp slivers of glass. Then resist the temptation to run your fingers over it to see if it is smooth.

• Keep the work area clean at all times. Brush glass chips, dust, and shards off the table with a stiff bench brush immediately after cutting glass, and sweep the floor frequently.

• Don't lean on your worktable with bare hands. Even the most vigorous brushing may not catch all the tiny chips of glass.

• Keep a first-aid kit at hand. Despite all your precautions, you may still receive an occasional glass scratch.

Working with Solder

In stained glass work soldering has the essential function of welding the lead strips or copper foil into a strong skeleton to support the glass composition. To construct this skeleton, it's helpful to understand the soldering process, as well as its particular application to stained glass work, which differs in some ways from other types of soldering.

Soldering joins metals by heating a solder alloy beyond its melting point, but below the melting point of the metals to be joined, so that the molten solder flows over and bonds with the metals. In order for this bonding to occur, several elements must be present—a solderable metal, flux, solder, and heat. This is true of both hard soldering and of soft, or common, soldering, the type used in stained glass work.

Lead and copper, both easily solderable, are the metals used primarily in assembling stained glass compositions. Brass, tin, bronze, and some steels can also be soldered, so that any needed parts—supporting bars, hooks, ties, for example—can be made of these metals and incorporated in the main lead or copper structure. There are other solderable metals, such as silver, gold, and platinum, that are not used in stained glass work, either because they are too expensive or because they require too volatile a flux.

Flux is a metal-cleaning agent that removes dirt and oxides that form on exposure to the air and prevents further oxidation during the soldering process, so that the molten solder and metal can adhere to each other. There are many types of fluxes available—all designed for different soldering jobs. Those that are suitable for soldering copper and lead in stained glass work may be quite dangerous if used to solder electrical or electronic circuits because the residue they leave can cause electrical short circuits.

Solder is an alloy, and in stained glass work and other soft soldering it is always a mixture of tin and lead. Hard solder contains other metals, primarily silver. In soft soldering, the solder flows and the bonding occurs at under 700° F; in hard soldering, at over 1000° F.

The fourth element in the process is heat,

which for stained glass work is supplied by a soldering iron. The iron transfers heat to the surface of the metal, rapidly raising its temperature about 100° above the melting point of the solder. Then the solder, following the heat and the flux, flows to the hot spot and bonds the metals together.

Tools and Supplies

Soldering irons are available in different weights and wattages, and with different shapes and kinds of tips. Depending on the size of the project and the metal to be soldered, irons for stained glass work are commonly between 25 and 175 watts, with 60- to 120-watt irons good all-purpose sizes. Low-wattage irons are best for soldering lead and for small-scale work in confined areas; high-wattage irons are useful for soldering copper foil and for large areas where speed of soldering is important. An iron with too small a capacity will take too long to heat and lose too much heat as you solder each joint; an iron with too large a capacity will get too hot and consume solder too quickly. The iron with the ideal capacity for a job will heat up quickly and retain its heat long enough to solder the joints without requiring frequent reheating. Irons do not usually have controls that main-

tain a constant temperature, or even on/off switches; they must be heated to the desired temperature and then unplugged.

The most versatile irons have replaceable heating elements and tips so you can change the temperature at which you are working and/or the size and style of the tip while using the same handle (see Figure 58). Sometimes the heating element is separate, sometimes it is part of the handle, and sometimes it is in the tip. In some models the tip is held in place by a set screw rather than screwed into the handle. Soldering guns don't have the versatility of soldering irons.

Whatever type or wattage soldering iron you choose, be sure it is light enough to hold easily and its handle is made of a material like wood or cork that won't get hot. The iron should have instructions on its use—especially on the care of the tips it accommodates.

Soldering iron tips are of two general types—copper and ironclad. Copper tips are cheaper than ironclad ones, but they require periodic cleaning, filing, and tinning because the copper oxidizes and pits. Ironclad tips are coated with an alloy—the working surfaces are iron plated over copper—and will not become eroded or pitted. The tips are pretinned and don't require periodic retinning. They need only minimal care—simply wipe the hot

Fig. 58   Fig. 59

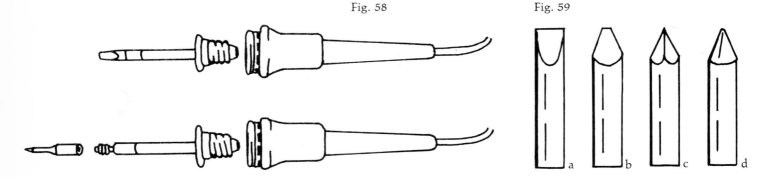

tip on a wet cellulose sponge to remove oxides and dirt—any additional abrasive cleaning or filing will damage the plated surface. For most craftsmen, the longer life and convenience of ironclad tips are more than worth their higher cost.

Both ironclad and copper tips are available in various sizes and tip shapes—chisel, semichisel, pyramid, cone (see Figure 59). They are used for different kinds of soldering. Small, thin tips provide greater control over delicate work and inside angles on projects like boxes and lamps. They are often preferred for soldering the narrow seams of copper foil. Large tips hold the heat longer and obviously cover a larger area more quickly. But essentially, the choice of a tip, both in kind and in size, is personal; try various tips to see which feel comfortable to use and do the job you require. Useful sizes are ⅛- to ¼-inch tips; the measurement refers to the width across the tip.

A *temperature regulator* attached to the soldering iron is a great convenience since most irons tend to get too hot as they are heat-ing up, then lose temperature when they are being used, requiring constant plugging and unplugging. You can solve both problems at the same time with a *rheostat*, which regulates the temperature and keeps the heat constant (see Figure 60). At a much lower cost you can install an *on/off switch* about 12 to 18 inches from the handle of the iron (see Figure 61) that will allow you to turn the heat off without unplugging the iron at the electrical outlet. However, it will not maintain a constant temperature.

An *iron stand* is sometimes supplied with the iron; if it is not, it is essential to get one. There are many types of stands (see Figure 62), and all of them perform the same basic function—keeping the hot iron off the table.

Fig. 61

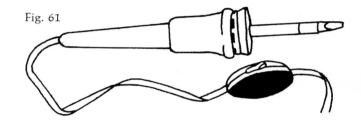

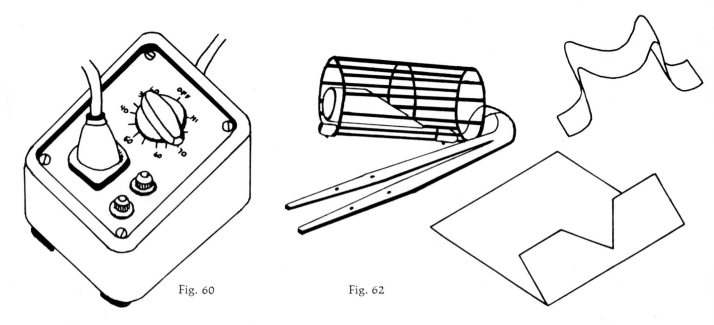

Fig. 60   Fig. 62

Flux for stained glass work is of two general types—corrosive and noncorrosive. Corrosive fluxes include zinc chloride, the most commonly used; ammonium chloride; and hydrochloric acid, also known commercially as muriatic acid. All of them are strong acids and must be used with care. Noncorrosive fluxes, as their name implies, are weaker than corrosive fluxes. Usually organic, they include olive oil, resin, and the most common of them for stained glass use, oleic acid, a fatty oil. They are less effective than corrosive fluxes in removing oxides, but on metals that are fairly clean to begin with, they prevent further oxidation and promote the flow of solder during the soldering process. Because they are based on fatty or oily substances, they are more time-consuming to clean than corrosive fluxes, which can be washed away with hot water.

When choosing a flux for stained glass work, select the mildest flux that does the job you want and is compatible with the metal you are soldering. Oleic acid is commonly used to flux lead because zinc chloride leaves a corrosive residue that eventually pits the metal. However, oleic acid doesn't penetrate and clean copper as well, so its use on foil is limited to special situations where zinc chloride might damage the materials—in soldering a foiled mirror, for example. Zinc chloride is the flux for copper foil. It usually comes in a muriatic acid base, but a less caustic, water-based zinc chloride flux is also available. When soldering lead and copper together, try to use oleic acid, the milder flux.

Flux is available in liquid, paste, or solid forms. Liquid flux is the easiest to use; you can scrub it into metal surfaces with a brush, dip small metal parts into it when necessary, and handle it easily. Avoid all spray-on fluxes, which are dangerous to inhale. Flux is also available combined with solder in a product called "cored solder," in which the flux is held in a hollow tube embedded in the center of wire solder (see Figure 63). This

Fig. 63

fluxed core can contain either rosin (noncorrosive) or acid (corrosive) flux. The acid-core solder, like other acid fluxes, should not be used with lead because it leaves a corrosive residue, and the rosin-core solder is not recommended for either lead or copper because the flux often oozes from the soldered joint, leaving the glass and metal gummy and hard to clean. So, despite the apparent convenience of having the flux an integral part of the solder, you would do well to keep flux and solder separate.

In small quantities, liquid flux is commonly sold in 2-, 4-, or 8-ounce bottles; paste flux usually in 2- or 4-ounce cans.

Solder for stained glass projects is usually mixed in the proportion of 60 percent tin to 40 percent lead and designated 60/40; occasionally it is half tin and half lead, called 50/50. The tin content is always listed first. 60/40 solder is more commonly used for two reasons: it is easier flowing, and it melts at a lower temperature than 50/50 solder, so there is less danger of melting the lead when you are melting the solder.

This difference in melting points—60/40 solder melts at 374° F. and 50/50 solder at 421° F.—is significant, although numerically small. Since lead alone melts at 621° F., you can see that the lower melting temperature of 60/40 solder gives you a little extra leeway when soldering lead, although the melting points of both solders are sufficiently lower than that of lead, so that with care there is little danger to the lead during soldering. The melting point of copper is so much higher— 1980° F.—that the copper is not in danger no matter how much heat is required to melt the solder.

Solder is sold in the form of wire on spools, and, less commonly, by the bar. Wire solder is more convenient since the solder can be held at the soldering point rather than having to be transported to it on the hot tip of a soldering iron. The most useful wire gauges for stained glass soldering are ⅛-inch and 1/16-inch diameter. The former is a good all-purpose size for general work that presents a bigger surface for heating, so a shorter length of the wire is needed to produce a neat sturdy joint. The latter is excellent for fine detail soldering. It uses less heat and melts faster, but its smaller diameter requires too long a strip of solder to cover most joints adequately.

Wire solders are also available with a center core of flux. Called cored solders to distinguish them from these solid solders, they are described under *Flux,* since their use is limited by the kind of flux they contain rather than by the solder.

You will find that the most commonly available solders are ⅛-inch and 1/16-inch solid wire, and ⅛-inch and 1/16-inch rosin-core solders, all 60/40; and ⅛-inch 50/50 solid wire. Most solders come in 1-pound spools, but you can sometimes find 5-pound spools at a lower price per pound. Bars of solder usually weigh a half pound. You can usually buy both kinds at a quantity discount.

Note: Liquid solder is not a true solder at all but a metallic powder in a cement base. It bonds without being heated. It is not used in stained glass work.

A *wire brush* with copper bristles is used to scrub away any oxidation that has formed on lead strips where you want to solder a joint. The bristles should be stiff but fairly soft so they will not gouge the lead. Don't use a steel brush, which will be too abrasive.

Steel wool or *fine sandpaper* can be used to burnish lead instead of the wire brush, or to clean copper soldering tips for retinning.

A *flux brush,* sometimes called an "acid" brush, has stiff bristles with which to scrub the flux into the metal. It is usually about 6 inches long and the bristles about ⅜- or ½-inch wide. You need separate brushes for oleic acid and zinc chloride.

Cellulose sponges for cleaning the soldering tips come in various styles: some sit in a simple plastic dish, some are mounted around or over a small reservoir of water which keeps the sponge wet, and may even have a base into which the soldering residues drop (see Figure 64), and some are incorporated into the soldering iron holder. A plastic sponge cannot be substituted.

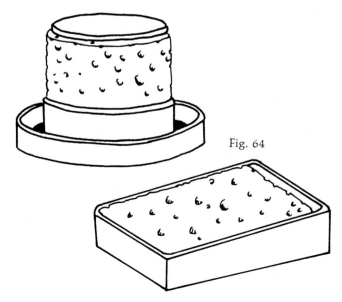

Fig. 64

Sal ammoniac, a small block of ammonium chloride usually about 2 inches square and an inch high, can also be used to wipe off the soldering residue from copper tips.

A *tinning lid* can be any metal receptacle—the bottom of a tin can, the inside of a jar lid—on or in which the hot tip of a soldering iron can be rotated as it is coated with melted solder. Since the molten solder makes the tin too hot to hold, many glassworkers nail a lid to a strip of wood, which becomes a handle for manipulating the hot lid during the tinning process (see Figure 65).

Fig. 65

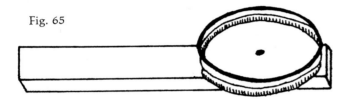

A *file* or *rasp* is used to file down any nicks or burrs on copper soldering tips and to remove encrusted soldering residues when cleaning them in preparation for retinning.

How to Solder

Even though lead is soldered only at its joints and copper foil along its entire surface, the same soldering techniques are used for both metals. You may want to vary the flux and change the soldering iron tip, but you can use the same soldering iron and the same solder, and certainly the same methods.

Choosing the soldering tips. Proper soldering starts with a clean and well-tinned tip of the right size and shape. Choose a tip that will deliver enough—but not too much—heat to the metal surface you are soldering. If you are soldering a broad, flat lead joint, for ex-

ample, use a tip with a proportionately large face (see Figure 66) so you can complete the joint as quickly as possible, without undue loss of heat from the soldering iron. If you are joining two copper-foiled pieces of glass, with only a thin band of copper showing on each edge, you will want a small narrow tip that presents a thin soldering surface (see Figure 67).

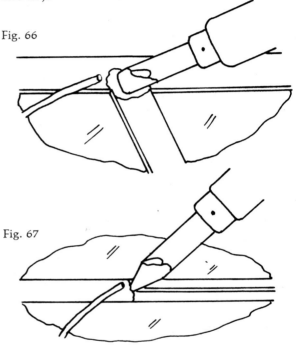

Fig. 66

Fig. 67

Heating the soldering iron. You want to heat the iron to a temperature that will melt the solder quickly and will heat the lead or copper enough so that the solder will bond with it, but not so hot that it will melt or burn the lead (the copper, with its higher melting point, is in no danger). Since the iron doesn't have a thermometer, you will have to gauge this temperature yourself. Test the hot iron on a small piece of solder; the solder will melt if the iron has reached or passed 374° F. (if you are using 60/40 solder, or 421° F. if you are using 50/50 solder). But don't start to solder lead before also testing the hot iron on a scrap of lead to be sure the iron hasn't heated so much (beyond 621° F.) that it will melt or burn the lead. If your iron is in the proper temperature range—that is, it will melt the solder but not the lead—you may want to unplug it while you actually solder so it doesn't get any hotter (the iron can be plugged in or not during soldering). Of course, if you are using a rheostat to keep the heat constant, you need not unplug the iron.

Cleaning the metal to be soldered. Because proper soldering depends on absolutely clean metal, you must clean the area just before soldering it, no matter how free of dirt or oxidation it appears to be. If there is little visible dirt and oxide, you can clean the metal chemically by simply applying flux (the same flux you will solder with). But if the metal looks dirty, or if you are repairing an already soldered joint, scrub the surfaces with a wire brush or fine sandpaper or steel wool until it shines. On badly oxidized lead, you may have to use a lead knife to scrape it down to its shiny—and solderable—surface.

Fluxing the metal. If you haven't already fluxed the metal in the cleaning process, you must do so now. With a stiff-bristle flux brush paint the flux on the metal where you will solder, covering the surfaces well but not lavishly. Since solder requires flux in order to effect the bond—and it tins those surfaces where it comes in contact with flux—you want to be sure both that there is sufficient flux exactly where you will solder and that there is none in adjacent areas where you don't want a bond. Since fluxed metals start to oxidize within a few hours, don't apply the flux until you are ready to solder.

Soldering the metal. If you have taken a lot of time to clean and flux the metal, recheck the heat of your soldering iron to be sure it hasn't cooled off or overheated during this interval.

Unroll a foot or two of wire solder and lay the end—no more than ¼ inch of it—over the fluxed metals (see Figure 68). Holding the soldering iron loosely in your other hand, lightly press the iron against the solder to melt the solder and heat the underlying metal (see Figure 69). Don't apply too much pressure; the

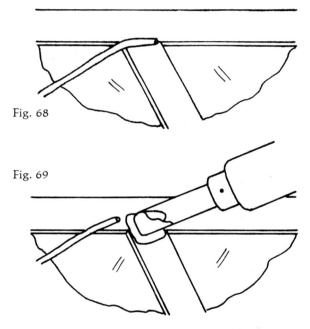

Fig. 68

Fig. 69

weight of the iron alone is sufficient. The molten solder will flow into the crack between the heated metals and form a properly soldered joint (see Figure 70). After a second or

Fig. 70

so, tip the handle of the iron so it is vertical, then lift it straight off the metal surface to prevent its leaving a mark on the molten solder. Let the solder cool and set, which will only take several seconds.

Some common soldering problems. Since successful soldering depends on several coordinating factors, there are various causes for poor soldering.

If you have a bumpy joint (see Figure 71), you may have used too much solder. Hold the hot iron on the excess solder, then pull the iron away; wipe off the soldering tip on a wet cellulose sponge and repeat the process if necessary. Don't flux the excess solder.

If you have a jagged joint, with points of solder pointing upward (see Figure 72), your iron wasn't hot enough to cause the solder to flow. To flatten the points, draw a hot iron lightly across the surface of the solder, without adding flux.

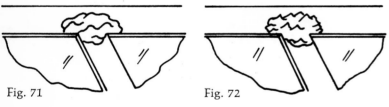

Fig. 71   Fig. 72

If the solder doesn't spread properly (see Figure 73), you haven't fluxed the metal well.

If the solder is thick and doesn't flow (see Figure 74), the soldering iron isn't hot enough to heat the metal or the solder.

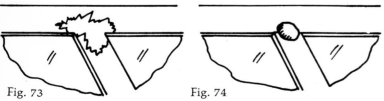

Fig. 73   Fig. 74

If the solder spatters or runs rather than flows, the soldering iron is too hot.

If the solder doesn't adhere, the lead strips

or copper foil may be oxidized and need cleaning, or the soldering iron tip may be dirty and need cleaning and retinning.

Removing the flux. As soon as you have finished soldering, remove all traces of flux—corrosive and noncorrosive—from your work because they may discolor the metals or leave gummy residues on the glass. Wash zinc chloride under hot running water, then wipe off remaining residue with a cloth. Remove the tacky residue from oleic acid with whiting, which is powdered calcium carbonate (chalk), or with plaster of Paris. Sprinkle the dry powder with a brush, then wipe off.

Note: Cleaning stained glass projects is explained fully in the following two chapters, "Working with Lead" and "Working with Copper Foil."

Care of Soldering Tips

Whether copper or ironclad, soldering tips tend to get dirty and oxidized from being used. Both kinds must be cleaned, and copper tips must be tinned periodically.

Cleaning tips. When soldering tips get dirty during work, and just as soon as you have finished soldering, wipe the hot tips off on a wet cellulose sponge to remove flux and solder residue. Then rinse the sponge out in water after working. Ironclad tips need no further care.

Copper tips, however, tend to get pitted from extended soldering, and must be cleaned more vigorously to remove the oxidation and to recapture a shiny copper surface. When they are cold, file the tips with a file or rasp, following the original shape of the tip and duplicating its angles. If a tip is not badly pitted, you can use sandpaper or steel wool, or even flux.

Retinning. When you have cleaned a copper tip, you should retin it at once, before it again becomes oxidized. Retinning is simply coating the hot tip with flux and solder, the very same process that takes place during soldering. There are several ways you can do this.

You can brush liquid flux—oleic acid—on the hot tip, touch a bit of solder to the tip, and, using the tinning lid, turn the tip quickly on all sides to coat it lightly with solder.

Or you can place a few drops of flux and an inch or so of solder in the tinning lid. Hold the hot tip in the solder—it will melt immediately—and coat the tip evenly with the solder and flux until it is shiny.

Or you can crumble a small piece of rosin in the tinning lid, add an inch or so of solder, then touch the hot tip to solder and flux and work the tip around, moving it across the surface, so all its sides are shiny and coated with solder. (You can use a rosin-core solder instead of the separate rosin and solder.)

No matter which method of tinning you choose, work quickly and use enough flux and solder. If the solder doesn't adhere to the tip—and the tip was clean—your iron was probably too hot. Let it cool and retin the tip.

Tips and Reminders for Soldering

• Clean all metal surfaces well before starting to solder, mechanically with a wire brush or steel wool or sandpaper, chemically with a flux.

• Use the mildest flux you can for the job.

• Use the right flux for the metal you are soldering. Generally, use oleic acid on lead and zinc chloride on copper foil.

• When applying flux, the brush should be moist but not wet. Try to keep the flux off metal surfaces that will not be soldered, since any solder that falls on fluxed metal may form a bond.

• Try to solder all joints as soon as possible after fluxing them, and certainly within a day. If the metals have oxidized because you didn't solder soon enough, apply more flux.

• Match the diameter of the solder wire to the size of the joint. Too thick a solder wire would dump too much solder and heat on the joint; too thin a wire would require too long a piece of solder for a good joint.

• Apply solder sparingly to avoid unsightly joints. Novices tend to use too much solder and, in trying to smooth out the excess, to hold the hot iron too long on the joint, which endangers the lead and even the glass.

• Work quickly when soldering so you won't apply too much heat if your iron is plugged in, or lose too much heat if the iron is unplugged.

• When soldering a long joint where two pieces of lead are in contact with each other for some distance, solder the entire line and not just one or two points of contact (see Figure 75).

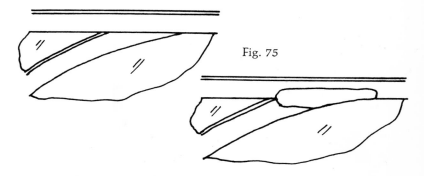

Fig. 75

• Since solder gets hot from contact with the iron, unroll a long enough piece of solder from the spool so that you can hold it where it is still cool. When you get down to a short end of solder, grasp it in the jaws of a pliers.

• When you're left with pieces of solder too small to use or hold in a pliers, save them for tinning.

• Don't be concerned over drops of solder that fall on your worktable or clothing during the soldering—the solder will only bond with a fluxed metal. Let the misplaced solder cool, then pick it off and discard it.

• Give your soldering iron the same reasonable care you give any small appliance. Don't knock it against the worktable lest you damage the heating element, and keep the cord from kinking.

• Remove the tip of the iron periodically and clean the tip, its shank, and the shaft it sits in. This will prevent the tip from freezing in the shaft, which sometimes happens if the iron overheats or the tips aren't cleaned well.

Safety Precautions

People new to glasswork believe glass to be the main source of danger, but flux, particularly zinc chloride and other acid fluxes, carries its own special risks.

• Use caustic fluxes only in well-ventilated areas or out-of-doors to eliminate the danger of inhaling toxic fumes, especially when the flux is heated. If your work area is not well ventilated, wear a surgical mask when soldering with an acid flux.

• Be sparing in the application of acid flux, using as little as will do the job, and avoid skin contact with it.

• Be sure your electrical outlet is adequate for the soldering iron you are using. Plug the iron directly into the outlet, or into a heavy-duty extension cord; do not use a lightweight extension.

• When not in use, keep your iron unplugged and in its stand.

• Always return a heated soldering iron to its stand. Never lay a hot iron on your worktable, where it can start a fire or char the surface or damage your design layouts.

Working with Lead

Historically, lead came is the traditional way of assembling glass into a panel, and the technique of leading glass has changed very little from the Middle Ages. For cutting glass, today's glass-cutting wheel has replaced the pointed heating iron; for nibbling away its jagged ends, grozing pliers do the work of the old slotted iron bar; and for soldering, the electric iron takes the place of the pointed iron heated in the fire. But even with these technical advances, a medieval glazier would feel quite at home in a contemporary glass workroom, no doubt pleased he need not cast his own lead strips or blow his own glass.

Tools and Supplies

The tools needed for working with lead are relatively simple, and many of them may already be part of your tool kit. Moreover, although you can buy special tools for leading, you can occasionally convert inexpensive household tools to this purpose.

A *lead knife* is used primarily to cut the lead strips, but it has many secondary uses—slipping glass into the lead channels, aligning glass and lead, even functioning as a hammer. It is available in a variety of shapes (see Figures 76a and 76d). One popular and useful style has a lead-inlaid handle for tapping glass into the lead channel during the leading-up process (see Figure 76d). You can use the knife upside down so its point can pry into tight corners, to align glass or lead strips, or to cut lead on the worktable when you don't have much room.

You can also cut lead just as well with a utility or mat knife (see Figure 76b). And if you have a fondness for hand-hewn tools, you can make your own lead cutter, using a rigid-bladed putty knife if you want a narrow blade, or a wall scraper if you want a wider blade (see Figure 76c). Choose tools with strong, thin, rigid blades. First grind the blade to a semicircle or straight edge, depending on your preference, then cut down the handle proportionately.

A *lead stretcher* takes the kinks out of lead strips and firms up the soft lead, removing any slack that will eventually cause the lead to

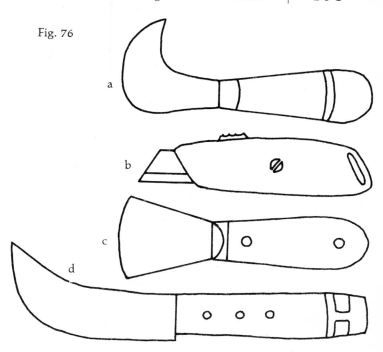

Fig. 76

sag and relax its tight grip on the glass pieces. A commercial lead stretcher grips one end of the lead with ribbed teeth while you pull the other end with pliers (see Figure 77). You can anchor the lead just as securely in a vise or by gripping it with a second pliers and then securing the pliers handles with two nails (see Figure 78) to keep them from opening.

A *lathekin,* also called lathkin and lathikin, opens the channels of the lead strip to accommodate the edge of the glass. This is often

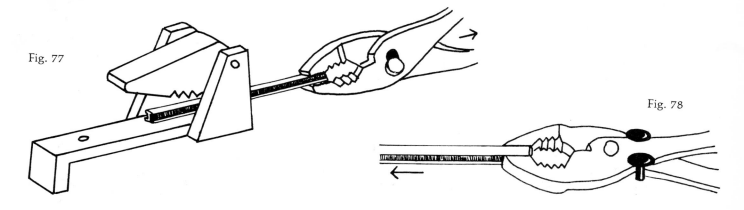

Fig. 77

Fig. 78

necessary after cutting, when the lead knife may crush or flatten the lead channels. Metal lathekins have a metal rod embedded in a handle and are available commercially with thick and thin rods to fit different sizes of lead strips (see Figures 79a and 79b). You can buy wood lathekins (see Figure 79c) or make your own out of hardwood by cutting it, shaping it to form a dull point, then sanding and oiling it. Or you can simply use the end of a ¼-inch wood dowel or the blunt end of a pencil.

Fig. 79

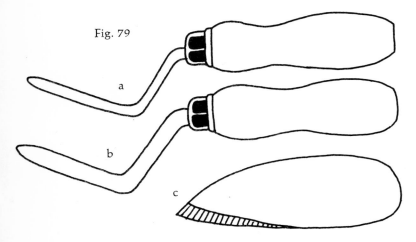

Nails are used to keep the glass sections in place while you lead up the design. Horseshoe nails (see Figure 80a) are about 2 inches long; they are easily hammered into and removed from the work bench, and their broad, flat sides prevent chipping of the glass. Leading nails (see Figure 80b) are an inch long, have round heads and long, tapered points

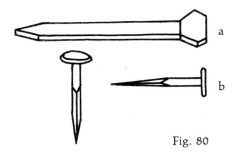

Fig. 80

which exert sufficient pressure against the side of the glass without the danger of chipping it. However, virtually any nail can be used to keep the glass locked in place against the lead strip if you first slide a remnant of lead against the exposed glass edge for protection (see Figure 81).

Fig. 81

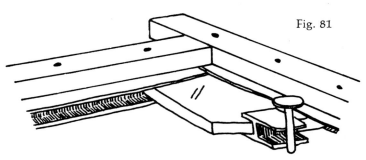

A *stopping knife* (see Figure 82a) with a bent blade is useful for prying up the flanges of the lead to insert or remove a section of glass. It can also be used for puttying the assembled panel and to crimp the lead flanges after puttying. You can make your own stopping knife by bending the blade of a straight putty knife (see Figure 82b).

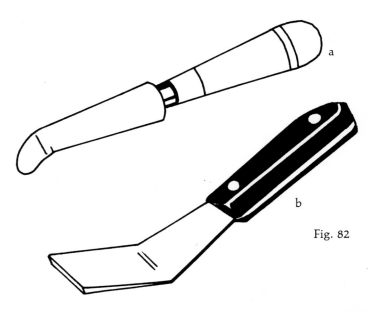

Fig. 82

Lathing strips of wood frame the design, bracing the lead and glass during the leading-up process and keeping them in alignment for soldering. With rectangular panels you will need four of them, each 1 to 2 by ½ inch, and a little longer than the sides of the design.

Putty, usually with a linseed oil base, reinforces the leaded project by cushioning the glass against the lead frame in which it sits and weatherproofing it. It comes in cans, already colored black or white, ready for application.

Stiff scrub brushes are used for sealing and weatherproofing the leaded panels.

Whiting, which is powdered calcium carbonate (chalk), is used to clean and polish the lead strips and glass after the panel has been sealed and weatherproofed with putty. It is available at drugstores.

A *Carborundum stone* is used to sharpen the cutting edges of lead knives. It can also smooth glass edges.

Lead Strips

Lead strips, called cames, have side channels to grip and hold pieces of glass together. They are strong enough to support the weight of the glass yet flexible enough to conform to the shape of most irregularly cut glass pieces.

Today lead strips are extruded commercially, but they were originally made by pouring hot metal into a long box lined with reeds. The casting was called a calm, or calme, in medieval England, after the mold in which the metal was poured, and today the lengths of channeled metal are still called calms (pronounced cams) in England and cames in the United States.

Cames are commonly made of pure lead, but some sizes and styles are available in a lead alloy, which is more expensive, somewhat more rigid, and stays shinier longer than the pure lead came and, for a beginner, is harder to handle. Cames are also made of copper, brass, and zinc—none of which can be cut with a lead knife, requiring instead a hacksaw or clippers.

In cross section, a general-purpose lead came looks somewhat like a small I beam, or a capital H on its side (see Figure 83), from which it is known as H came. A crossbar, called the heart of the came, connects the top and bottom faces, forming channels on either side which grip the glass and separate each piece from its neighbor.

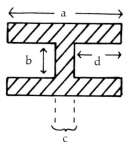

Fig. 83

The size of the lead came is expressed in terms of the width of its face (see Figure 83a), the top surface that is visible once the glass design has been leaded up; ¼-inch came, for example, has a face about ¼ inch wide. The width of the face determines how much lead will overlap the surface of the glass; since the heart of the came (see Figure 83c) remains fairly constant, the wider the face of the lead, the wider will be the flange—also called the lip or leaf—of each channel.

The depth of the channel (see Figure 83b) is measured between the top and bottom flanges of the came, and is actually the height of the heart. Although the depth can vary according to the size of the came, it is usually between 1/8 and 1/4 inch deep to accommodate the most common thicknesses of glass. The soft lead channel can be opened to receive a glass of a little greater thickness, or pinched together to grip a thinner pane of glass. For extra-thick glass, special cames with high hearts are used.

The heart of the came (see Figure 83c) is usually about 1/32 inch thick, but you allow for a 1/16-inch gap between glass pieces to give you latitude in cutting and leading up. This 1/16 inch is an important measurement which you must plan for in your working layout so that the finished project comes out the same size as the original design for it. If the heart of the came you are using is appreciably thicker, make the necessary adjustment when you come to make your assembly diagram.

The flanges or lips (see Figure 83d) of the top and bottom faces grip the glass and, together with the heart of the came, form the channels.

Types of Lead Came

Lead is made with a variety of profiles, but the most common have flat or round faces (see Figure 84a). They are available in a variety of sizes (which designate the width of the face), ranging from 1/16 inch wide for fine leadwork to 1/2-inch-wide came, which is generally the widest lead used by stained glass hobbyists. Professionals often use wider leads of 5/8, 3/4, 1, and 1 1/2 inches in large installations, but these sizes are hard to handle and have little use in most home workshops.

In addition to the choice of face, lead came is also available with a single channel rather than a double channel, and called U came (see Figure 84b). U came is primarily used along the edges of a project where its finished ap-

pearance makes a trim neat border. It can have a round or flat face.

Came also is made in other special-purpose shapes to solve different problems in glass design and assembly.

Off-center came, sometimes called *eccentric came* (see Figure 84c) has one channel wider than the other. It is used for abutting a large piece of glass next to a narrow piece (you set the narrow piece into the narrow channel where the lead flange won't cover too much of the glass surface).

High-heart came (see Figure 84d) has a channel of extra height to accommodate overly thick glass or to mount two pieces of glass back to back in what is called double glazing.

Angled came (see Figure 84e) is used to mount panels of glass in lamp shades or to turn corners in other projects. It is available with a 90° angle and with a 120° angle.

Ribbon came (see Figure 84f) is a flat strip of lead with no channel at all. It is laid across the face of already leaded glass, then soldered to abutting leads at each end. It is used to simulate a lead line, to emphasize design elements, or to strengthen a weak piece of glass.

Open-heart or reinforced came (see Figure 84g) has a double, or hollow, heart that can

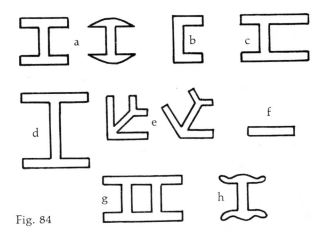

Fig. 84

carry a steel rod for additional support. If the reinforcing rod is already in place in the hollow core, you must cut the came with a hacksaw rather than a regular lead knife. This came is used only for large panels that require additional support, and for straight-edged glass, since the reinforcing rod has very little flexibility with which to follow curved edges. Naturally, its double heart is wider than the heart of most other came, so you must make allowance for the increased width in planning your working layout.

Colonial came (see Figure 84h) has an ornamental face, usually with a beaded top. Since its decorative façade calls attention from the glass, it must be used sparingly.

Selecting Leads

As you settle on the style, type, and size of came for a project, you will have to balance competing interests.

Style. On straight-line cuts, both flat and round leads are equally easy to use. Flat came is harder to work around curves, but it is easier to handle at joints. Round came is more maneuverable on curved edges of glass, but is more difficult to cut because of the greater thickness of the domed face. Beginners will find flat lead easier to learn on.

Unlike lead sizes, which can be happily combined in the same project—and indeed, enhance it—lead styles should generally not be mixed. The one opportunity for diversity of style is in the border where you might want to finish a flat-leaded panel with a round or beaded edge. Otherwise, exercise restraint in combining different styles within one panel, unless you are striving for special effect.

Types. In general, the position of the glass in the composition will dictate whether to use H or U came. H came is used in the interior, where two pieces of glass abut. U came is used along the exterior edges, where its single channel grips the border glass and neatly frames the project.

However, there are circumstances when you will want to bend these rules. For example, if you plan to install a glass window panel into a wooden frame or sash, you would use H came around the edges of the panel so that the unused outside channel can be sunk into the putty to give you a footing (see Figure 85); if you used U came in this installation, the putty would encroach on the glass area. Moreover, the extra unused flange gives you some latitude in installing the panel; if your panel is tight for its space, you can cut the empty flange down to fit the opening.

Fig. 85

On other occasions, you may want to include U came within the interior of a glass panel. For example, you might want to wrap a small, sharply angeled piece of glass with an extremely narrow and flexible U came, then solder it back-to-back to an adjoining piece of glass similarly wrapped. This technique is particularly appropriate for small free-form projects rather than rectangular panels.

Size. Thicker lead has a wider flange which can hide the uneven glass cuts that beginners are apt to make, but it is less flexible than thinner lead, and thus is more useful for straight-line cuts. Thinner leads are more easily worked around acute angles and small pieces of glass, but, naturally, they are less stable than thicker leads.

Novice glassworkers will probably be most comfortable with leads $3/16$, $1/4$, and $3/8$ inch wide. The first is delicate yet stable, the third is strong yet flexible, the second—$1/4$-inch came—is a good all-purpose size. As you solve different design problems, you may, in fact, want to combine different sizes of leading in the same project.

In addition to structural considerations, you will want to weigh the aesthetic impact of different leads on your design. Leading, first of all, must be appropriate to the spirit of the design, to the dimensions of the project, and to the size of the glass pieces that compose it. You don't want to overwhelm a small panel with heavy leads, or crowd small pieces of glass with too much leading, or assemble large pieces of glass with narrow came, giving the appearance of structural instability.

Your task in deciding on the leading will be somewhat eased by the fact that not all styles and types of came come in all sizes, and that your supplier will probably have a limited selection in any case. Rely on your stained glass supplier or hobby shop to help you choose the came most appropriate for your project.

Buying and Storing Lead

Lead cames are usually sold by the pound and in 6-foot lengths. Wider came, containing more lead in each strand than narrow came, costs a little more, and special-purpose cames are higher still. Some suppliers require a minimum order of five or ten strands; others sell came by the box and may require a minimum order of 25, 50, or 100 or more pounds.

If you buy your came in bulk, you will get a better price. When buying by weight, keep in mind that the number of lead cames per pound will vary, depending on the style and size of the came. Some styles are thinner and lighter than others of the same general dimensions, and therefore will have more cames, or at least more total length of came, in the pound. Store the lead flat in its shipping box, or wrap it tightly to prevent exposure to the air and to retard the oxidation that prevents a sturdy solder joint.

How to Work with Lead

Stretching lead strips. Before using any lead strips, you must remove any kinks and bends, and firm up the soft lead by stretching it. Using a lead stretcher or a pair of pliers, pull the strip until its channels are straight and you can feel the lead become taut. A 6-foot strand will stretch 4, 8, or even 12 inches. Be careful not to overstretch the lead, which will weaken the came and narrow the channels. If the lead is badly kinked, you may have to untwist the strand between pulls.

Stretch the lead just prior to using it, not earlier. If you let an already stretched strand lie around and become twisted, you will have a hard time straightening it, since you will already have stretched it to its limit.

Cutting the lead. Since lead is soft and pliant, you will have no trouble cutting it. Lay the came on the worktable on one of its faces, and gently work the curved blade of the lead knife from side to side over the came so as not to damage the lead or collapse the channels. You will find that the weight of the knife and the sharpness of the blade alone are almost enough to cut through narrow and light-weight cames, and that very little additional pressure is needed to slice heavier cames. Be sure the knife makes a clean vertical cut.

If either end of the lead has been crushed during stretching by the lead stretcher or pliers, cut it off before measuring for the individual lead sections. To cut each piece of lead to size, measure the strip against your assembly diagram, then score the cut line with a nail or your thumbnail. Move the lead to an open area on your worktable and cut it as marked. For a well-fitting lead skeleton, measure and cut the lead pieces only as you lead them up.

Sharpen the lead knife occasionally on a Carborundum stone because use will dull its cutting edge. Lift the knife handle about an inch off the surface of the stone and push the blade forward along the surface of the stone, keeping the handle at a steady angle. Repeat a few times on one side of the blade, then sharpen the other side of the blade in the same manner.

Making lead joints. Lead came is cut wherever it meets another came, either straight across or at an angle. Then the two pieces are soldered together at the joint. There are two common types of joints: a butt

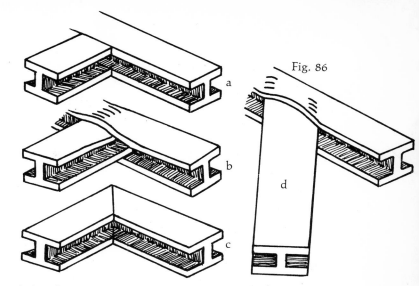

Fig. 86

joint (see Figures 86a and 86c) and an overlap joint (see Figures 86b and 86d). Both can be made at any angle at which the two pieces of lead meet.

A *butt joint* can be made with flat, round, or any of the ornate cames. Both pieces of lead must fit edge to edge, whether they meet at right angles or on the diagonal (see Figure 87). Whether straight or angled, make clean vertical cuts through the lead so that the edges will fit neatly and snugly together. If

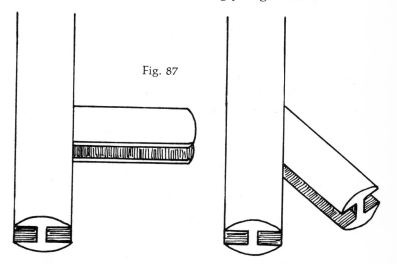

Fig. 87

your cuts are at a slant, the leads will meet at the top (or bottom) but not through the cross section (see Figure 88, next page). If there are any gaps at the joint, plug them with strips of lead cut to fit (see Figure 89) before soldering the joint. With the glass already in place, you

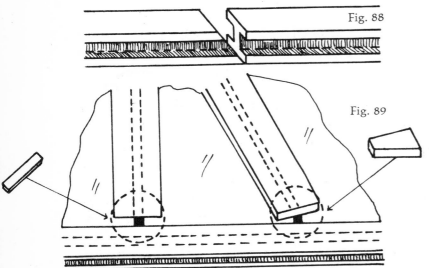

Fig. 88

Fig. 89

won't be able to fit H came into the gap, so cut the plugs out of ribbon came, or slice the face off your H came.

An *overlap joint* can be made with flat

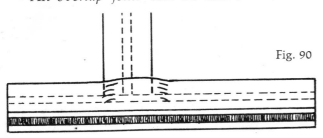

Fig. 90

came only. In this joint, the end of one strip of lead fits into the channel of the second strip of lead (see Figure 90). To make a tight fit, the flanges of the receiving lead must be opened a little at the joint. The overlap joint results in a strong bond, but the double thickness of lead forms a slight hump at the joint.

Opening the lead channels. Obviously, the channels of the lead came must be wide enough to receive the glass pieces they will encase. If you flattened the flanges during

cutting or narrowed the channel during stretching, open them with a lathekin. And if you are working with glass of variable thickness, a characteristic of much hand-blown glass, you may have to enlarge certain parts of the channel still further. In any event, it's good practice to use the lathekin before leading up each piece of glass, even if the channels look sufficiently wide.

Leading Up the Glass

After you have cut the glass, stretched the lead, and opened the lead channels to receive the glass, you are ready to assemble lead and glass in a process called leading up, or glazing. This process starts with planning the metal skeleton.

Planning the lead layout. Since lead tends to weaken and stretch with time, it is important to plan the structure of the soldering joints for maximum stability. Although the basic lead skeleton was set when you worked out your glass design, you will still have choices in the leading sequence.

In order to get the maximum structural support for your project, it is helpful to understand the behavior of lead cames, especially when they are hung vertically and subject to the pressures of gravity. When you plan the lead joints, keep the following in mind:

• One continuous length of came is stronger structurally if it runs vertically rather than horizontally (see Figure 91).

• Short and medium lengths of came that crisscross in a basket-weave pattern are structurally sounder than one length of came that runs from one side to the other (see Figure 92).

• Lead joints that intersect at right angles

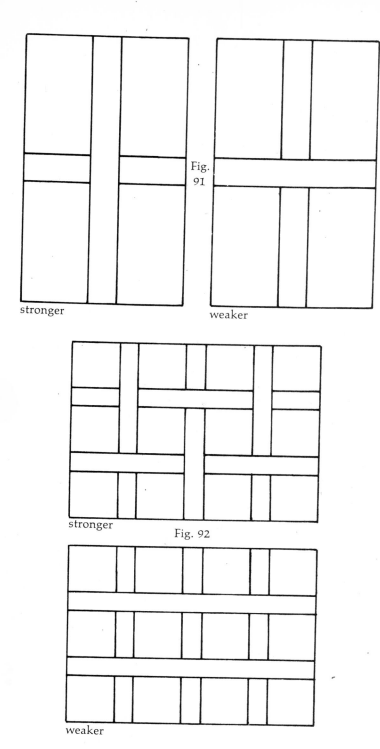

stronger   weaker

Fig. 91

stronger   Fig. 92

weaker

are stronger than joints that converge at acute angles.

These general guidelines suggest choices you can make that will lend stability to the project. Naturally, you don't want to eliminate all the acute angles that occur in your design, but you may want to be careful about clustering too many of them in one area. And if your design depends on a large number of acute angles, you may want to support the project with reinforcing bars.

Even if your glass pieces are already cut, look over the lead layout carefully. If you find that changes in the glass design will result in a stronger, or more interesting, lead structure, recut the glass at this point. It is still relatively easy to improve the glass pattern or lead layout. As soon as you start leading up the glass and soldering the joints, it will be difficult and frustrating to make corrections.

Checking the glass assembly. Each glass pattern on your cartoon, cutting pattern, and assembly diagram is numbered in its general order of assembly. Now that you have worked out the position of all the lead joints and cut lines, double-check this glazing sequence. Since each piece of glass must be slid into its lead channel—rather than dropped into place like a jigsaw puzzle—be sure you have a logical sequence for leading up the glass. This always requires one open side of sufficient width to accommodate the glass, no matter how odd or irregular its shape, for there are many situations in which an unwary glassworker can be caught, unable to insert the next piece of glass into its lead frame (see Figure 93, next page). Often the only solution is to disassemble those glass pieces that block the leading-up sequence and reassemble them in a more logical order.

To avoid any such glazing problems, re-

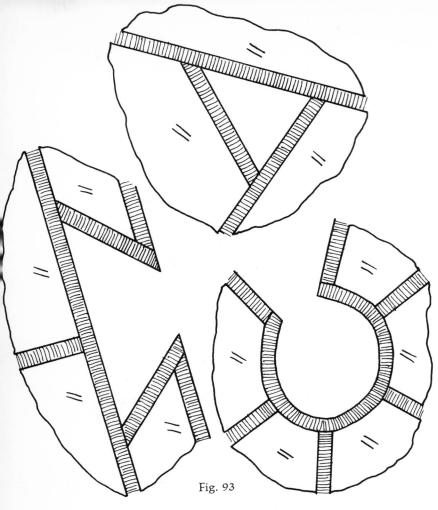

Fig. 93

When your glazing sequence is set, mark on the assembly diagram the order in which you will install the leads (see Figure 94). Note it in a different manner—for example, circle the leading numbers—from the glass sequence already designated there. (Figure 94 shows only the leading sequence; the glass sequence was eliminated for the sake of clarity.)

Setting up the worktable. It is important to keep your pattern pieces and glass pieces in manageable order, particularly if your design includes many pieces of similar shape and size. This is the reason for numbering each pattern piece on the assembly diagram and on the cartoon, and even on each piece of glass. You should also keep track of all the glass pieces themselves. The best way to do that is to lay the cartoon on a flat board or, better yet, in the bottom of a tray, then place all the glass pieces, cut and grozed to their

Fig. 94

check the sequence of your glass layout, starting at the lower left corner of a rectangular panel and fanning out, or in the center of a free-form design. As you note the sequence of each piece of glass, verify each glass number on your assembly diagram. The sequence as marked will probably be correct, but you cannot afford to skip this step. Occasionally, an irregularly shaped piece of glass or a particular leading sequence will change the order in which you originally thought you would lead up the project. Naturally, as you fit lead and glass together, follow any revised sequence of numbers. And if you have numbered the actual pieces of glass, remember to keep those numbers in agreement with a new glazing sequence.

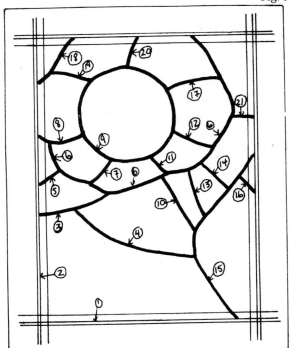

finished shape, on top of the cartoon, each in its proper position. What you will have is the design in glass—without the leading, of course—which gives you one more opportunity to check the fit of the glass components. Then, after you have completed the project, you can file the cartoon for future reference.

Now tape the assembly diagram to your worktable. If you don't have a permanent worktable, set up a temporary one, using a composition board like Homasote or a soft wood board about ½ or ¾-inch thick and at least a few inches larger all around than your project. In either case, tape the assembly diagram a few inches in from both the bottom and the left side of the work surface.

Leading Up a Rectangular Panel

The following instructions are for a rectangular panel, which can be braced against two wood strips. Instructions for leading up free-form designs are given on page 145.

Place one of the four lathing strips on the assembly diagram, lining up its inner edge on the "full-size" border line at the bottom of the assembly diagram (see Figure 95). Tack it in place, nailing through the assembly diagram and partially into the work surface for easy removal after glazing.

Place another lathing strip on the assembly diagram, lining up its inside edge on the "full-size" border at the left side of the assembly diagram and butting one end of the strip at right angles to the side of the first lathing strip (see Figure 96). Tack this lathing strip in place in the same manner. One end of this strip will extend beyond the side of the de-

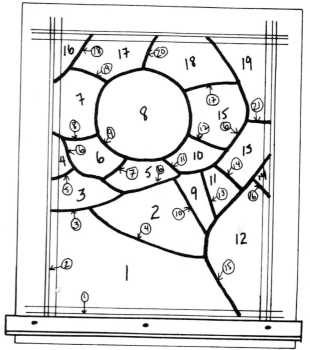

Fig. 95

Fig. 96

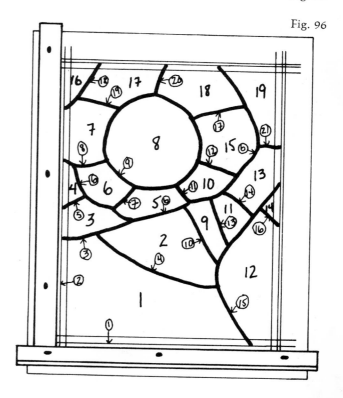

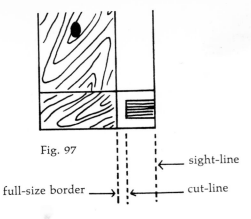

Fig. 97

sight-line

full-size border ⟶ cut-line

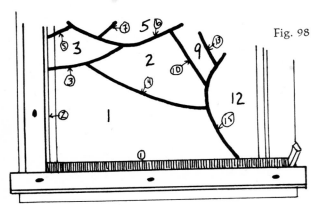

Fig. 98

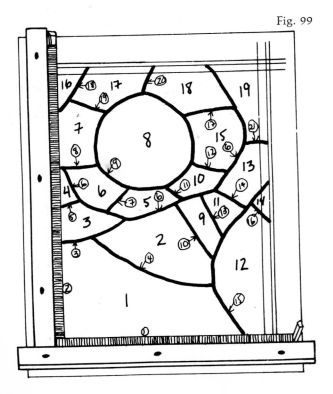

Fig. 99

sign, as one end of the first strip will extend beyond the bottom of the design.

Installing the border leads. Cut one length of lead about an inch longer than the bottom of the design. (Remember to use U came if the edges of the project will be exposed and you want a neat finish.) If your cut has flattened the flanges, open them with the lathekin. Lay the lead against the inside of the horizontal lathing strip with its channel facing in (see Figure 97); the edges of the flanges should come up to the "sight line" on the assembly diagram. Butt one end of the border lead against the vertical lathing strip and tack a horseshoe nail at the other end to hold the lead tightly in place (see Figure 98).

Cut another length of border lead about an inch longer than the left edge of the design, and open its channel if necessary. Lay this lead against the inside of the vertical lathing strip, its channel facing in and its lower end butted against the horizontal lead now in position at the bottom (see Figure 99). This will give you a butt joint at the lower left corner of the border. If you want an overlap joint, open the channel of the horizontal lead slightly and slip the flanges of the vertical lead down into it. Whichever joint you choose, tack a nail at the upper end of the second lead to hold it in place (see Figure 99).

Seating the glass in the lead. Fit the glass piece marked "1" into the corner where the two leads meet, tapping it carefully into place with the weight end of the lead knife. If the channel is too tight for the edge of glass, pry up the flanges with the stopping knife—it will be hard to work the lathekin through the channel when the lead is on its side—then fit the glass into the channel. If the edge of the glass catches on the edge of the bottom flange as you are working it into place, lift the glass

Fig. 100

slightly with the leading or stopping knife so the glass can clear the lower flange (see Figure 100).

When the glass is properly seated, its exposed edge or edges will exactly match the corresponding outline on the assembly diagram on which you are working (see Figure 101). If the glass fits well but its edge still extends beyond the line on the assembly diagram, remove the glass piece and check it against its cutting pattern, then groze where necessary. If it is just slightly too small for its designated space, you can slip a sliver of lead into the channel of the came before fitting the glass back into it. But if the piece of glass is appreciably smaller than its pattern, you will have to cut a new piece of glass the right size. Under no circumstances should you proceed with the leading up if you cannot make the first—or any subsequent—piece fit properly. An ill-fitting glass is difficult to weatherproof and seal, and it may fall out if the lead stretches at a later time.

The glazing sequence. When the first piece of glass has been properly fitted into the corner cames, slip a piece of scrap lead onto the exposed edge and anchor it with a horse-shoe nail (see Figure 102); you may need to secure the glass on more than one edge. Following the leading plan marked on the assembly diagram underneath your work, cut the next strip of lead. (Remember to switch to H came if you used U came for the border leads.) Sometimes a lead extends beyond the edge of the glass (see Figure 103). Fit one channel of this newly cut lead around the exposed edge of glass, and butt one end against a border lead, then slip a piece of wood or

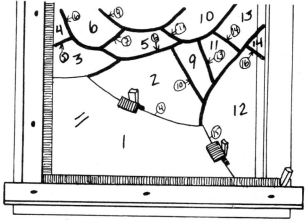

Fig. 102

Fig. 103

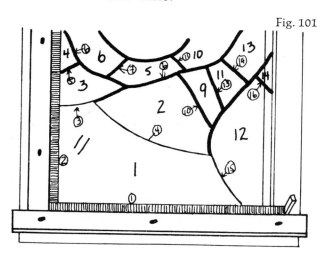

Fig. 101

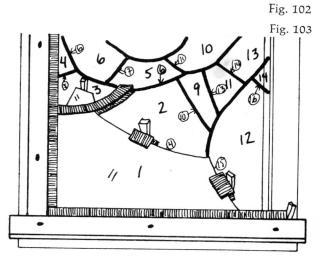

scrap glass into the opposite (empty) channel and secure it with a nail (see Figure 103). At this time ignore the end that extends beyond the glass; it will be fitted to the neighboring glass as you work your way through the glazing sequence.

Remove the nail and scrap lead that secures the glass along the next glass edge to be leaded, then cut that next piece of lead according to the assembly diagram. Install the lead and hold it in place with a piece of wood or scrap glass and a nail (see Figure 104). Note

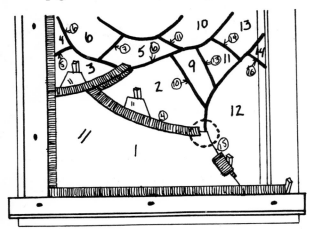

Fig. 104

that this piece, like all interior leads, is cut about $1/16$ inch shorter at each end than the glass edge it encases, to allow room for the flange of the adjoining lead.

Continue to fit glass and lead strips together, following the sequences marked on the assembly diagram. After installing each lead and each piece of glass, check the diagram to see that your work continues to match the outlines of the design. Don't proceed to the next piece of glass or lead until you are satisfied that the glazing is correct.

As you fit each successive piece of glass, tack a piece of scrap came against its edge while you measure and cut the next strip of lead; then remove that nail and scrap lead in order to install the next lead strip, securing that in succession with a piece of wood or scrap glass and a nail. In this way, tacking and retacking the glass and lead as you fit the design together, you can keep the components in alignment.

Occasionally your assembly diagram will designate a long lead that is to hold several pieces of glass, and not all of them may be in place when you first lead up the strip. Measure the lead for its entire length, then lead up the glass pieces in sequence, letting the unfitted portion of the lead fall freely on the worktable until needed (see Figure 105, in which No. 6 lead, already partially leaded in place, awaits the installation of No. 15 and No. 18 glass pieces). As each piece of glass is installed, you can anchor another segment of the lead strip against its edge.

When you have fitted all the glass pieces tightly in place, but before you install the last two border leads, inspect all the exposed glass along these two open sides to be sure they are aligned with the cut line (the center of the three border lines). Groze or recut any ill-fitting glass so that these edges and the border leads that will hold them will form straight lines.

When the border glass fits properly, cut the top and right border cames according to the type of joint—overlap or butt—you want at the three remaining corners. Fit the border came around the edges of the glass; their flanges should coincide with the "full-size" lines on the assembly diagram (see Figure 106). Now trim the ends of the bottom and left border leads flush with these newly installed leads.

Nail the two remaining lathing strips along the right side and the top, as you did

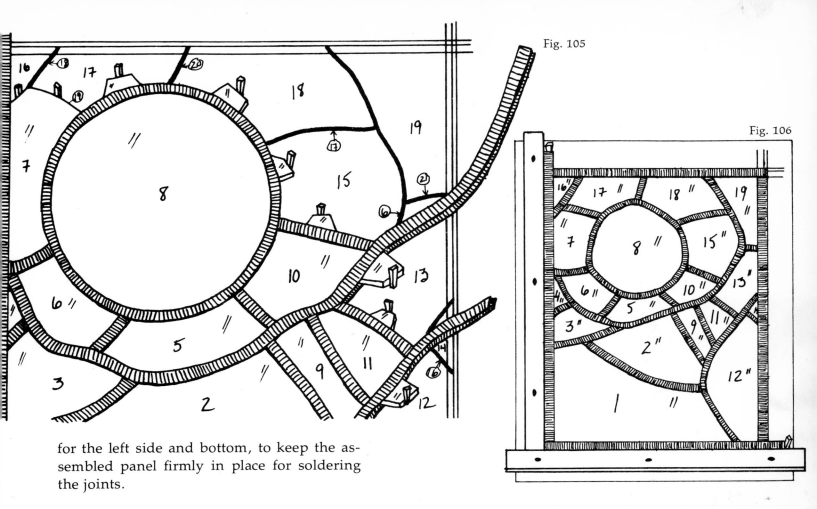

Fig. 105

Fig. 106

for the left side and bottom, to keep the assembled panel firmly in place for soldering the joints.

Leading Up Free-Form Designs

The basic techniques for leading up free-form designs are the same as they are for leading up rectangular panels, with two main differences: you start leading in the center of a free-form design and fan out, rather than starting at the lower left corner and moving to the right and up; and since there are no lathing strips to hold the assembly in position as you work, you solder each joint as you lead it up rather than wait to the end to solder all the joints at once.

Mark the assembly diagram with the leading sequence, as well as the order in which you will lead up the glass pieces (see Figure 107, next page). The first piece to be leaded will be somewhere in the interior of the design; then the contiguous pieces, working your way to the outer edges. Remember that you must always be able to slide each glass piece into the already leaded structure (see Figure 93 for some pitfalls in leading layouts). When you have numbered the assembly diagram, tape it to your work surface.

Lead the first piece of glass and solder the joint. Position it on the assembly diagram and secure it with horseshoe nails and a scrap of wood or glass (see Figure 108, next page). Follow the assembly diagram, fit the next piece of glass, then lead, in place, keeping

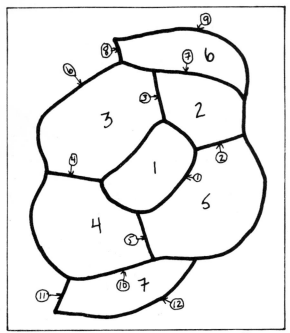

Fig. 107

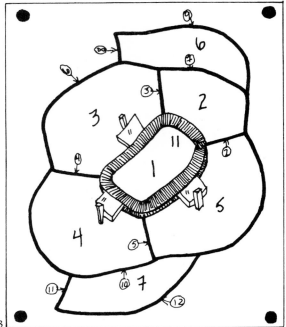

Fig. 108

them aligned with horseshoe nails and protecting the lead with a piece of wood or glass, and the glass with a remnant of lead.

As you work, fitting glass and leads together, and soldering as you go, check the fit and shape of each glass piece against the assembly diagram taped underneath. Any discrepancy will throw the entire composition out of kilter, and once you have soldered in a mistake, you will have a hard time correcting it.

On free-form pieces, just as on rectangular panels, use U came around the outer edges for a neatly finished appearance. Occasionally your leading layout may call for a lead to run from the interior out and around part of the border (see the No. 6 lead in Figure 109). In such cases, use U came even though it will extend into the interior of the design. Then use another piece of the same U came on any contiguous interior edges (see No. 7 lead in Figures 109 and 110). Solder those U cames

back-to-back, creating, in effect, one H came.

Note: Since free-form designs have irregular outlines, they usually cannot be braced by lathing strips. Sometimes, however, you can rig up a frame for a geometric shape, like an octagon or hexagon (see Figure 111). If possible, try to devise one to keep your design tightly assembled.

Tips and Reminders for Leading Up

• Cut the came in place on the assembly diagram when that is easier for you, using the curved lead knife upside down if you need to get into tight places. Don't worry about mutilating the paper assembly diagram; it will be riddled with nail holes and you will discard it after leading up the design. You can keep the original cartoon for reference and filing.

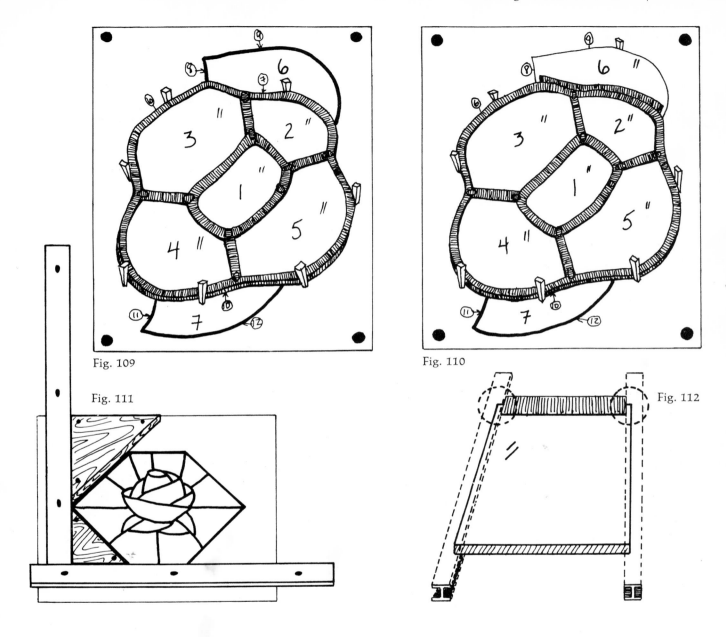

Fig. 109

Fig. 110

Fig. 111

Fig. 112

• Keep scraps of lead to use in anchoring the glass pieces during glazing.

• Every time you cut lead, make it a habit to open the flanges with a lathekin, even if the came doesn't appear to need it. If you take this precaution, the glass will always enter the channels easily during glazing.

• In general, when you are using butt joints and fairly straight-edged pieces of glass, you can cut each lead strip about $1/8$ inch shorter than the length of the glass edge it encloses. This will allow $1/16$ inch on each end to abut the flanges of the adjoining leads (see Figure 112).

• When leading curves or circles or irregular shapes, cut the came about an inch longer than needed (see Figure 113a). As you shape the lead to the contours of the glass, you will see that the extra length gives you needed flexibility. Then trim the came to size, allowing for either overlap or butt joints on contiguous leads (see Figure 113b).

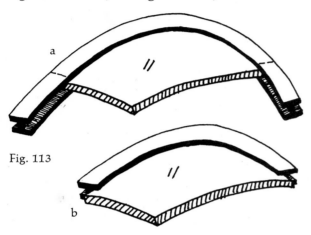

Fig. 113

• When leading a circle or oval, cut the lead an inch or two longer than the circumference of the glass, then bend the lead strip into a circle, with the two ends overlapping each other. Score the cut line on the top piece of lead, then carefully slice through both layers of the came (see Figure 114). You will have a neater joint using this method than if you make a separate cut on each end of the lead, then join them in a circle.

• When leading curves, mold the came carefully to the edges of the glass, and move your fingers slowly along the came to prevent the lead from kinking.

• If you are leading around a sharper curve than your lead can negotiate without bunching up, cut a triangular wedge out of the flanges (see Figure 115). Close up the dart and solder as you would a butt joint.

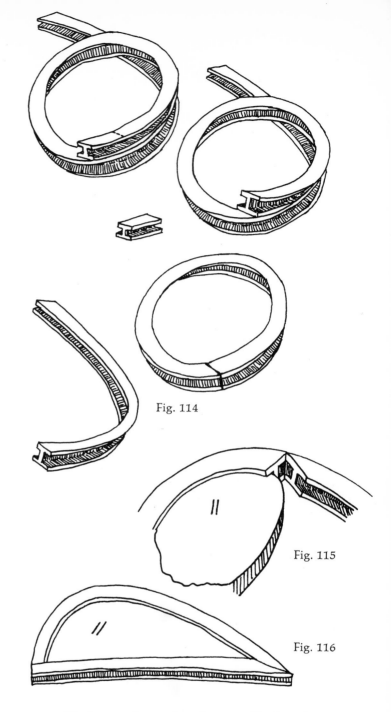

Fig. 114

Fig. 115

Fig. 116

• If the outline of a shape calls for sharp crisp edges—the point of a star or leaf, or a diamond, for example—cut the lead rather than bend it so you can make mitered butt joints that will form the angle you want (see Figure 116).

• When you want to create the impression of having leaded up two contiguous pieces of glass without actually cutting them, use ribbon came to traverse the surface of the one piece. Cut it to fit between two other leads, then solder it at each end (see Figure 117).

Fig. 118

Fig. 119

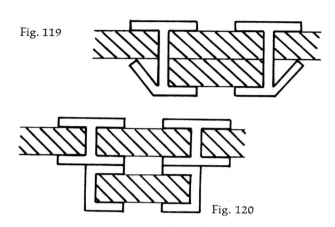
Fig. 120

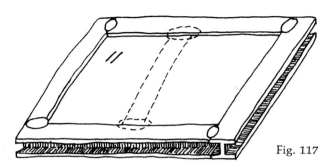
Fig. 117

• You can simulate ribbon came by slicing the face off flat H came, or by opening the flanges of U came until it lies flat. You can also cut ribbon came lengthwise into narrower strips.

• If you are leading two pieces of contiguous glass, one thinner than the other, and you want a flat surface, raise the thinner piece so it is flush with its neighbor. Keep it in place temporarily with a scrap of cardboard wedged between the underside of the glass and the flange. As soon as you have entirely leaded around the thinner piece of glass, remove the cardboard and crimp the bottom flange so that the glass is flush with the upper flange (see Figure 118). If you want to recess a thin piece of glass, mount the glass flush with the bottom flange, following the same procedure.

• If you want to blend glass colors visually, mount two pieces of glass back-to-back in high-heart came (see Figure 119). Or you can lead up the top layer of glass traditionally, then solder a second lead piece to the back of the first (see Figure 120), using H or U

came. This last method can be done at the time of the original leading, but it can also be done after the panel has been completed, an obvious advantage if you want to change or correct the color or tone of a piece of glass. The technique is called doubling, or double-glazing.

Soldering the Lead Joints

Inspect all joints carefully to be sure they abut tightly. If there are any gaps, fill them with slivers of lead came (see Figure 89). If you are working with flat lead came, hammer out any bulges or unevenness at each joint. Then scrub all the joints to a newly minted shine with a wire brush or steel wool to remove oxidation. Finally, plug in your soldering iron and, as the iron is heating, flux the joints with oleic acid.

Solder all the joints on one side of the panel, then turn the panel over carefully and solder the other side. Wipe the excess flux from the glass with a rag (see "Cleaning the Project," page 153).

Note: Complete instructions for soldering are given in the preceding chapter, "Working with Solder."

Turning Over Large Panels

Turn all panels over with care, particularly when only one side has been soldered. The weight of the glass and the lead may cause the unsupported panel to sag and the lead to release its firm grip on the glass pieces. Use the following procedure to turn all panels under 2½ feet square; larger panels require even more caution.

Remove the wood lathing strips that hold the panel in alignment. Slide the glass panel to the edge of the worktable and then out over the edge until you can tip it vertically—that is, perpendicular to the floor. Holding the panel vertically, rotate it so that the soldered side is now facing the table. Position the vertical panel so that its upper half extends above the rim of the table (see Figure 121). Using the

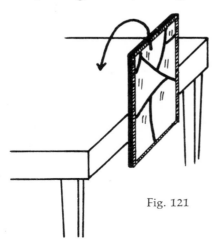

Fig. 121

edge of the table as a fulcrum, tip the panel horizontally until its top half rests on the table, then slide it all the way onto the table. The unsoldered side of the panel will be facing up.

If you are making a panel larger than 2½ feet square, you should take extra precautions. First, you would do well to have another person help you. Then, before starting to turn the panel, slip a plywood board between the panel and the table, working it under the glass from one corner only; at this point, don't lift two corners of the leaded glass at the same time. Lay another board over the glass to make a glass sandwich, as it were. The two boards will support the panel as you turn it, following the instructions above.

Use the supporting boards through the entire turn, removing them only after the panel is again back on the worktable. Slip the bottom board out just as carefully as you inserted it, picking up just one corner of the panel.

Reinforcing Large Panels

A leaded panel more than 3 or 4 feet tall should be reinforced with horizontal bars every foot or two to buttress the lead against gravitational pull that may cause it to sag. This is just as true for a hanging or freestanding panel as it is for a panel installed in a window.

Plan the support bars where they will be least disturbing visually, preferably behind some horizontal leading. Remember that even though the bars will be at the back of the panel, light coming through the glass will silhouette them. With a hacksaw cut the support bars the width of the panel out of ½-inch-round metal bars—galvanized steel, for example—and set them aside until the panel has been completed. However, the copper ties that will hold the bars to the project should be soldered in place while you are soldering the lead joints.

You will need copper ties to hold each bar at every point where the bar crosses a lead came; this will be at each border lead and probably at one or more points across the panel (see Figure 122). For each tie cut a piece of 16- or 18-gauge copper wire about 4 to 5 inches long. At their points of contact, scrub wire and lead clean with a brush, then apply oleic acid or zinc chloride flux.

Solder the center inch of each copper wire to the lead, applying a small amount of pressure with the hot soldering iron to embed each heated copper tie in the lead came. Mount the copper ties vertically—or as upright as the direction of the lead cames permits—so that the ends of the copper ties can be twisted around the metal bar easily (see Figure 123).

Loops for Hanging

If you want to hang a leaded panel, you will have to solder hooks to the project. These hooks are usually made of copper wire of a gauge suited to the weight of the panel; 18-gauge wire is a good all-purpose weight. For a particularly heavy panel use a thicker wire (lower gauge number), and for a lightweight piece you can use a thinner wire (higher gauge number).

Form the copper loops in either of the fol-

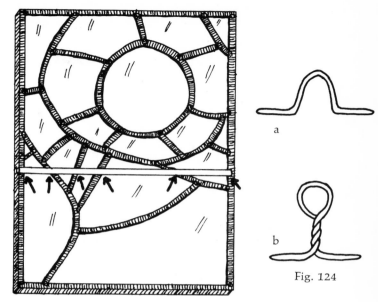

Fig. 122

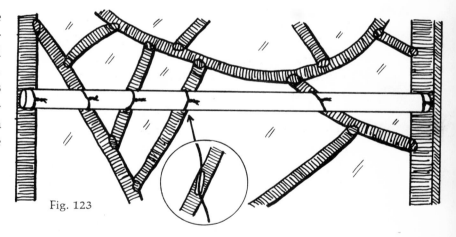

Fig. 124

Fig. 123

lowing ways. You can bend a 2-inch length of wire into a semicircle with outstretched arms (see Figure 124a). Or you can fold a 3- to 4-inch length of copper wire in half, insert in the bend a pencil, a nail, or the shaft of a screwdriver, then twist the wire ends together with a pliers or your fingers. Leave at least a half inch at each end of the wire which you can pull apart and flatten (see Figure 124b).

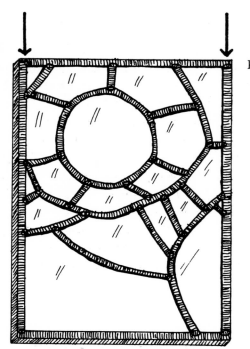

Fig. 125

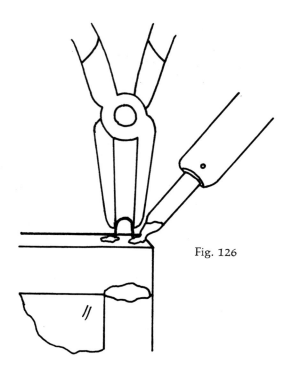

Fig. 126

Solder hooks only at points where leads run from top to bottom in the panel. The weight of the panel should rest only on vertical leads and not at other points where the pull of gravity could cause leads to sag and relax their grip on the glass pieces. In many projects, this dictates the placement of the hooks at the two top corners—above the vertical border leads (see Figure 125)—but if there are other upright leads that run through the entire panel, you may attach hooks at those points.

Prop the panel upright to avoid possible solder drips on the sides of your work. At the soldering points, scrub the lead with a wire brush, then paint with oleic acid or zinc chloride flux. Hold each copper loop with a pair of pliers and dip it into the flux. With the hot tip of your soldering iron, lay some solder over the wire ends of the hook as you press them into the lead came (see Figure 126).

Puttying

After the lead joints are soldered, the project should be puttied. The putty fills the cracks between the glass and the lead channels, stabilizing the glass in its frame and actually weatherproofing the panel—an important consideration if you are making an exterior window.

To facilitate cleaning up and to cushion the panel as you work, lay the project on a few thicknesses of newsprint. Take a small amount of putty in your hands and force it into the channels of the lead came between the flanges and the glass. As you work along the length of one lead, you will find you can push the putty under the flange on the near side with your thumb while you draw it under the flange on the far side with another finger (see Figure 127). The lead channels must be well puttied, and if you have dif-

Fig. 127

ficulty working the putty deep into them, lift the flanges slightly with the stopping knife. Don't forget to putty the border leads as well as the interior leads, taking care not to push them off the border glass with the vigor of the application.

When you have puttied all the leads on the first side of the panel, crimp the flanges against the glass with the stopping knife or a bent putty knife. This will force some excess putty out of the channels. Now draw a pointed stick along the glass at the side of the lead to force some putty back under the flanges and at the same time cut the excess putty away so you can discard it as you proceed.

After you have completed one side, turn the panel over in the manner described above and putty the second side in the same way. Forcing the putty into the channels and crimping the flanges on the second side may well cause some of the putty to ooze out of the flanges on the first side, so when you complete the second side, turn the panel over and check the original puttying. You may have to clean the edges of the leads again with the pointed stick.

The putty may continue to seep out of the lead flanges for a short while. During this period, keep the glass wiped clean with a rag because the putty forms a crust that is hard to remove when entirely dry.

Note: You can remove putty from your hands with linseed oil.

Cleaning the Project

Clean the glass and the leading with Spanish whiting (calcium carbonate), which will absorb any remaining linseed oil from the putty and any residues from the oleic acid flux. Sprinkle one side of the panel with the powder, then scrub the surface well with a stiff brush. Tip the panel to remove the powder, then wipe off any remaining whiting with rags or paper toweling. Inspect the panel carefully, and if the glass is still dirty repeat the whiting treatment on this side.

Turn the panel over carefully and clean the other side in the same way.

Antiquing Lead Came

If you like the soft look of pewter, leave the lead cames and soldered joints alone. But if you want an antique finish, you can use gun blue, a commercially prepared solution available at many sports stores. With a small brush, apply the solution first to the soldered joints only, letting it stand for 2 or 3 minutes. Apply a second coat to both leads and soldered joints, letting this application stand no more than 2 minutes. Rinse the panel well with water, then wash it with water and a mild detergent.

Note: Keep the glass free of gun blue, which will stain it.

You can concoct your own antiquing solution by mixing muriatic acid with acetic acid, a wetting agent; a stronger solution will produce a darker color. Brush the solution on the leading, then wash it off—the color depends on the strength of the solution and not on how long it sits on the lead.

Repairing Cracked Glass

Sometimes you can repair a simple glass crack without reglazing by using ribbon came like a lead splint. Cut the came to fit over the fracture and between the nearest lead strips on either end of the fracture—even if the crack itself doesn't extend the entire distance between those leads. Then solder them together in butt joints (see Figure 117). You may want to lead the other side of the cracked glass in the same way to reinforce the break.

If the fracture is so compound that it cannot be repaired by a single lead, you can replace the entire piece if the original leading had a flat face (round-face lead is much more difficult to manipulate in this procedure). If you don't have the original cutting pattern with which to make a replacement glass, turn the damaged section into a cutting pattern by taping its cracked surface with masking tape while it is still held by the leading. Cut the flat lead came holding the cracked section diagonally at the joints, then pry open the flanges to release the damaged glass.

Using your original cutting pattern, or the taped section of glass, cut the replacement glass, matching the color and texture of the original if you can. If all else fails, you can make a new cutting pattern from a piece of oak tag. Tape the oak tag to the back of the project behind the now empty section, and trace its outline. Since the tracing represents only the visible glass area—the sight line—you must add about ⅛ inch all around for the cut line, to account for the glass which will lie under the flange.

Before soldering the replacement glass in place, clean the surrounding leads carefully with a wire brush and steel wool. Drop the new glass in place, press the pried-up flanges back against the glass, and solder at the cuts.

Safety Precautions for Working with Lead

• Keep your work area well ventilated at all times, especially during soldering.

• Flush your hands well with warm water immediately after working with lead. This will open the pores so the lead particles will rinse away. Then wash well with soap.

• Don't touch your hands to your face, especially around your mouth, or pick up food while working with lead. Slight exposure to lead fumes or particles will not cause damage, but prolonged exposure has a cumulative effect and may cause lead poisoning, which is characterized by the following symptoms: upset stomach, abdominal cramps, numbness and tingling of hands and feet, headache, and irritability. See your doctor if you experience any of these symptoms.

Working with Copper Foil

Copper foil, a newcomer compared to lead came, with its medieval origins, has been in use about 100 years as a means of joining glass pieces together. And its technique, made more convenient by the development of adhesive-backed foil, is still basically the same as that practiced by the glass artisans of the late nineteenth century who first recognized its potential.

Tools and Supplies

The equipment needed for working with copper foil is simplicity itself—little more than the foil and something to cut it with. Plus, of course, a soldering kit to transform the flexible metal strips into a sturdy skeleton for the glass.

A *utility knife, single-edged razor blade,* or a cutting tool like an *X-acto knife* are used to cut foil. They make cleaner cuts than do scissors, although scissors can be used if necessary.

A *metal straightedge* guides the knife or razor blade when cutting foil. Any straightedge can be used, but you will find that a metal one will withstand the nicks that are likely to be inflicted by the cutting tool. Since you will probably want foil strips about 18 to 24 inches long, your straightedge should measure at least 2 feet.

A *burnisher* rubs the copper foil against the glass edges to remove any air bubbles that may have been trapped while you wrapped and crimped the foil. Some craftsmen like a smooth and polished piece of wood for this purpose, but you can actually use anything at all—the handle of your knife, the side of a pencil, even the top of your fingernail.

A *wire brush* cleans dirty and oxidized copper foil so it can be soldered properly.

Needle-nose pliers (see Figure 128) have long narrow jaws for forming loops out of copper wire.

Nails keep the glass sections in position while you tack-solder them together. Horse-

Fig. 128

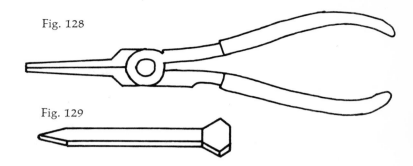

Fig. 129

shoe nails (see Figure 129) are about 2 inches long; they are easily hammered into and removed from the work surface, and their broad, flat sides won't nick the foil as sharp-sided nails are likely to do.

Lathing strips frame rectangular designs, bracing the foil-wrapped glass and keeping the pieces in position as you tack-solder them together. With rectangular panels you will need four lathing strips, each 1 to 2 inches by ½ inch.

#000 steel wool is used to remove the oxidation from the soldered seams and to buff them for a silvery finish.

Copper sulphate is applied to the soldered foil for a coppery patina. It comes already in solution or in the form of crystals, to be mixed with hot water.

Tinner's fluid is applied to the soldered foil for a pewterlike patina. You can buy it at hardware stores.

Whiting, which is powdered calcium carbonate (chalk), is used to clean soldered foil if you have used oleic acid as the flux.

Copper Foil

Copper foil is sold in lengths or sheets by the pound and with adhesive backing in narrow rolls of various precut widths. Sheet foil is usually available 6 or 12 inches wide and in thicknesses ranging from .005 inches for heavy work to .001 inches for fine work. A pound of .005-inch foil, 12 inches wide, is about 4 feet long; a half pound of .001-inch foil, 6 inches wide, is about 21 feet long.

More expensive but much more convenient are the already cut rolls of adhesive-backed foil that adheres to the glass edges and greatly simplifies the wrapping process. These rolls are 36 yards long, about .015 inch thick, and are available in a variety of useful widths—$^3/_{16}$, $^7/_{32}$, $^1/_4$, $^5/_{16}$, $^3/_8$, and $^1/_2$ inch. Some suppliers offer kits with samples of each width of foil.

When buying copper foil, your choice will usually be between the higher cost and greater convenience of the precut, adhesive-backed rolls and the less expensive foil sheets which do not have adhesive backing and which must be cut into strips. However, if your work requires a heavier (thicker) foil for stability, or if you need wider foil than you can find in the roll, you will obviously have to cut your own. In whatever form you purchase the foil, store it in plastic bags, brown paper, or another airtight package in a dry place to retard oxidizing.

Selecting the right foil. The width of the copper foil will be determined by the thickness of the glass to be wrapped, since the strips of foil should be slightly wider than the edges of the glass they enclose. The precise amount of this overhang on top and bottom glass surfaces can vary, as long as there is sufficient foil to retain a good grip on the glass. Thin edgings of foil create an airy gossamer look and appear more appropriate to smaller pieces of glass; wider surface bands lend a look of strength and stability, and seem better suited to larger pieces and longer spans of glass—although the actual strength of the foil has little relation to its width. When tinned—that is, soldered over its entire surface—even the narrowest foil becomes strong and capable of supporting a heavy glass structure.

A good rule of thumb is to choose foil that is twice or, at most, three times as wide as the thickness of the glass. Since much of your glass will be about $^1/_8$ inch thick, you'll find that $^1/_4$-inch foil is a good width for general use. But don't hesitate to vary foil widths, not only to accommodate glass of different thicknesses but also for decorative interest. However, when deciding how much foil to show on the face of the glass, remember that all foiled edgings, wide or narrow, will double in width as soon as similarly foiled pieces of glass are set next to them.

How to Work with Copper Foil

Cutting a foil sheet into strips. Start with a piece of foil the length you want your individual strips to be, probably between 18 and 24 inches. Don't work with a longer piece than you need since foil strips tend to tangle. Lay the foil sheet on newsprint or cardboard and secure it across the short ends with tape. Mark each tape in the widths you want your strips. Following the markings, hold a utility knife or single-edged razor blade against the side of a straightedge, and cut the foil in one continuous motion from side to side (see Figure 130). Discard one tape by slicing across the cut strips, then affix the remaining tape to the side of your worktable or to a wall (see Figure 131), letting the foil strips hang neatly out of the way (copper strips tend to tangle

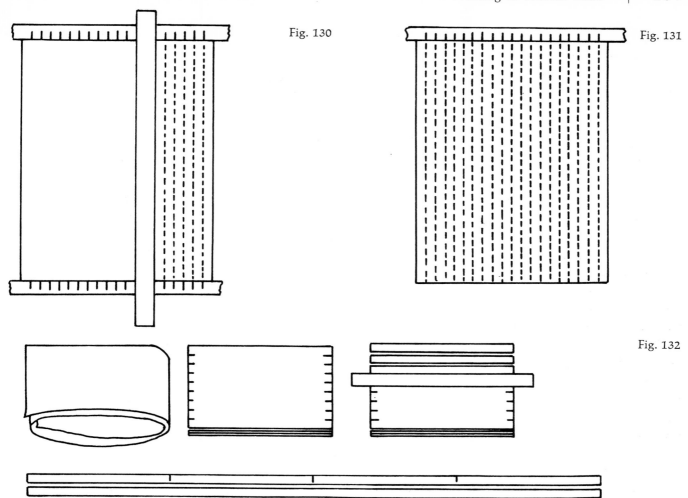

Fig. 130

Fig. 131

Fig. 132

and tear if left on a flat surface). As you wrap the glass, peel off foil strips as needed.

If your foil sheet is longer than your worktable, fold it over a few times. Carefully mark the folded foil in the widths needed, then cut cleanly through the multiple thicknesses and unfold each long strip (see Figure 132). The markings on each side must match each other accurately so the long strips will be uniformly wide when spread out.

Wrapping the glass in foil. Before working with foil strips, wash and dry your hands and the glass so the foil will adhere well.

Unroll about a foot of precut foil and peel

the protective paper off the adhesive backing; if you have cut your own strips, take a length in one hand. Hold the glass in your other hand and center the foil over one edge of the glass (see Figure 133, next page). You can start foiling anywhere along an edge, but not at a corner or point, and not along the outside edges of border pieces. Wrap the foil around all the edges of the glass. Keep the foil taut with one hand and guide the foil around the glass with the other (see Figure 134, next page). As you work your way around the glass, be sure that the foil remains centered on the glass edges so the overhang on each side is exactly

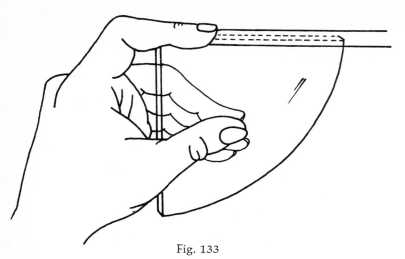

Fig. 133

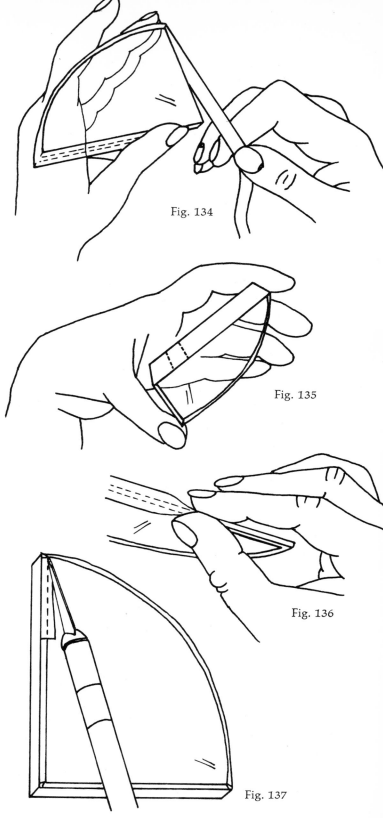

Fig. 134

Fig. 135

Fig. 136

Fig. 137

the same width. If the foil moves off center, correct the deviation immediately.

When you reach the point where you started, overlap the ends of the foil about ¼ inch, then cut the strip of foil off neatly (see Figure 135). Adhesive-backed foil will stick nicely to the glass, but if you are using plain foil, secure the overlapping joint with flux and a drop of solder so the foil will not slip off the glass edges.

After you have wrapped the glass, press the overhanging foil tightly against each side of the glass to form neat margins of foil. Using thumb and first finger, you will be able to crimp both sides in the same motion (see Figure 136). Work your way around the piece of glass, making neat tucks at the corners to take up the slack. If the foil margins don't meet evenly at the overlap, or if the foil was not always centered on the glass edges, you can trim excess foil right on the glass with a razor blade or X-acto knife (see Figure 137).

Rub all the foil surfaces—front, back, and on the edges—with a burnisher, the handle of the glass cutter, a fingernail, or a piece of wood to press them tightly to the glass. The taut, neatly crimped, and burnished foil now makes a form-fitting U channel, as it were, around the glass.

If any strips of foil become tangled or torn during the wrapping or crimping procedure, replace them and refoil the piece of glass. Except for the slight overlap where the ends of foil meet each other, don't lay one strip of foil over another.

Setting Up the Worktable

It is helpful to keep your glass pieces in manageable order, especially if your design includes many pieces of similar shape and size. This is the reason for numbering each pattern and piece of glass and for indicating the corresponding numbers on the assembly diagram and cartoon. You will also want to keep track of the foiled glass pieces, and the easiest way to do that is to set the cartoon on a flat board or in the bottom of a tray.

As you foil each piece of glass, place it on the cartoon in its designated area (see Figure 138). When all the pieces of glass have been foiled and laid in position on the cartoon, you will be able to see the assembled project before soldering it. Now is the time to check the fit of each foiled glass, matching it against its individual outline and making sure that all glass sections nest snugly together.

Even though each piece of glass has been cut and grozed to match its pattern precisely, you may well find that after it has been foiled it no longer fits tightly into the design layout. This may be because the foil was not wrapped tautly—leaving some crinkled, bunched, or slack foil—or because the foil was not crimped and burnished well. Whatever the reason, correct it by refoiling the piece before soldering the project. Since you should not

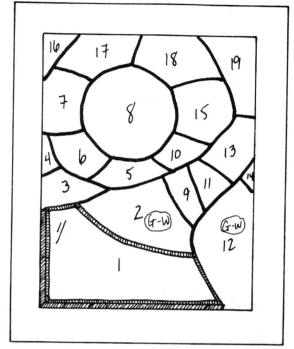

Fig. 138

reuse foil, peel the foil off the edges and rewrap more carefully with new foil.

When you are satisfied that the foiled pieces fit properly, tape or pin the assembly diagram to your worktable, a few inches in from the bottom and left side. If you don't have a permanent worktable, you can set up a temporary work area, using a composition board like Homasote about ¼ or ¾ inch thick, and at least a few inches larger all around than your design.

Assembling a Foiled Project

Free-form designs. Transfer the foiled pieces from the cartoon to the worktable, placing each in its proper position on the assembly diagram. As you assemble the design, hold the individual pieces tightly in place, one against the other, with push pins or horseshoe nails (see Figure 139).

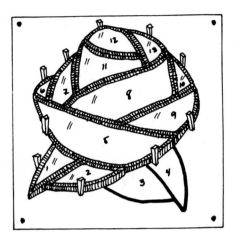

Fig. 139

Rectangular panels. If your design is rectangular, you may find it easier to brace the project against wood lathing strips than to keep it aligned with nails. Place one of the four lathing strips on the assembly diagram and line up its inner edge on the bottom border of the diagram (see Figure 140). Tack it in place, nailing it through the paper and partially into the work surface for easy removal after assembly.

Place a second lathing strip on the assembly diagram, lining up its inner edge on the left border of the diagram and abutting its bottom end at right angles to the side of the first lathing strip (see Figure 140). Tack this lathing strip as you did the first.

Transfer the foiled pieces from the cartoon to the assembly diagram, working from the bottom left corner of the design and placing each piece in its designated position. Hold the individual pieces tightly in place with push pins or horseshoe nails, tacking and retacking them as you extend the design (see Figure 141). When all the foiled pieces are laid

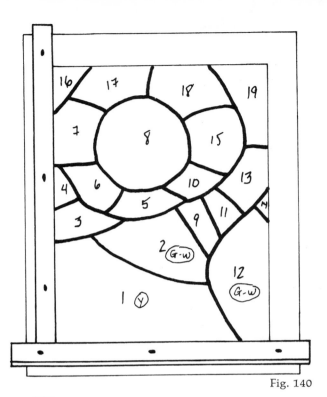

Fig. 140

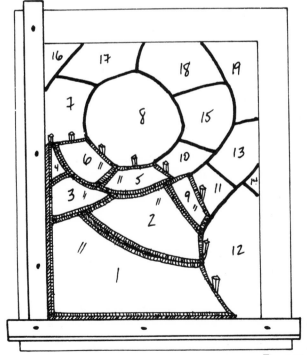

Fig. 141

down, nail a lathing strip along the right side, and another across the top, just as you did on the left side and bottom (see Figure 142).

When the project is assembled and held firmly in place with horseshoe nails, push pins, or lathing strips, it is ready to be soldered.

Soldering Foiled Projects

Unlike lead came, which is soldered only at its joints, copper foil is soldered all along its surface so that no foil at all remains visible. Moreover, a second soldering, called "beading," follows the first soldering, or "tinning," and it lays a high rounded ridge on the tinned skeleton that adds needed strength and stability to the project as well as a nicely finished look. Before the initial soldering, however, the foiled pieces are "tacked" together at strategic points with drops of solder so that you can remove the nails or lathing strips that hold the project in place. Tacking, tinning, and beading are done on both sides of a project in the following order: tack and tin the first side, then turn the project over and tack, tin, and bead the second side, then turn the project over again and bead the first side.

Note: Complete information about soldering is given in the chapter, "Working with Solder."

Tack-soldering. Wherever you want to tack the project together, brush the joint with flux, then over it melt a dollop of 60/40 solder with a hot soldering iron (see Figure 143). The solder tacks should be fairly flat for the tinning procedure that follows; if any are bumpy, "iron" them with a hot soldering

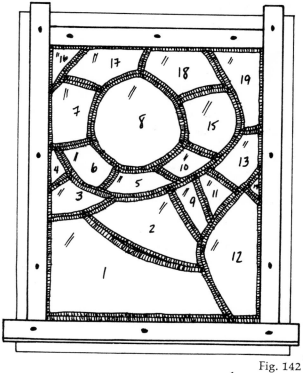

Fig. 142

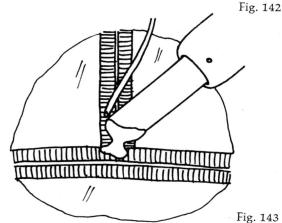

Fig. 143

iron without adding flux. Tack the first side, but don't move the project until this tacked side has been tinned, because tacks alone have only a loose hold on the panel.

At this point you can remove the horseshoe nails or lathing strips that brace the project if you find they get in the way of your soldering. If you want to make the same design another time, you should also carefully remove the assembly diagram underneath the panel before it gets messy or torn during the tinning or beading.

Tinning. Tinning lays a thin coat of solder over the copper foil, filling in any small crevices between the separately foiled pieces of glass and transforming the flexible foil into a fairly rigid metal that retains a strong grip on the glass. If, despite careful glass cutting and foiling, there are still wide gaps between the individually foiled pieces of glass, stuff them with bits of copper foil before tinning the project (see Figure 144).

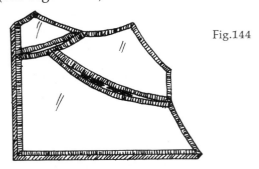

Fig.144

To tin the project, brush flux all over the copper foil, including the already tacked joints. Hold the solder wire in one hand, just below and ahead of the hot soldering tip. Move the solder and the soldering tip together over the copper foil seams so the hot solder can flow over the foil as you simultaneously feed the wire solder and heat it with the iron (see Figure 145). Don't let the solder-

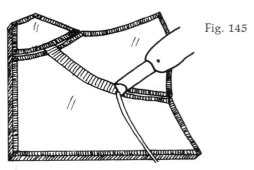

Fig. 145

ing iron get too hot or the solder will fall through to the opposite side of the project, and don't keep a hot iron in one spot for more than a moment because the heat can break the glass. However, since copper melts at a much higher temperature than the lead and tin in the solder, a hot iron is not likely to endanger the copper foil itself.

As you move the solder and the iron over the foiled seams, be sure to plug the small crevices with solder and to see that the larger gaps, which you have filled with crumpled foil, are well soldered. Hold and use the soldering iron lightly so the tip doesn't push and dislodge the pieces of glass or tear the foil. When you have completed this soldering— that is, tinning—properly, the copper bands edging the glass pieces will be entirely covered by neat, flat solder seams.

Beading. Beading is the most difficult of the soldering procedures, especially for the novice. Not only is it hard to form and maintain a nicely rounded bead—the solder tends to flatten out as in the initial tinning—but you run the risk of melting and destroying the firm, neat tinning job you have just completed.

To build a high, rounded line of beading, work quickly with a moderately hot iron. If you have a rheostat control on your soldering iron, set it to about half or three-fourths the line voltage; if you don't have a temperature control, turn the iron on and off, maintaining as cool a temperature as possible that will still soften the solder and pull it up.

Without fluxing the tinned seams, lay down the solder with the iron, connecting continuous drops of solder while trying to keep them from melting and flattening out. Keep the tip of the iron slightly raised, rather than dragging it through the solder, so that it can pull or push the solder into an elevated ridge—that is, float a bead—along the previously tinned seam (see Figure 146). Try to complete each bead in one draw.

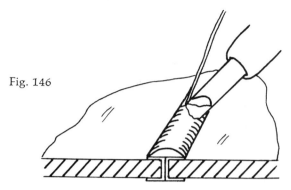

Fig. 146

Bead all the lines in the same direction, working from one edge of the project across to another. Then float the beading in the opposite direction, interrupting this second ridge when you come to a previously beaded line (see Figure 147). Rather than pulling one bead across another, connect the two lines of beading with a separate drop of solder (see Figure 148).

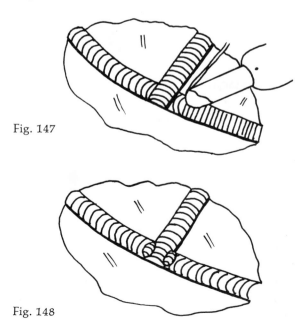

Fig. 147

Fig. 148

Because of the difficulty in mastering the beading technique, you may have to rework your initial beading at least once, if not several times. Use essentially the same technique for subsequent beadings as you did for the first, but use very little solder and a cool iron. Start at an outside edge and work across to the opposite side, keeping the iron slightly raised so that its tip can smooth out the bumps and crags of the previously beaded line and pull them into a rounded ridge (see Figure 149).

Fig. 149

Finishing Edges

After both sides of the project have been tinned and beaded, you must finish the outer edges along the rim (see Figure 150). There are several ways to do this: you can bead the edges just as you beaded the foiled seams; you can encircle the outer rim with copper wire; or you can edge the project with lead came or a brass channel. All require soldering.

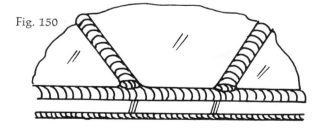

Fig. 150

Beaded edges. When you bead the rim of a project, you will, in effect, connect the beads you have already laid down on the outer edges of the front and back panels (see Figure 151). Stand the project absolutely upright, so the rim to be beaded is horizontal and the solder is less likely to drip down either side and mar previously soldered work. As an added precaution, before starting to bead the rim wipe excess flux from all previously soldered lines so that the flux cannot catch and hold any inadvertent solder drips. To stand the project vertically, you can hold it in a vise, or wedge it between a chair and a table (see Figure 152), or rig up some other way to brace it.

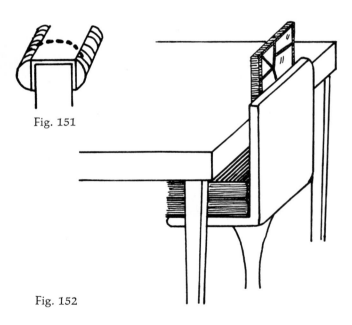

Fig. 151

Fig. 152

Flux the rim of the project, then bead it, using a cooler iron and a smaller amount of solder than you used for other beading. Carefully connect the beads on either side of the panel, forming a nicely rounded three-dimensional edge.

Edging with copper wire. Encircling the rim of a project with copper wire gives you a ready-made beading, as it were (see Figure 153). Use 18- or 20-gauge copper wire for most projects, and wrap the outer edge as if it were one large piece of glass. When you come to your starting point, cut the wire to fit and connect the two ends with a drop of flux and solder (see Figure 154). Stand the project vertically (as described above), then flux and solder the entire wire edging, connecting the wire to the previously beaded sides to form one rounded three-dimensional perimeter (see Figure 155).

Copper wire makes an attractive rounded edging even if the beading on either side has flattened and lost its ridge. Wrap the project in wire as described above, then flux and solder the wire to the sides (see Figure 156). If you want a flat rather than round edging, you can substitute flat copper strips for the wire and use the same technique.

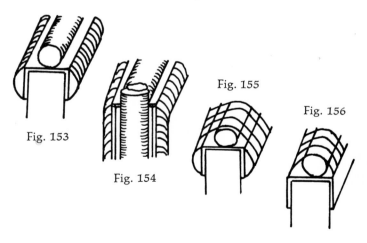

Fig. 153

Fig. 154

Fig. 155

Fig. 156

Edging with copper foil. Since copper U channels are not made, if you want to frame your edges with copper, you must use foil in a wider strip than you used for foiling each piece of glass. You can wrap this wider foil right over the existing (narrower) foil, but you should do it before beading. Then tin and bead the wider foil at the same time as you solder the other foil seams. Be sure to solder the rim as well as the front and back of the strip.

Edging with lead or brass U channels. Since different metals can be combined happily in the same project, there is no reason why you shouldn't finish a copper-foiled piece with lead or brass channels. You can slip the channels right over a foiled edge, after it has been tinned but before it has been beaded. If you want a beaded look, choose one of the round lead U cames (see Figure 157). If you want a flat edge, you can use brass U channels, flat lead U came, or lead ribbon came cut to a width that approximates the thickness of the glass. Cut each length of edging to size, solder at all joints where one end of the metal meets another end, as well as to each foiled and soldered seam it crosses on both front and back (see Figure 158).

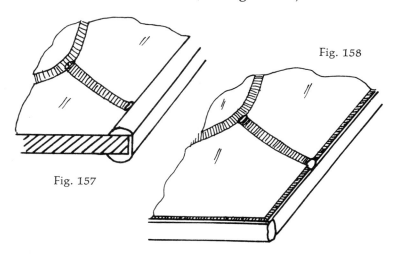

Fig. 158

Fig. 157

Three-Dimensional Projects

All the assembling and soldering techniques needed for flat projects will be used in three-dimensional ones, with the added challenge of bracing the project, sometimes in awkward positions, so that all surfaces are parallel to your worktable when they are to be soldered. This is important, because if the soldering were done at an angle the hot solder would run off its copper foil track.

Since each project presents its own unique bracing problems, only a general idea of some solutions can be offered (see Figure 159). A collection of wood blocks of varying sizes and shapes will come in handy, and a large measure of ingenuity.

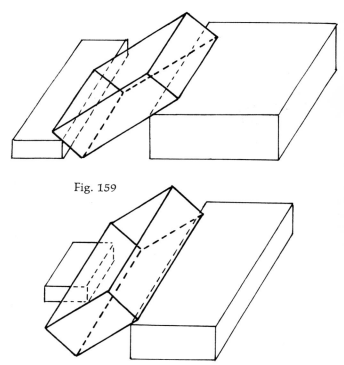

Fig. 159

When soldering three-dimensional projects, try first to assemble a number of pieces into larger components—especially if they can be soldered as flat units—then solder these larger elements together. This will be much easier than dealing with a greater number of smaller pieces. (In a foiled project, you can assemble and solder the foiled pieces in any order.)

Tips and Reminders for Working with Copper Foil

• Before foiling, check each piece of glass carefully for poor glass cuts and stray slivers of glass that will prevent the copper foil from fitting tightly and contiguous glass pieces from nesting snugly together.

• For best adhesion, keep both glass and foil free of skin oil. Start with clean glass, handle the foil carefully, and once the glass pieces are foiled try not to handle them too much.

• Dirty or oxidized foil won't accept solder easily. Before cutting sheet copper, clean it with a wire brush, and before soldering clean wrapped strips the same way, maneuvering the bristles of the wire brush into the crevices. Or you can rely on the flux to clean the strips. Whenever solder doesn't adhere to the foil, check to see if dirt or oxidation is the cause.

• Don't use twisted or torn foil strips. If foil that has already been wrapped around glass becomes damaged, remove it and rewrap the glass in another piece of foil.

• If you want to correct or reduce a margin of already applied foil without having to rewrap the glass, you can cut the foil right on the glass with a single-edged razor blade or X-acto knife (see Figure 160).

• Crimp and burnish the edges of the wrapped foil well so they will grip the glass tightly. Poorly crimped foil tends to release its hold on the glass.

• If you are foiling different thicknesses of glass and want to maintain the same width of foil on the face of the project, simply use (or

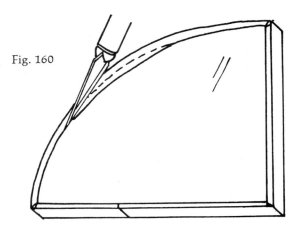

Fig. 160

cut) wider or narrower foil to accommodate the difference in the glass thickness.

• When you want to create the impression of having joined two contiguous pieces of glass without actually cutting them, you can use a flat copper strip to traverse the surface of the glass. Cut it to fit between two foiled seams, then solder it at each end, tin it across its length to make it rigid, and bead it (see Figure 161).

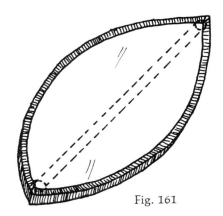

Fig. 161

• When soldering long lines of copper foil, use long pieces of wire solder. Save the short ends for tack-soldering.

• If you are soldering two pieces of foiled glass, one thinner than the other, prop the thinner piece up with one or more pieces of cardboard so its top surface is flush with its neighbor while you solder their contiguous seams together (see Figure 162). If you want to recess the thinner piece of glass, let both pieces of foiled glass rest on the work surface, then solder their contiguous seams together, holding the solder wire so it can bridge both foiled edges (see Figure 163). In fact, the thicker piece of glass need not be soldered flush with either surface, but mounted so both its surfaces protrude (see Figure 164).

• If you want to blend glass color, you can mount two pieces of glass back to back, using foil of sufficient width to encompass both the double thickness of glass and the visible margins on the front and the back (see Figure 165). Before joining this double-glazed sec-

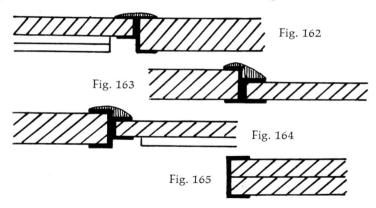

Fig. 162

Fig. 163

Fig. 164

Fig. 165

tion to another piece of glass, tin the entire copper surface, applying flux, solder, and heat to the top and bottom surfaces and the edge to make the foil rigid. Then, since the doubled glass will be thicker than its neighbors, mount it in one of the ways described above (see Figures 162, 163, 164).

Loops for Hanging

From large panels to smaller mobiles to earrings and pendants, many foiled projects require wire loops for their attractive display.

Any metal that can be soldered can be used for the loops, the most common being copper wire. Select wire of sufficient thickness to support your project; 18-gauge wire is a good all-purpose gauge. Use a thicker wire (lower gauge number) for a heavy object and a thinner wire (higher gauge number) for a lighter piece.

There are two simple ways to form a hook. You can bend a 2-inch length of metal into a semicircle with outstretched arms (see Figure 166a). Or you can bend a 3- to 4-inch copper wire in half, insert a pencil or the shaft of a screwdriver into the fold, then twist its two ends together two or three times with a pliers or your fingers to form a loop; leave at least a ½-inch tail at each end of the wire and pull them apart (see Figure 166b).

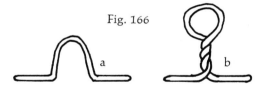

Fig. 166

a

b

If your foiled project is edged with copper foil or copper wire, these hooks can be soldered at any point along the rim; since the copper has been soldered along its entire surface, one point is as strong as any other. However, if the foiled project has been edged with lead came, solder hooks only at points that have been previously soldered—that is, at any place the lead came crosses and is soldered to a tinned copper seam (see Figure 167, next page); except at soldered junctions, the lead is not as stable as tinned copper, and the pull of a heavy object might cause the came to sag and relax its grip on the border glass. When you are attaching just one hook to a foiled piece, naturally place it so that the project will balance.

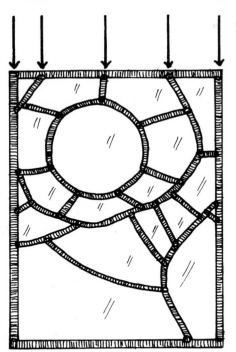

Fig. 167

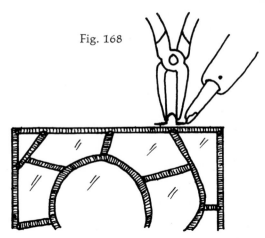

Fig. 168

Prop the project upright while you solder the hooks in place so that solder won't drip down one side. You can anchor small projects in an empty can or partially embed them in a container or in a can of sand or dirt.

Hold the loop with your pliers and dip it into the flux. If your edging is lead, clean and flux the came at the point of contact. Hold the fluxed hook in position and, with a drop of solder and a hot iron, fuse its legs into the edging (see Figure 168).

Reinforcing Copper-Foiled Projects

A properly foiled and soldered project will be extremely firm and rigid throughout its structure, but occasionally you may want to reinforce your work—perhaps at certain points of stress or to bridge a particularly large piece of glass. You can reinforce your work with any solderable metal—copper wire or strips, brass strips, lead came, even straightened paper clips—that can be laid between two points that can also be fluxed, soldered, and heated. You can make the reinforcing metal a decorative element on the face of your projects (see Figure 169a) or a hidden support at the back (see Figure 169b).

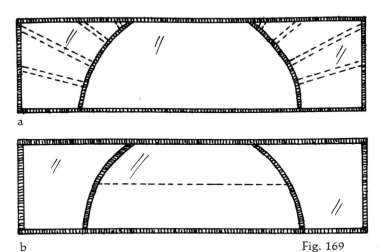

a

b

Fig. 169

Cleaning

After you have completed all the soldering, clean the project. The method will depend on the flux. If you used zinc chloride, just wash in soapy water with some ammonia added—you can scrub stubborn dirt with a toothbrush—then dry and polish the piece.

If you used oleic acid flux, sprinkle whiting (calcium carbonate) on one side of your work to absorb excess flux residue, then scrub the soldered seams and glass pieces with a stiff brush or fine steel wool. This will polish the glass and burnish the seams to a silver finish. Repeat for the other side, then brush or wipe the cleaning agent off. If you want to put a glossier shine on the glass, wash with a commercial window cleaner or with a water–ammonia solution.

Antiquing

There are three types of finishes for soldered copper seams: the first looks like silver, the second like copper, and the third like pewter. For a silvery finish, rub the soldered seams with #000 steel wool, then apply a commercial metal polish to retain the finish.

For a coppery look, use a solution of copper sulfate in the ratio of 2 ounces of copper sulfate crystals dissolved in 4 ounces of hot water. Buff the soldered seams with steel wool to remove any oxidation, then, wearing rubber gloves, apply hot copper sulfate solution with a brush or paper toweling. Each application will turn the solder a darker copper color. When the solder has reached the desired finish, stop the action by holding the project under running water and wash with soap or detergent. Let your work dry on paper toweling or newsprint.

For a dull gray pewterlike finish, apply tinner's fluid with a paper towel. Wear rubber gloves and wipe any drips off the glass at once with water. Stop the chemical action by washing with water. Be especially careful in handling this liquid.

Repairing Foiled Glass

You can sometimes repair a simple glass crack in a foiled piece by applying a strip of adhesive-backed foil over the crack. Cut the foil to fit between two foiled pieces of glass—even if the crack itself doesn't extend all the way between them—then solder this foiled splint at each end to the contiguous foiled bands. Finally, tin the strip across its length and carefully solder a bead over it. (Figure 161 illustrates the technique.) You may want to foil, tin, and bead the other side of the cracked glass for reinforcement. If this splint won't hold the cracked glass together, you will have to replace the broken section.

To remove a piece of glass from a foiled project, you have to melt the surrounding solder—you cannot pry up a soldered foil seam as you can a strip of lead. Hold a hot soldering iron over the affected foiled and soldered seams and work the iron back and forth until the solder flows freely; the hot iron will attract and lift the solder away. Periodically wipe your soldering tip on a cellulose sponge to remove melted solder. In this way draw the solder from both sides of the project—the hot iron will cause the melting solder to run through from the first side to the second—until you can pry out the broken glass. Clean out the inside area with the hot soldering iron and refoil all the exposed edges of glass.

Cut a new piece of glass. You can use your original cutting pattern if you still have it, or the cracked glass, if you can tape it together for a pattern, or you can use the area just vacated as a template. Refoil and insert the replacement glass in the project, then tin and bead the foiled seams. If the cracked glass has broken into relatively few neat fragments, you can wrap each one in foil, tin and bead them together, then insert the repaired section into the project. Naturally, this will add more seam lines to the design, which may or may not be acceptable.

PART 3

STAINED GLASS DESIGNS

Using the Design Workbook

The following pages offer a medley of stained glass designs. Some of them are single objects, to be used alone or as components in a larger composition. They are drawn to a scale that makes them usable right from the pages of the book, without further enlarging. Others are complete designs that require enlargement. All of them are intended to stimulate your imagination and enthusiasm for working in glass and to tide you over until you start creating your own glass designs. Moreover, they can be adapted to the stained glass projects in Part IV (each of which offers its own design).

Single Objects

The individual objects—flowers, fruits, shells, and the rest—can be used alone in a free-form project. For example, a flower can be worn as a pendant (see Figure 170), a butterfly hung high in a window, as if alighting from flight; a rose can become a window shade pull, transmitting light all day (see Figure 171, next page). Or one of these single designs can form the central focus of a simple panel to be displayed in front of a window (see Figure 172, next page).

You will have at least as much fun, however, if you use these single objects as compo-nents in a design where you can group them, repeat them, tilt them, reverse them, flip them—in short, combine them in all kinds of ways that make your stained glass compositions uniquely your own. There are borders to frame them, numbers to date them, alphabets to sign and label them.

You might want to group some seashells in a composition; you can use each shell in this section once, or repeat one or more of them, or assemble other combinations of shell forms (see Figure 173, next page). If you live in a beach house, you can set the shells against a background of clear glass through which to see the sand beyond, giving the impression of shells nesting in their own environment. If you don't have a beach view, you can mount the shells in a sea of blue-green glass. If you are charmed by flowers, plant a stained glass garden to be viewed against a real-life lawn or woods outside (see Figure 174, next page), and even add a peacock to your scene. Although your compositions need not utilize the outside environment, its inclusion brings richness and depth to the design, as well as an appealing playfulness.

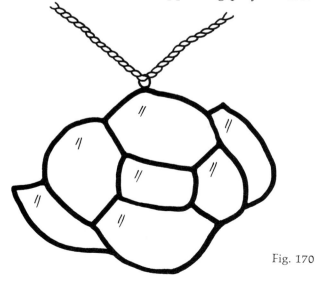

Fig. 170

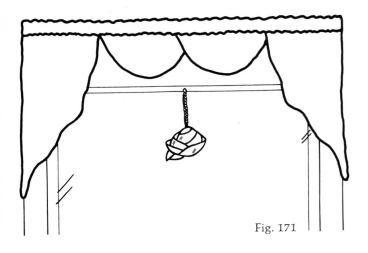

Fig. 171

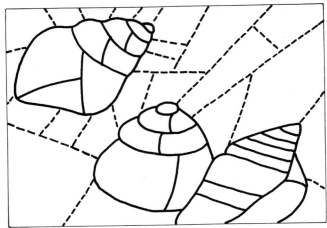

Fig. 173

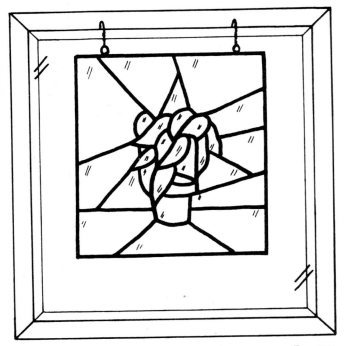

Fig. 172

Fig. 174

Working with the Designs

Whether you use these single objects alone or in combination, the first step is to trace them. If you are using a design alone, the tracing will become your cartoon. If you are combining several, you will group the traced components into a composition, then make a master tracing, which will become your cartoon (combining designs is explained below).

Tracing the designs. You will note that the color areas on each design are separated by heavy black lines. These are exactly $1/16$ inch thick, and represent the heart of the lead came. If you are going to lead your project, trace the design with a thick marker that duplicates the lead line (see Figure 175). When you cut the separate glass patterns out, the $1/16$-inch thickness will fall away in order to allow room for the lead came. If you are going to use copper foil, ignore the heavy line (foil does not require the $1/16$-inch allowance), and trace the design in the center of the heavy line with a fine pencil or marker (see Figure 176). Whether you are going to lead or foil the design, you can use the tracing in a variety of ways. For example, you can reverse it, repeat it, tilt it to any angle (see Figure 177).

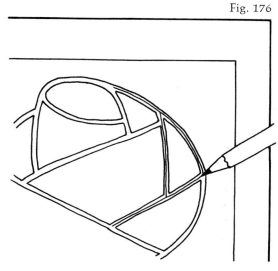

Fig. 176

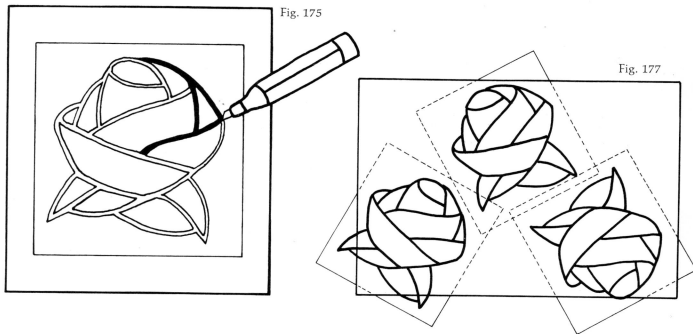

Fig. 175

Fig. 177

Combining designs. To design a composition using one or more of the components, first outline the desired shape of the finished stained glass project on a large sheet of tracing paper, then set aside this master tracing.

On small, separate sheets of tracing paper, trace each of the designs you want to include (see Figure 178). Move these design components around within the area of your project outline, trying out different patterns and relationships (see Figure 179).

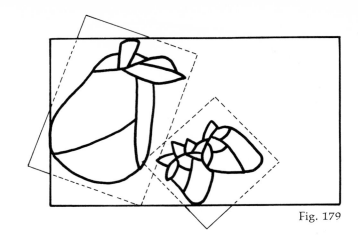

Fig. 179

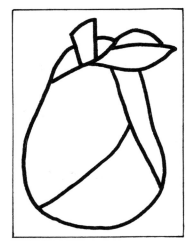

Fig. 178

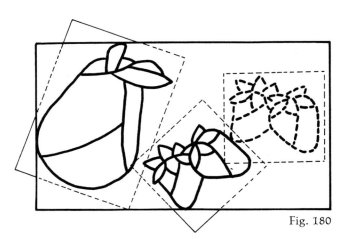

Fig. 180

If you want to use the same component more than once, trace it in one position, then move it, and trace it onto the master tracing in a second position (see Figure 180). Repeat this process as many times as needed.

If you want to reverse a design and use its mirror image, turn it over and then trace it onto the master tracing (see Figure 181). You will be able to see its outline from either side of the tracing paper.

If you want to superimpose one component over another, lay one on the other and trace both of the motifs, omitting that portion of the underlying motif that falls beneath the top one (see Figure 182).

Fig. 181

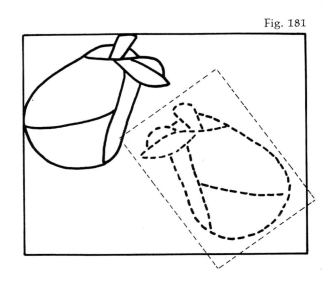

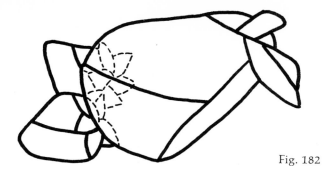

Fig. 182

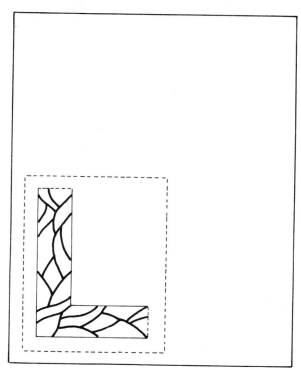

Fig. 183

Fig. 184

When you are satisfied with the configuration of motifs, lay the master tracing over the individual tracings and trace the new composition onto the master, project-size paper. This master tracing is, in effect, your cartoon. You need not transfer it to heavier paper—although you may, of course—and you should proceed to make your cutting pattern and assembly diagram from it as described in the chapter "From Design to Working Drawings."

Borders

For reasons of space, each border design is presented only as a quadrant—a corner section—so you must "flop" it in order for you to get a complete four-sided pattern. First make a tracing of the corner section given in the book, then position it under one quadrant of a large sheet of tracing paper and trace it off (see Figure 183). Flop—that is, turn over—the border tracing so its lines abut and match the already traced border on the master tracing, and trace it again on the master (see Figure 184). Continue this procedure two more times, until you have traced the design in all four quadrants of the master tracing to complete the border (see Figure 185, next page).

If you want to extend either or both pairs of sides in the border to fit the dimensions of

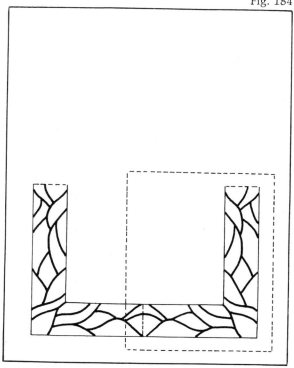

Fig. 185

Fig. 186

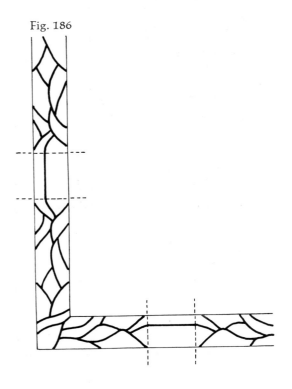

a specific project, you should use the design inserts that appear with each border motif. These are planned to be inserted at the extended dotted lines in each border design (see Figures 185 and 186). Borders I and II have one insert per side; Border III has two inserts per side (pages 208-213), and since they don't intersect a design area, you can make them any length you want, as long as both are identical so that the overall design remains symmetrical. As you can see, the inserts make a smooth bridge as they enlarge the border. You can repeat the inserts at the extended dotted lines as many times as needed, but, naturally, plan opposite sides of the border to match.

Complete Designs

Unlike design components, which are project size and can be traced right from the book, the complete designs must be enlarged before you can work them.

First make an outline of the finished project on a large piece of paper; this will eventually be your cartoon, so be sure the outline is accurate.

An easy way to enlarge the outline in proportion is as follows. Take one dimension—either the bottom or the left side—and draw it with a straightedge on the cartoon paper; then draw both of the sides perpendicular to it (see Figure 187), making them longer than you think they will be. Into one of the right angles fit the dimensions of the design as they appear in the book (see Figure 188). Draw a diagonal line from the inside corner of the small book-page design through its opposite corner, and extend it until it hits one of the perpendicular side lines (see Figure 189). At that point, draw a line parallel to the original

Fig. 187   Fig. 188   Fig. 189

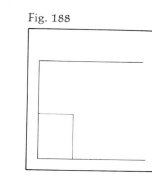 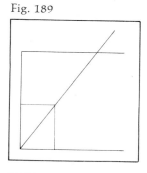  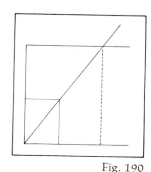

Fig. 190

line you drew (see Figure 190). This is the outline of your project, in exact proportion to the design in the book.

Enlarging the design. One simple way to enlarge and transfer your design to the cartoon is by the box method.

Divide the design in the book into boxes, roughly one inch square; the precise dimensions of the square do not matter. You can draw the boxes lightly over the design—right on the book page—connecting the markings along all sides of the design (see Figure 191). If you don't want to mark up the book, you can make the grid on a sheet of tracing paper laid over the design in the book. You don't need to trace the design itself on the tracing paper since you will be able to see it through the grid.

On the cartoon paper, divide the enlarged outline you have just made into the same number of boxes as the small grid, laying them out in the same configuration as they appear on the book design. For instance, if the book design has four boxes horizontally and five vertically, divide the enlarged outline into four horizontal squares and five vertical squares. As you will see, although you have the same number of boxes in the enlarged outline, they are much bigger than those in the book design.

Now transcribe the design from the book to the enlarged outline, working box by box (see Figure 192). When you have transferred

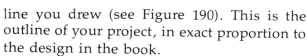

Fig. 191

Fig. 192

the entire design, you will have a complete cartoon for your stained glass work. When you eventually use the cartoon to make the cutting and assembly diagrams, simply ignore the grid.

Using this same method, you can reduce any of the designs—including the numbers and letters—by making the corresponding boxes smaller rather than larger. And you can likewise enlarge or reduce any of the design components.

Note: An easier but more expensive way to enlarge the designs is to have them photostated at a photocopy store. Just indicate the finished dimensions of your project, and ask for a positive print, which will show dark lines on light paper, or you will get a negative.

Color Key

All the designs—both project-size components and complete compositions—are offered with suggested color schemes. The color schemes accompany the designs. The color of the glass is identified by the name it is sold under, as in "yellow/white opalescent."

Please regard the colorways only as a guide, for the great fun is choosing your own glass in your own colors. You may love green skies, blue snails, and fiery lions—and your projects will be all the more delightful for it. Moreover, you may find that you cannot obtain all the glass colors you want at your supplier, and this alone will force you to stretch your color horizons.

1. *Above*: Often called the finest glass in the world, the mid-twelfth-century Tree of Jesse window in Chartres Cathedral makes marvelous use of blue glass, the color of light; the glass fragments in the borders echo all the colors in the main panels. Closely modeled on the first Jesse window at St.-Denis, the central vertical panels are the most important, with the reclining figure of Jesse at the bottom supporting the tree trunk, on whose branches sit four kings, the Virgin, and, finally, Christ surrounded by seven doves. Seven prophets in half-medallions flank the figures on each side.

2. *Right*: Resa is one of the remaining figures from the great twelfth-century Ancestry of Christ windows in Canterbury Cathedral, a genealogical series of eighty-four figures from Adam to Christ and the Virgin that originally ringed the choir clerestory. Many have been lost or mutilated and some were moved to other locations in the cathedral.

large circular medallion. *Above*: The parable of the sower, from one of the Poor Man's Bible windows, showing a farmer dressed for work in the fields, carrying his seeds in a two-handled basket. Photo courtesy Council for Places of Worship, London

3. Canterbury Cathedral is a treasury of thirteenth-century medallion windows. *Above*: Characteristic color, scenes, backgrounds, and borders of a whole window. *Top right*: Four scenes from the life and miracles of Thomas à Becket in Trinity Chapel in a

Characteristic French medallions of the thirteenth century.

4. *Above left and right*: Six of the forty medallions in Ste.-Chapelle, Paris, that tell the story of Judith. The lower four show the invasion by the army of Holofernes, the upper two Achior being questioned and bound.

5. *Right*: The moneylenders, donors of a window in the Lady Chapel of Le Mans Cathedral, represented by five bankers standing behind a table full of money, the scales for weighing it behind them.

6. *Top left*: The great north rose window of Chartres Cathedral is dedicated to the Virgin, who is surrounded by angels, prophets, kings, and doves in the tracery shapes. Called the Rose of France by Henry Adams, the window was the gift of Blanche of Castile in the early thirteenth century, and her castles of Castile appear, alternating with the fleur-de-lis of France and her son, Louis IX (St.-Louis).

7. *Top right*: The kaleidoscopic brilliance of thirteenth-century French glass focuses on the Virgin and Child in the center of the north rose window of the Cathedral of Notre Dame, Paris, and radiates out to the scenes and figures that seem to rotate around them.

8. *Left center*: In the center of the graceful, petallike Flamboyant tracery of the fifteenth-century rose window of Ste.-Chapelle, Paris, God, with a sword in his mouth, sits among seven candlesticks, surrounded by the seven churches of Asia.

9. *Above left and right*: The fifteenth-century south rose of Angers Cathedral (above left) centers on "Christ in Majesty," from whom radiate twenty-four scenes which include the twelve signs of the zodiac in the upper half. It faces the fifteenth-century north rose (above right) with the central figure of Christ and the twelve labors of the months among the surrounding sixteen scenes.

10. *Above*: Typical of the fourteenth century is a figure beneath a simple canopy. In this window in the Priory Church, Deerhurst, England, St.Catherine holds the wheel of her martyrdom, which is stained yellow like her crown and the flowers on the quarries.

11. *Top and bottom right*: Two fifteenth-century windows from All Saints' Church, York, are particularly interesting for their subjects. *Top right*: The last fifteen days of the world are depicted in "The Pricke of Conscience," with the donor family praying beneath the daily catastrophes. Reading from left to right, from bottom to top, among the early catastrophes are floods, sea monsters, and fire; later the graves open, the coffins are full of skeletons, every person dies, and finally, on the last day, flames devour everything. *Bottom right*: "Acts of Mercy" shows six of the seven merciful deeds. In this detail, the red-robed donors pray beneath the scene "Visiting Those in Prison." Yellow stain colors the side columns, the visitor's robes, and the stock to which the prisoners are chained.

12. A group of Tiffany lamps made in the first two decades of the twentieth century. *Above*: A blue-gray wisteria lamp, 27 inches high, its shade 18½ inches in diameter. The bronze stand is formed like the trunk of a tree, including its roots; the shade shows the top branches, from which the delicately foiled glass pieces cascade in a graceful pattern that resembles the vine. *Top right*: A flowering peony lamp 30 inches high, with a shade 22 inches in diameter. The pictorial subtleties of its leaves and petals are represented by the polychromatic Tiffany-made glass. *Center right*: A red oriental poppy floor lamp, 6 feet 4½ inches high, with the shade 26½ inches in diameter. *Bottom right*: A red and green hanging-head dragonfly lamp, 28½ inches high, with a shade 21¾ inches in diameter, set with oval jewels. Applied metal filigree simulates the net-veined wings; the background glass is suggestively leaded.

13. Two of the twelve windows by Marc Chagall at Hadassah-Hebrew University Medical Center in Jerusalem. *Above*: Crouching by the ramparts of Jerusalem is the lion of Judah, tribe of priestly rulers, with its kingly crown at the top. *Top right*: Uniting all other tribes and windows in a swirl of color and orbs is the window of Benjamin. A wolf, symbol of the tribe, stands over his prey at the bottom of the window, in front of a gleaming city of Jerusalem. Like the window of Levi, this window includes the four heraldic animals that symbolize Jewish faith.

Photos courtesy Hadassah. ©Hadassah Medical Relief Association, Inc., 1961.

14. *Bottom right*: Marc Chagall's narrative window in Reims Cathedral depicts events in the lives of French kings that occurred there—St.-Louis dispensing justice, top left; Charles VII crowned before Joan of Arc, top right; the baptism of Clovis, bottom left; the coronation of St.-Louis, bottom right. Although completely contemporary and personal in style, the window, designed in the middle of the twentieth century, lives harmoniously among the medieval glass of the cathedral.

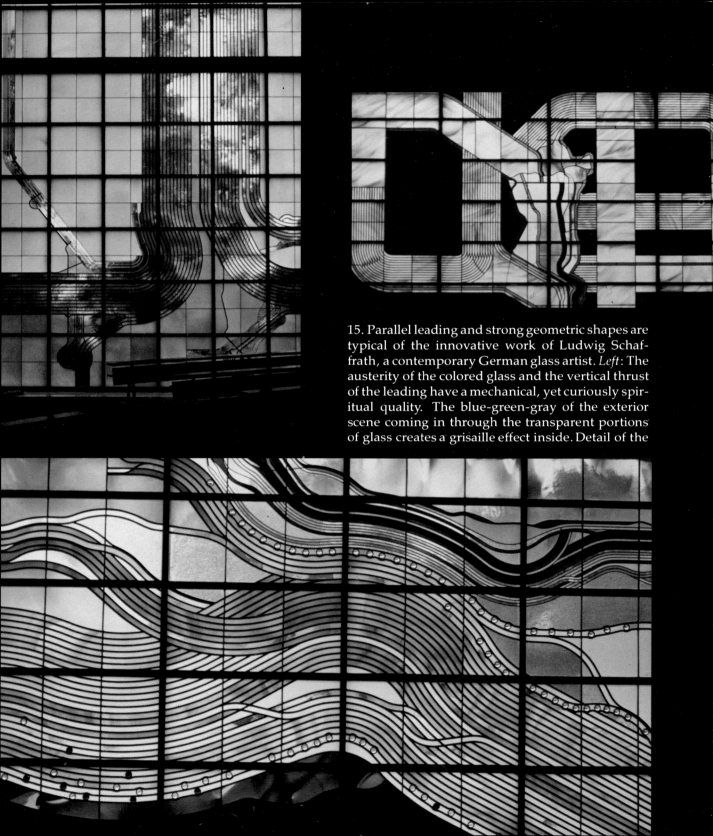

15. Parallel leading and strong geometric shapes are typical of the innovative work of Ludwig Schaffrath, a contemporary German glass artist. *Left*: The austerity of the colored glass and the vertical thrust of the leading have a mechanical, yet curiously spiritual quality. The blue-green-gray of the exterior scene coming in through the transparent portions of glass creates a grisaille effect inside. Detail of the

east window of St. Maria Church, Bad Zwisch-enahn. *Opposite top right*: A window wall of the cemetery chapel, Übach-Palenberg. *Opposite bottom*: Schaffrath uses his characteristic style to suggest waves, water in motion, even bubbles with the glass jewels embedded in the glass in the entrance-way to the public pool in Übach-Palenberg. *Above*: A window in St. Anthony's Hospital, Eschweiler.

Above: A window in the cemetery chapel at Halen. *Below*: A large gable window in St. Peter and Paul Roman Catholic Parish Church in Selfkant-Schalbuch, in which the leading echoes the wooden ceiling.
Photos by Inge Bartholome, from *Ludwig Schaffrath, Stained Glass and Mosaic,* © C. & R. Loo, Inc., Emery-ville, Calif.

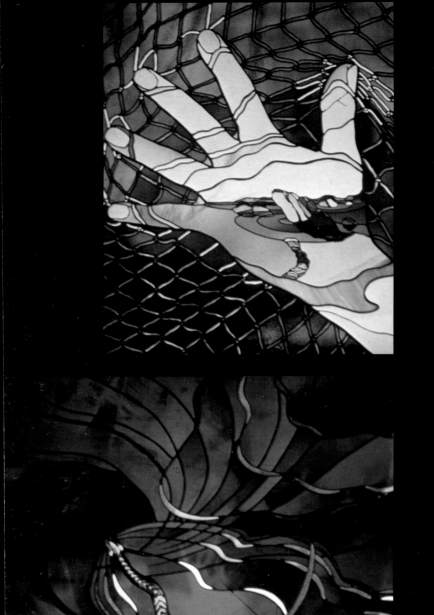

16. The compositions of Kathie Bunnell, a talented young American glass artist, have grace and delicacy. *Top left*: Almost a thousand pieces of glass are foiled or leaded in "Envisioning a Marriage." A variety of antique and opalescent glass contributes to the liquidity and delicacy of the poetic composition (3 by 4 feet, 1975). *Bottom left*: In "Moving Through Darkness," Bunnell used an obsidian arrowhead (volcanic glass) in the head of the snake, and sandblasted the skin markings. Variations and texture of dark-blue flashed glass give depth to the night sky, which is punctuated with opalescent arcs (35½ by 36½ inches, 1975). *Above*: Double-glazing and sandblasted glass modify the colors in "Childhood Icon," which is based on a crayon drawing by the artist at age seven (27 by 39½ inches, 1975). *Opposite*: "Young Buckeye" contrasts large shapes of light-tinted glass that partially reveal the outside environment with the smaller, more brilliant shapes of young buds and branches. The panel is set into a doorway at the Zen Center, Muir Beach, Calif. (28 by 61½ inches, 1974).
Photos courtesy of the artist

17. *Below*: Use of unorthodox material characterizes the innovative work of Paul Marioni, who incorporates a doll's plastic arm and a photographic transparency in "Howling at the Moon." From the collection of Sy and Theo Portnoy

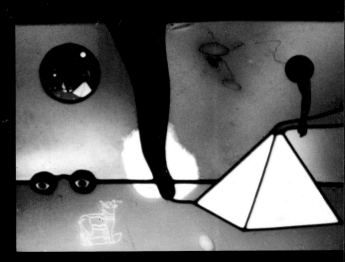

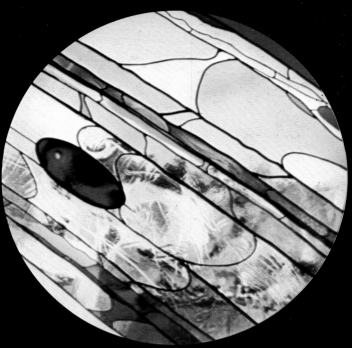

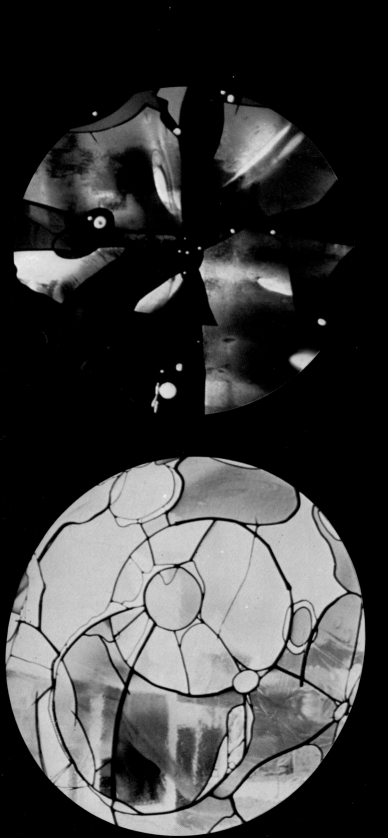

18. Narcissus Quagliata has a commitment to architectural stained glass in public environments and works as well in a personal mode that is often expressed in large figure panels. In the Commodore Sloat Elementary School's Media Center in San Francisco, three windows—"A Galaxy" (top left), "Jupiter" (top right), and "Moon" (bottom left)— present a view of the universe. All three windows are 5 feet 6 inches in diameter and made of handblown antique glass (1976–77). *Opposite*: Two details from the clerestory windows in a private residence, in which the artist examines the idea of liquidity in glass.

Photos courtesy of the artist,

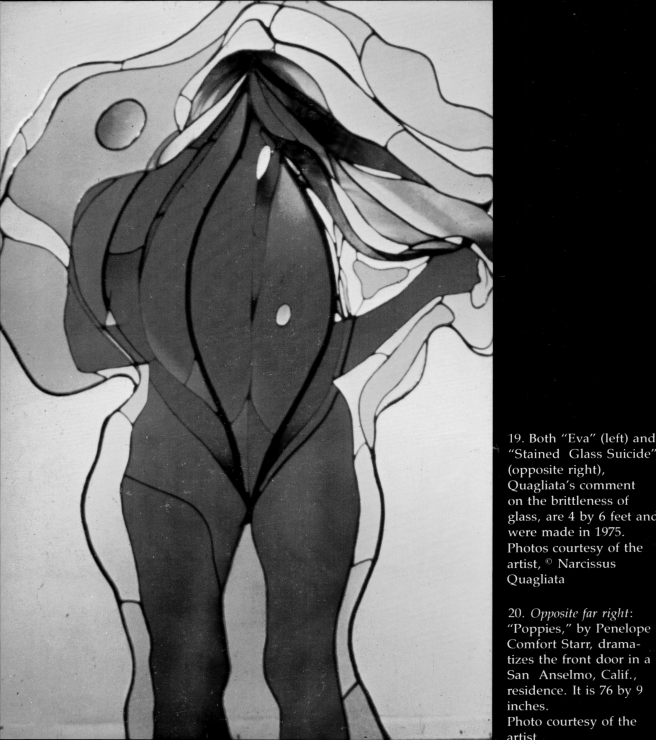

19. Both "Eva" (left) and "Stained Glass Suicide" (opposite right), Quagliata's comment on the brittleness of glass, are 4 by 6 feet and were made in 1975. Photos courtesy of the artist, © Narcissus Quagliata

20. *Opposite far right*: "Poppies," by Penelope Comfort Starr, dramatizes the front door in a San Anselmo, Calif., residence. It is 76 by 9 inches.
Photo courtesy of the artist.

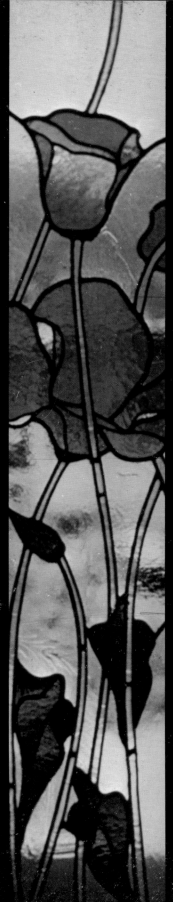

21. *Left*: In "Orange and Blue Convergence," Elizabeth Quantock uses wide and narrow leading with antique glass (25 by 18 inches, 1974–75).
Photo courtesy of the artist

root beer/dark
brown
(opalescent)

dark amber/
white
(opalescent)

aquamarine
(transparent)

pale yellow
(transparent)

light amber
(transparent)

opaque white
(milk glass)

opaque white
(milk glass)

dark amber
(transparent)

medium
amber
(transparent)

light amber
(transparent)

green
(transparent)

blue/white
(opalescent)

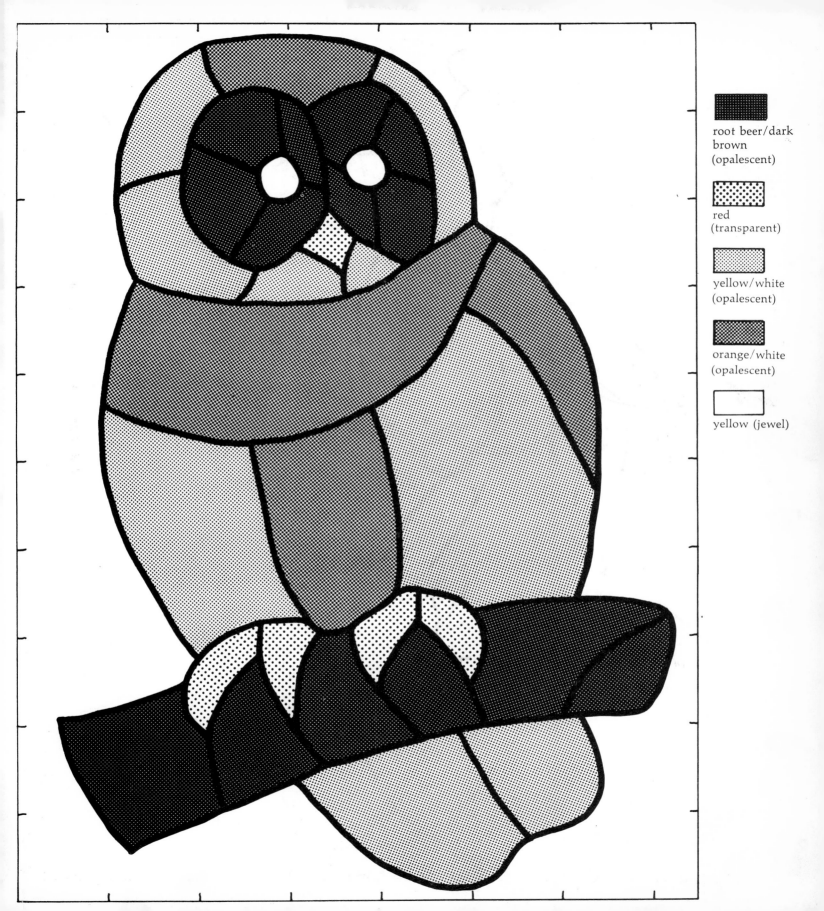

root beer/dark
brown
(opalescent)

red
(transparent)

yellow/white
(opalescent)

orange/white
(opalescent)

yellow (jewel)

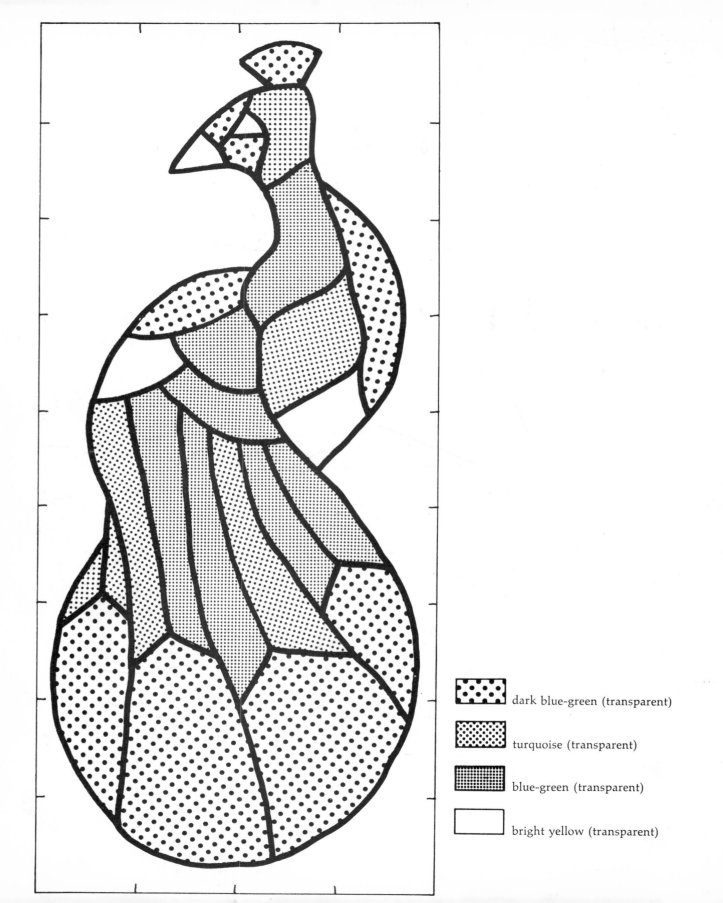

dark blue-green (transparent)

turquoise (transparent)

blue-green (transparent)

bright yellow (transparent)

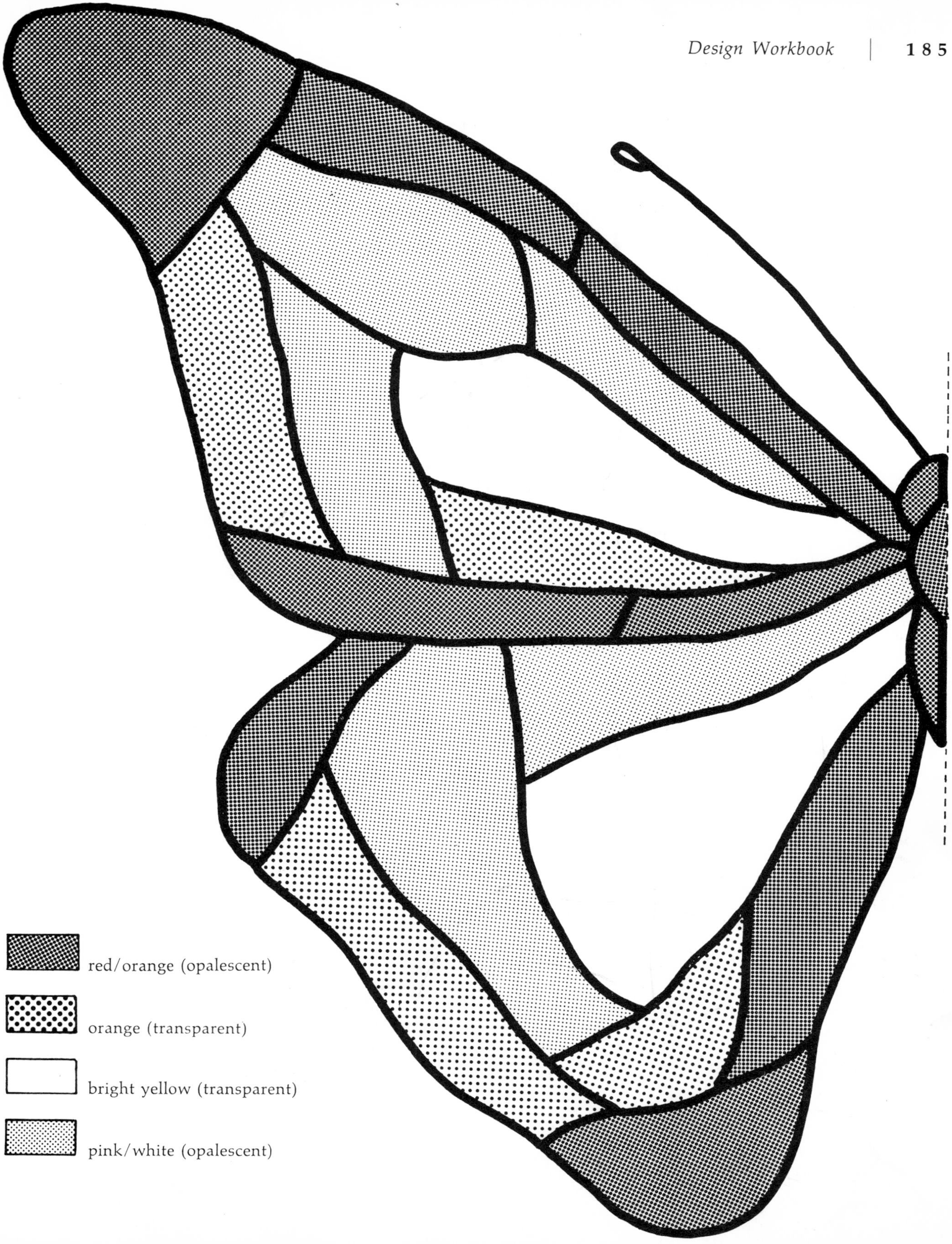

red/orange (opalescent)

orange (transparent)

bright yellow (transparent)

pink/white (opalescent)

red
(transparent)

orange
(transparent)

yellow
(transparent)

medium amber
(transparent)

red (transparent)

orange (transparent)

yellow (transparent)

medium amber (transparent)

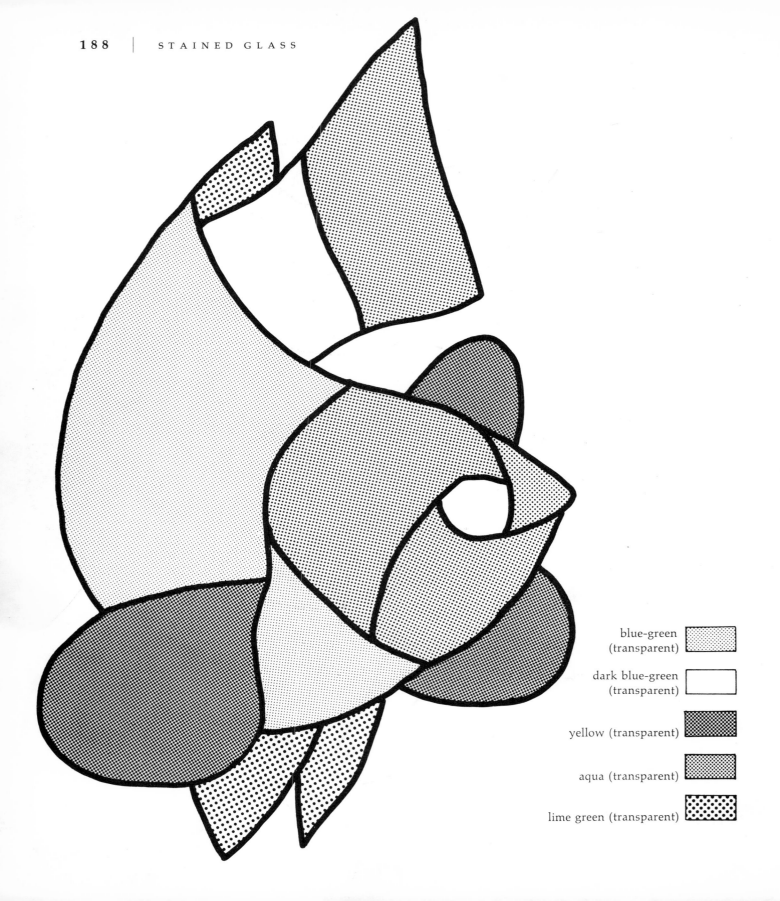

blue-green
(transparent)

dark blue-green
(transparent)

yellow (transparent)

aqua (transparent)

lime green (transparent)

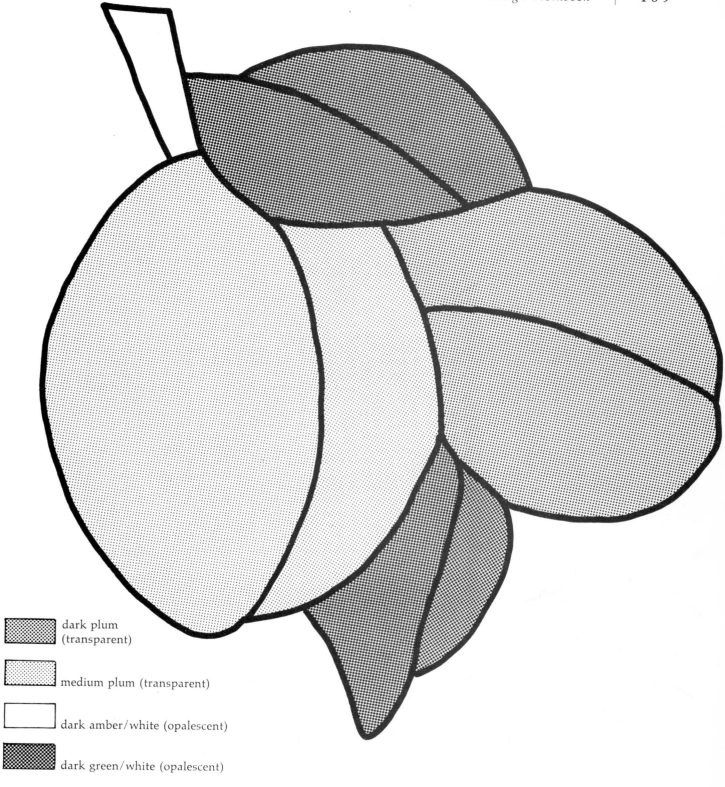

dark plum
(transparent)

medium plum (transparent)

dark amber/white (opalescent)

dark green/white (opalescent)

 ruby red (transparent)

 green (transparent)

lime green (transparent)

ruby red (transparent)

green (transparent)

lime green (transparent)

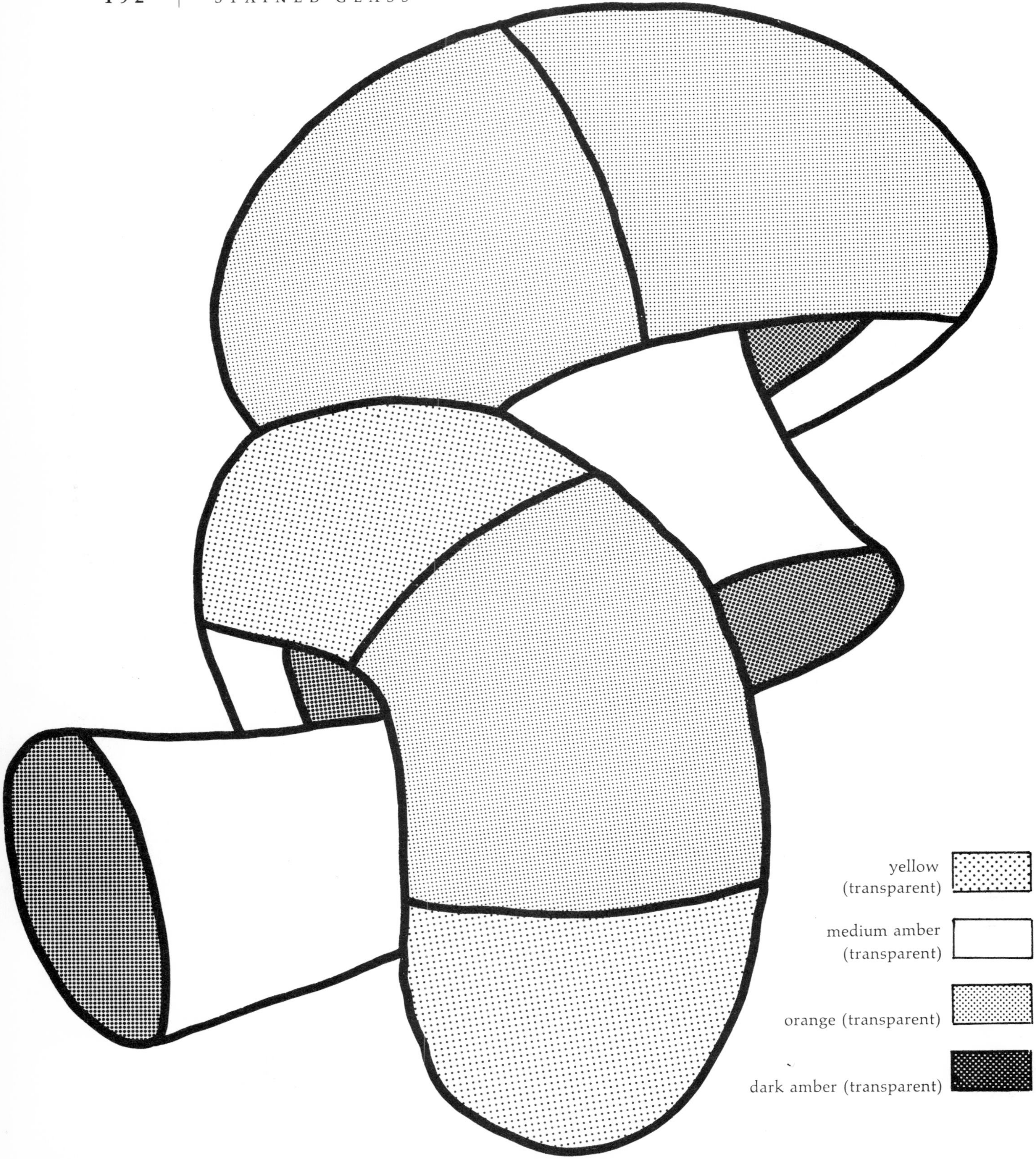

yellow
(transparent)

medium amber
(transparent)

orange (transparent)

dark amber (transparent)

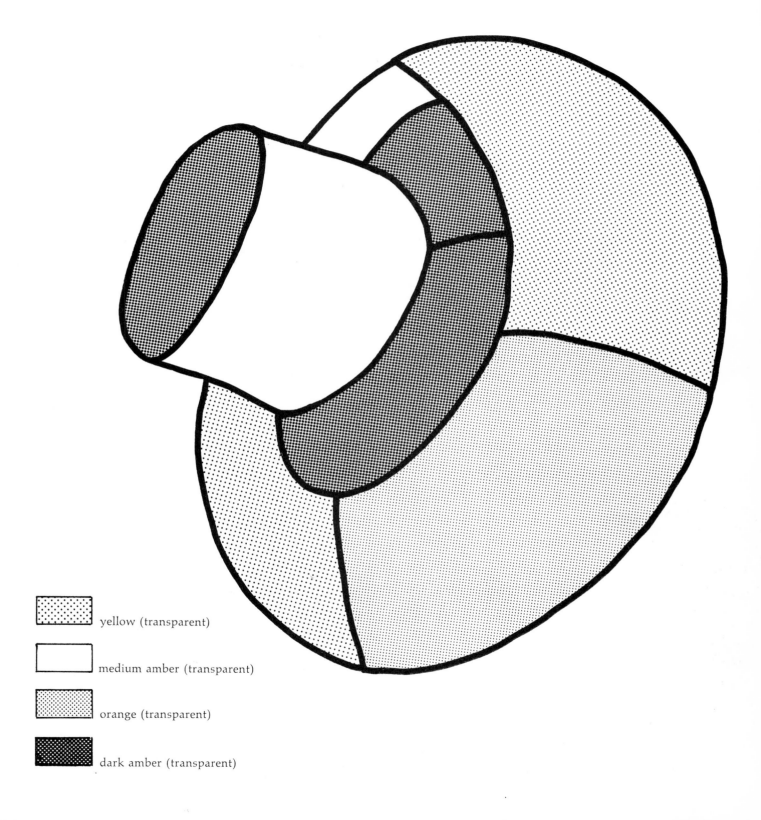

yellow (transparent)

medium amber (transparent)

orange (transparent)

dark amber (transparent)

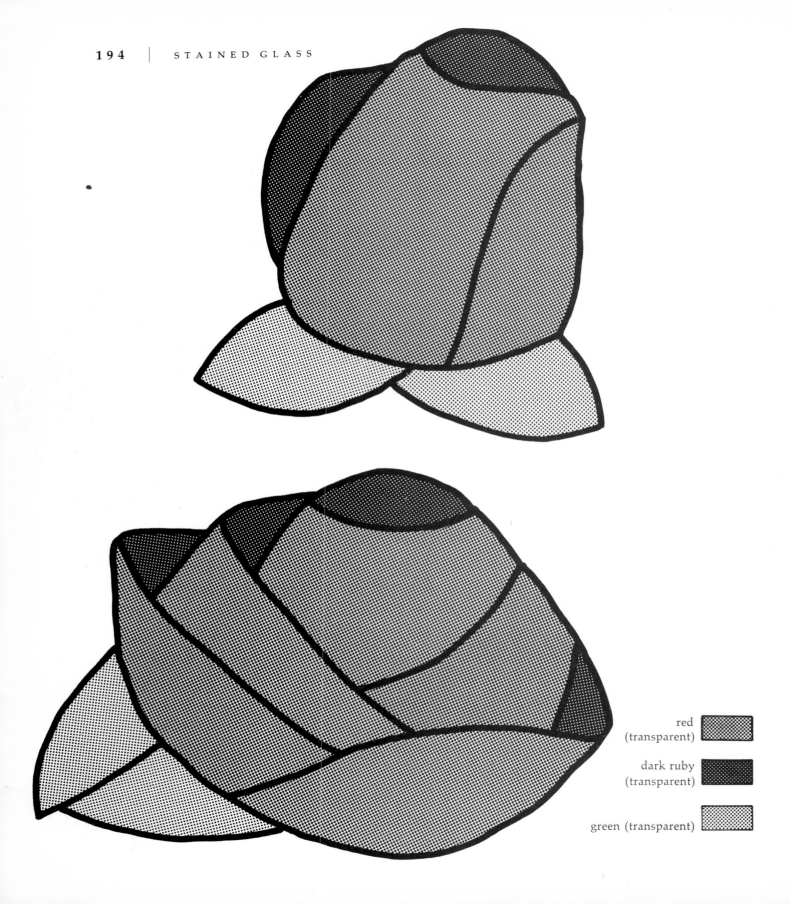

red
(transparent)

dark ruby
(transparent)

green (transparent)

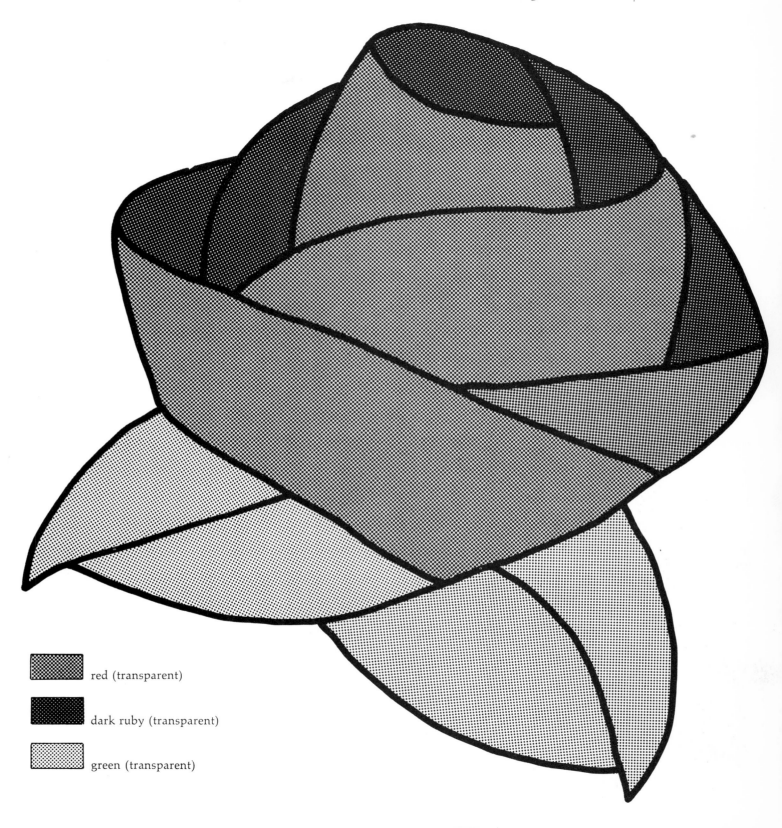

red (transparent)

dark ruby (transparent)

green (transparent)

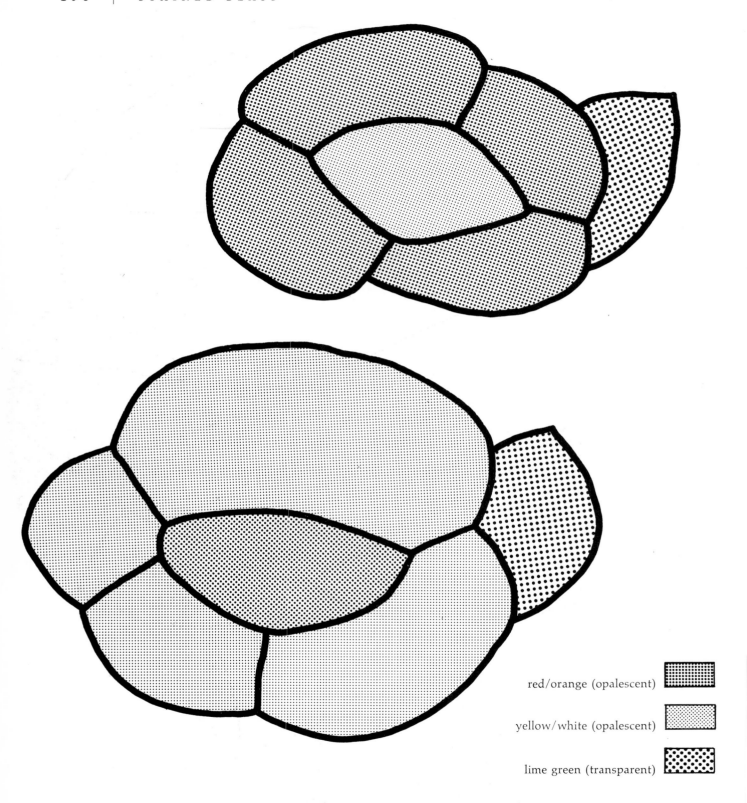

red/orange (opalescent)

yellow/white (opalescent)

lime green (transparent)

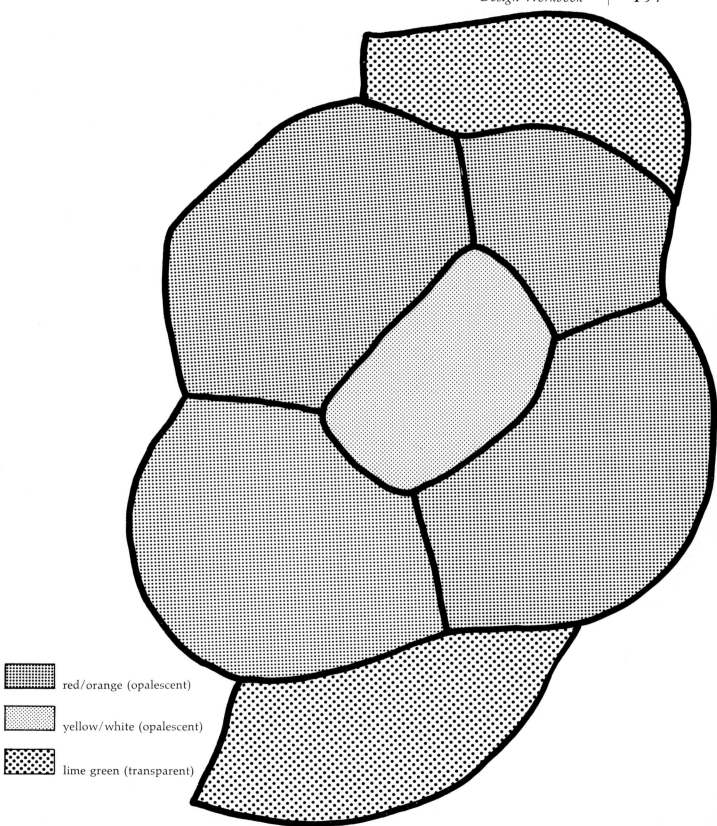

red/orange (opalescent)

yellow/white (opalescent)

lime green (transparent)

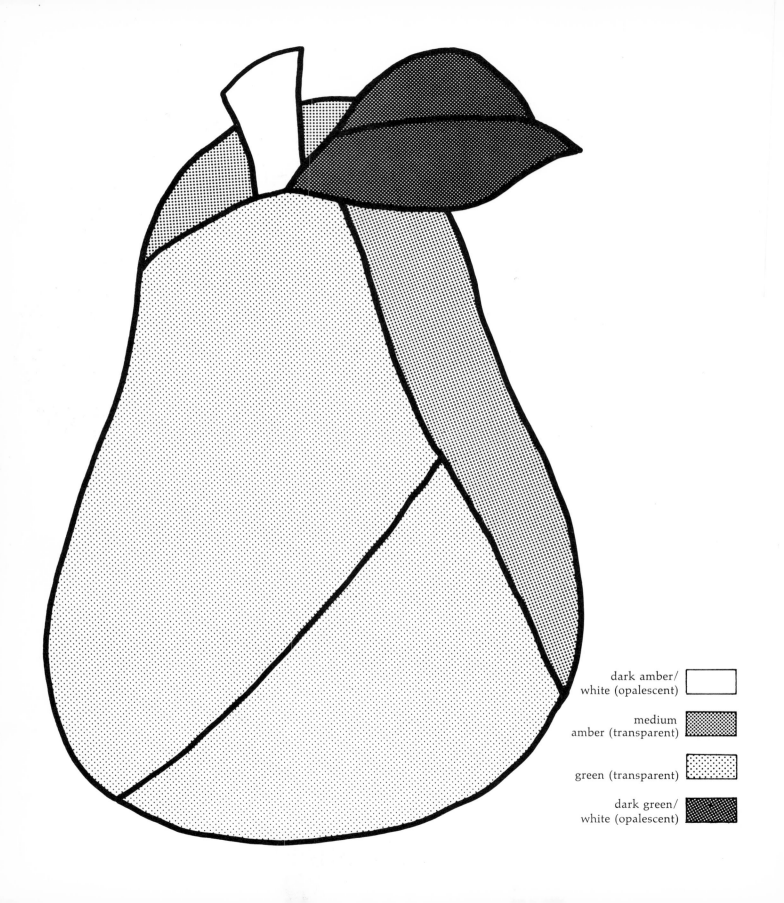

dark amber/
white (opalescent)

medium
amber (transparent)

green (transparent)

dark green/
white (opalescent)

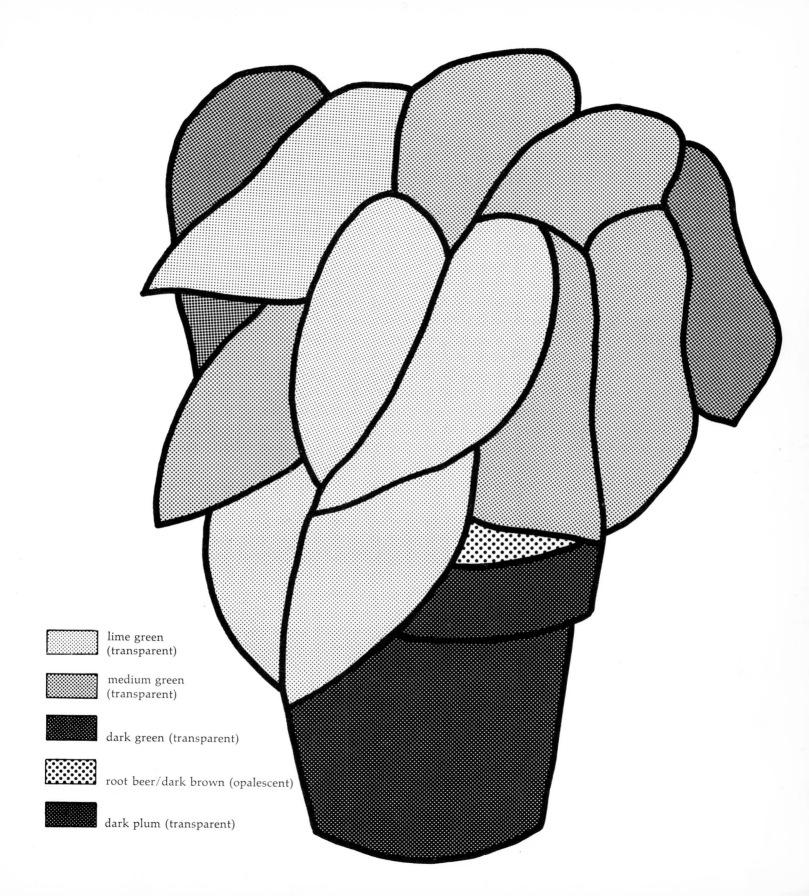

lime green
(transparent)

medium green
(transparent)

dark green (transparent)

root beer/dark brown (opalescent)

dark plum (transparent)

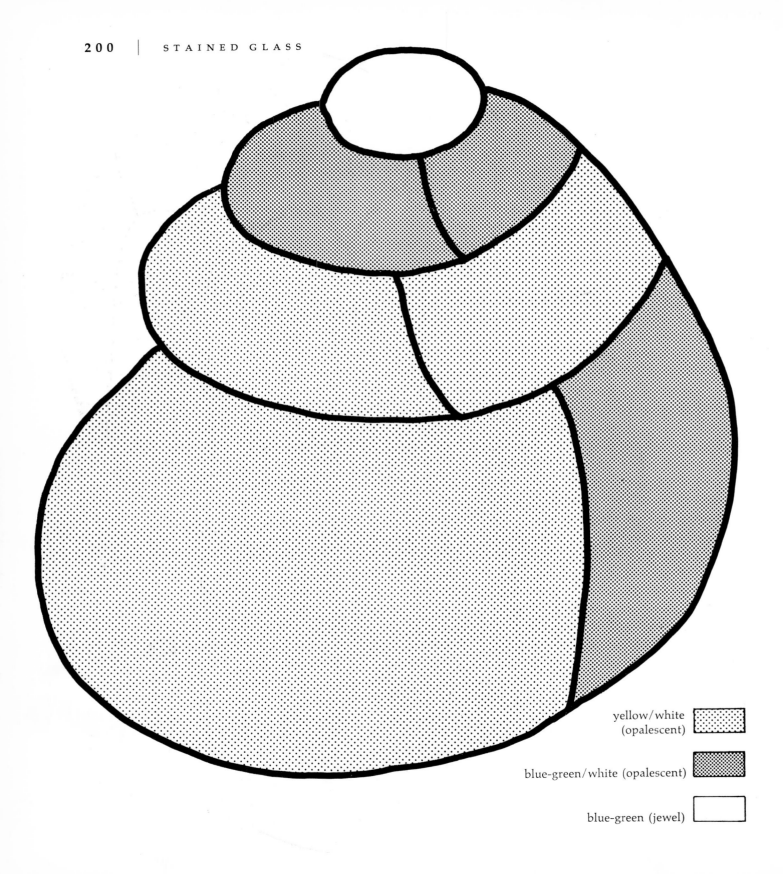

yellow/white
(opalescent)

blue-green/white (opalescent)

blue-green (jewel)

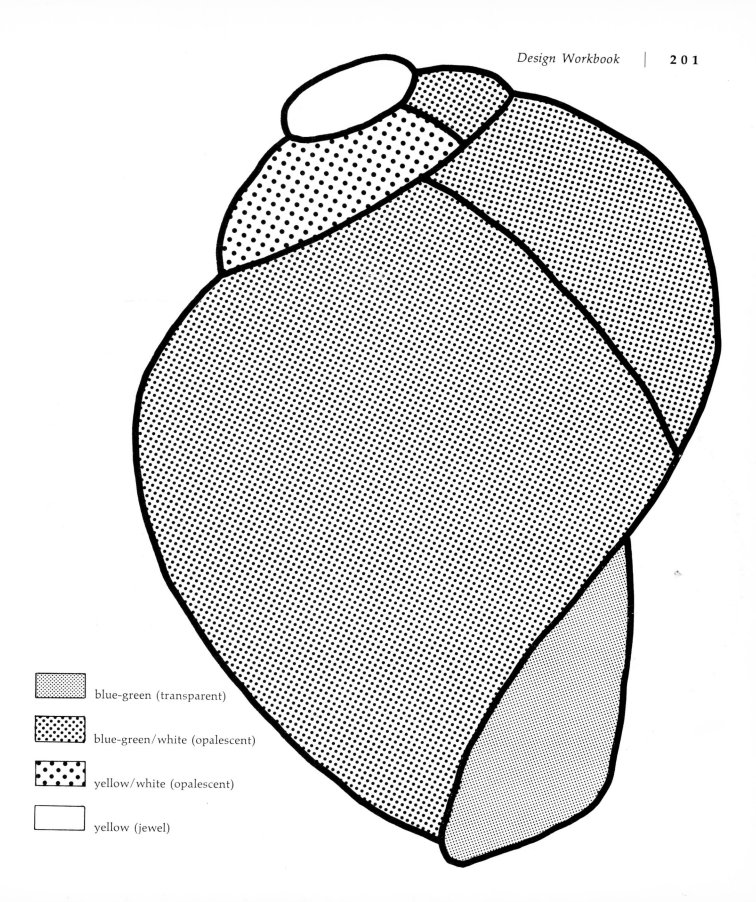

blue-green (transparent)

blue-green/white (opalescent)

yellow/white (opalescent)

yellow (jewel)

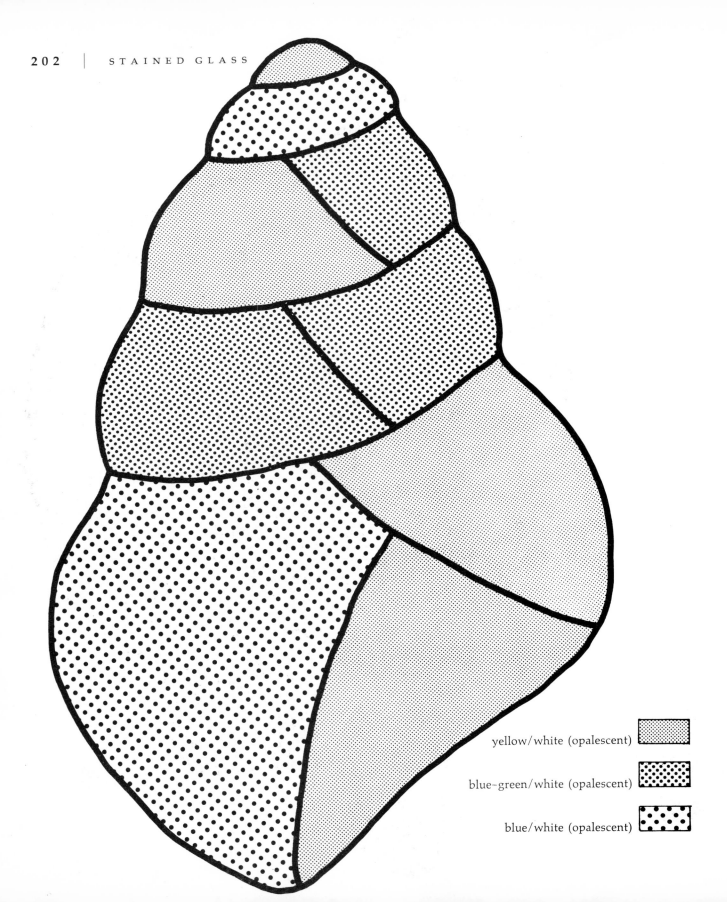

yellow/white (opalescent)

blue–green/white (opalescent)

blue/white (opalescent)

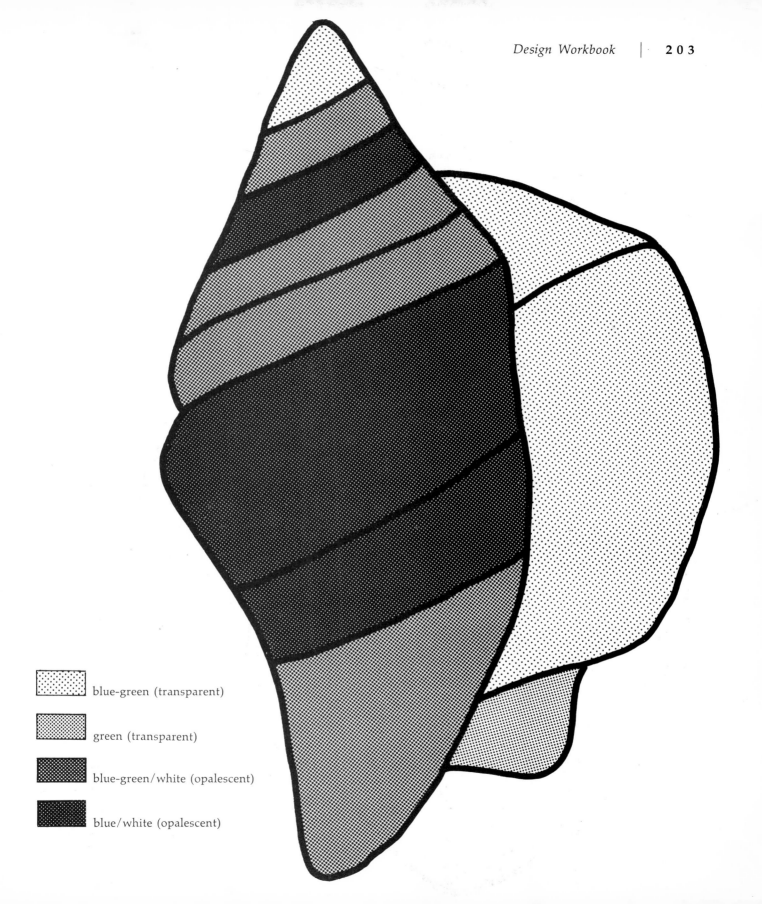

blue-green (transparent)

green (transparent)

blue-green/white (opalescent)

blue/white (opalescent)

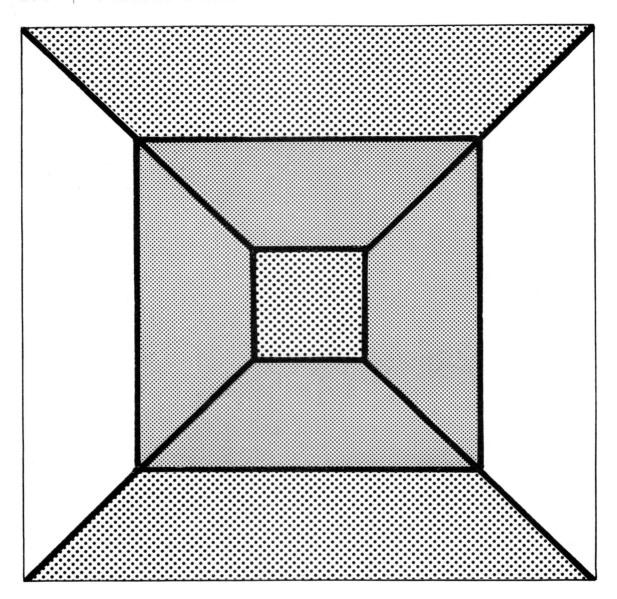

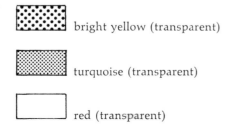 bright yellow (transparent)

turquoise (transparent)

red (transparent)

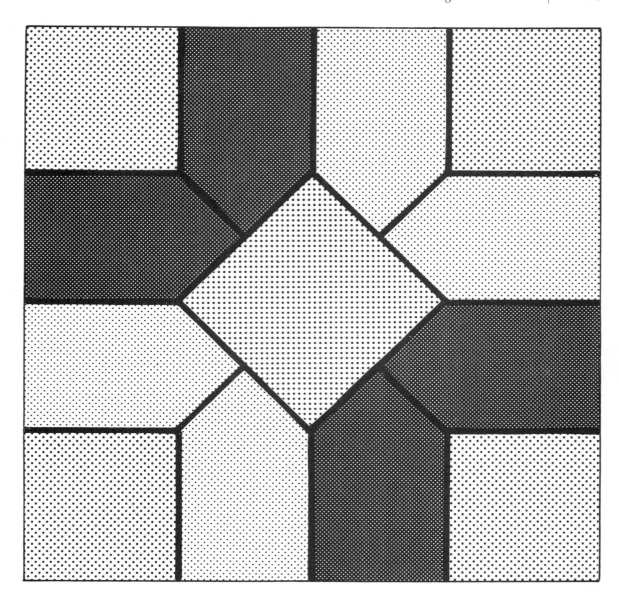

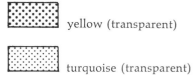 yellow (transparent)

turquoise (transparent)

 dark blue-green (transparent)

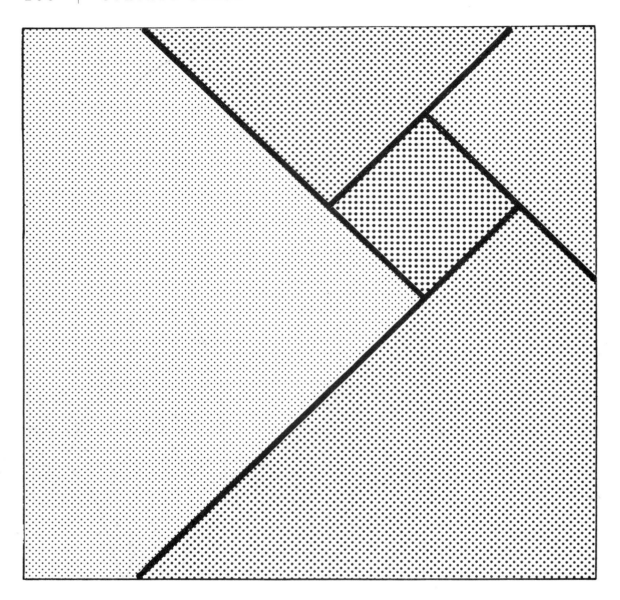

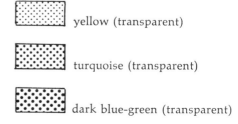 yellow (transparent)

turquoise (transparent)

dark blue-green (transparent)

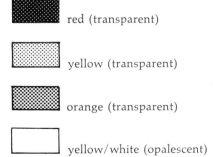 red (transparent)

yellow (transparent)

orange (transparent)

yellow/white (opalescent)

border I

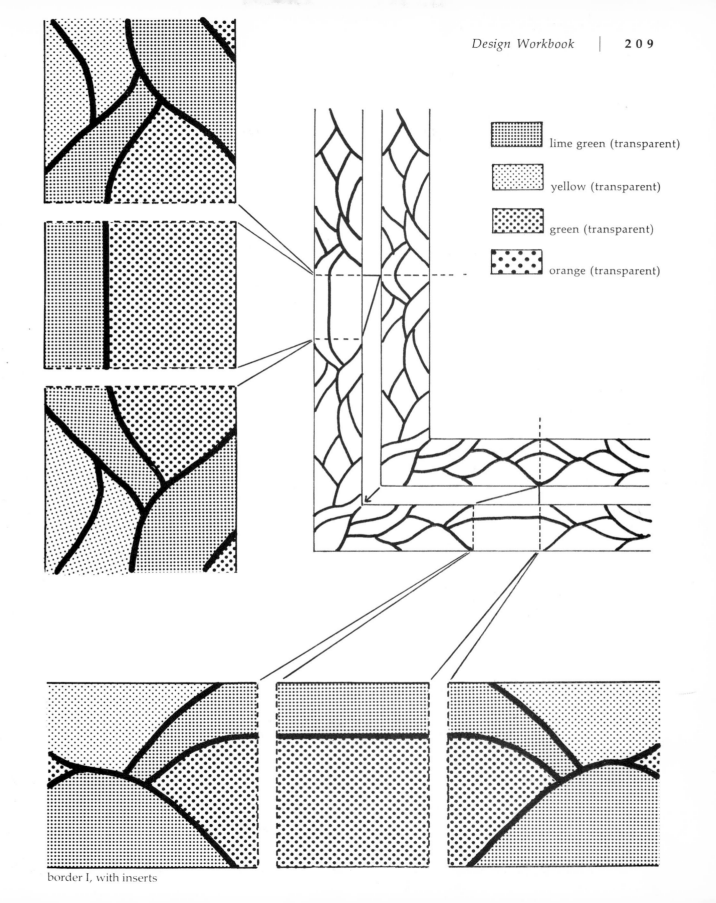

lime green (transparent)

yellow (transparent)

green (transparent)

orange (transparent)

border I, with inserts

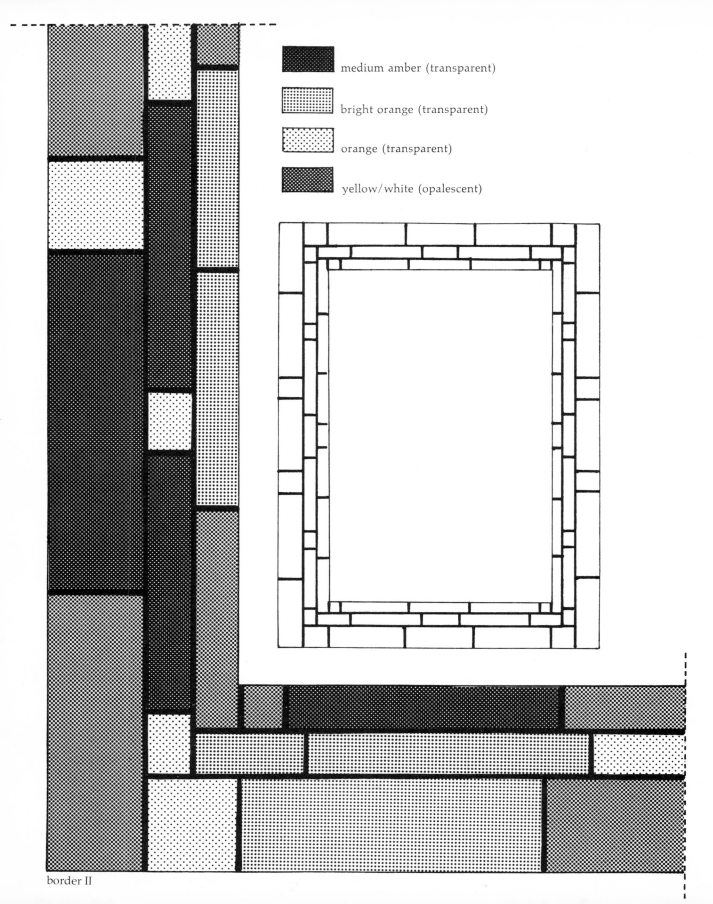

medium amber (transparent)

bright orange (transparent)

orange (transparent)

yellow/white (opalescent)

border II

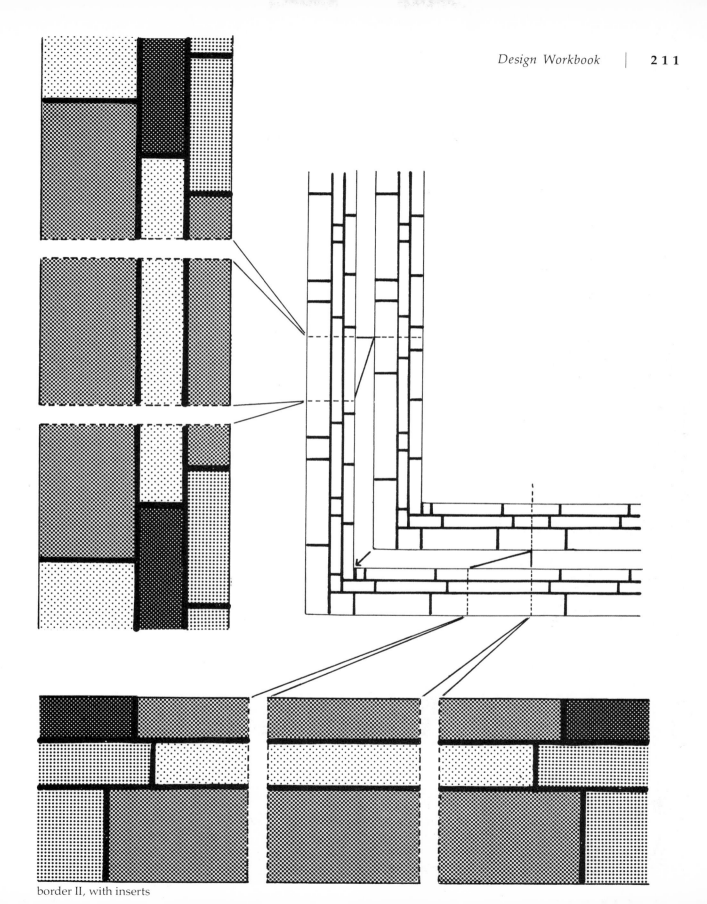

border II, with inserts

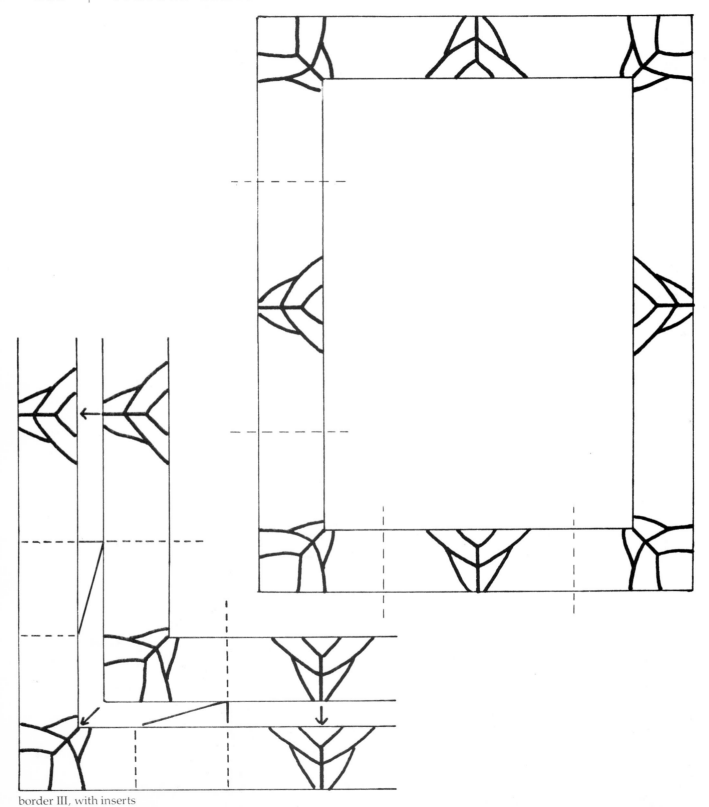

border III, with inserts

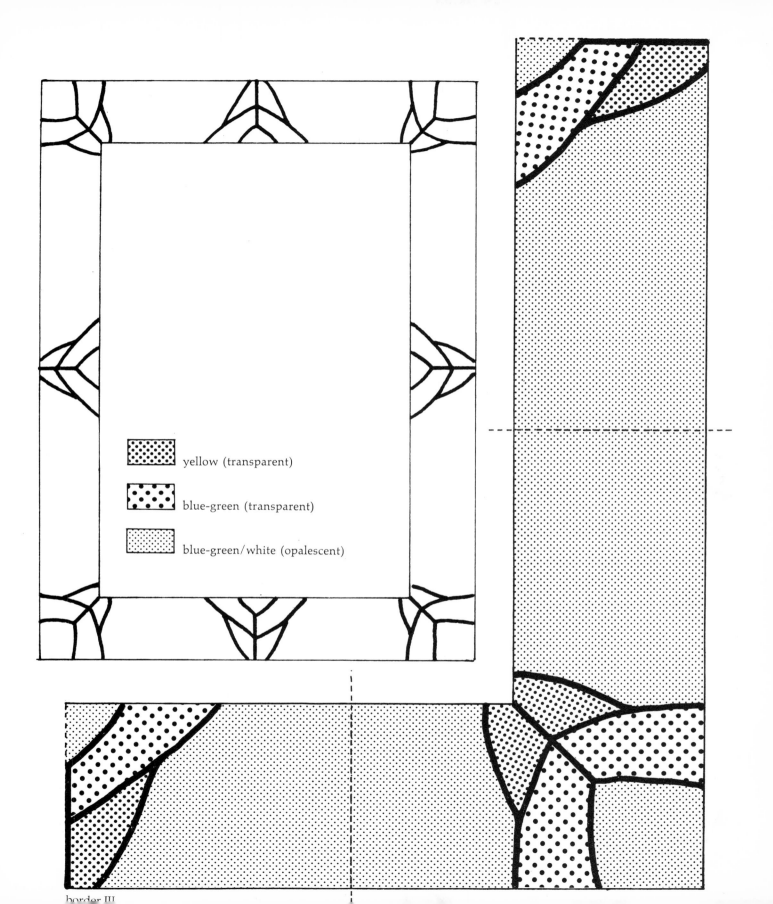

yellow (transparent)

blue-green (transparent)

blue-green/white (opalescent)

border III

JKL
MN
OPQ

PART 4

STAINED GLASS PROJECTS

Window Panels

Window panels can be displayed in several ways. The easiest is to suspend the panel from the top window trim or the ceiling by wire threaded through two loops soldered to the top edge. This type of mounting allows you to open and close the window, and also accommodates panels of any shape and size. Soldering loops to leaded projects is described on pages 151–52, to copper-foiled work on pages 167–68.

You can also mount a panel within the window opening, either in front of or in place of the existing window. The precise installation depends on the type of window you have and on whether the panel is leaded or copper foiled. In any case, however, you should plan and assemble the panel only after you have measured the available space for it.

Copper foil panel. A foiled panel is often thin enough to fit into the existing window assembly, replacing the glass pane (most window glass is ⅛ inch thick). For this kind of installation, simply remove the window glass and replace it with the foiled panel, anchoring it with a strip of molding mitered at the four corners (see Figure 1).

If your foiled panel won't quite fit into the existing frame, or if you have a multipane window that obviously can't accommodate the single stained glass panel, you can remove the entire window frame and replace it with a frame custom made to fit the panel and still function in the window.

Leaded panels. Leaded panels are rarely

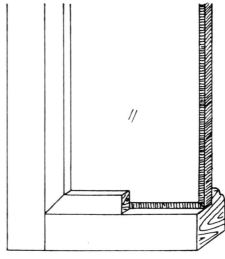

Fig. 1

window panels

installed directly into existing window frames because they are usually much thicker than the glass panes they would replace. Instead, they are customarily set in a made-to-order frame and then mounted in front of the existing window on the inside sill.

To make such a frame, use wood molding that is about an inch deeper than the depth of the panel (it will be about 1¼ inches deep). Cut the molding to fit so that the leaded panel will sit inside the frame, then butt the lengths at the corners to form the frame (see Figure 2a, next page); do not make mitered corners.

Cut four strips of wood, ½ inch by ½ inch, and nail them inside the wood frame, flush with one side of the frame (see Figure 2b). These stopping strips should be mitered at the corners.

For a weatherproof seal lay a bed of putty on the inside of the stopping strips and on a narrow strip of the frame where the panel will sit (see Figure 2). Then set the stained glass panel into the frame against the stopping strips at the rear. If one side of the panel looks better than the other, set the inferior side into the puttied stopping strips: this will face out.

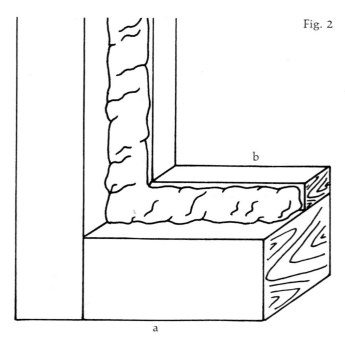

Fig. 2

Now nail a second set of stopping strips over the panel, fitting them into the frame and mitering them at the corners (see Figure 3). These strips, as well as the front of the frame, may be faced with decorative molding if you like (see Figure 4a).

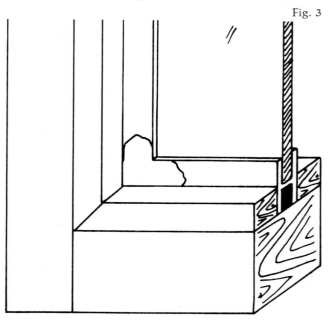

Fig. 3

If the frame you build is barely deeper than the depth of the panel, you should provide a space between the panel and the glass of the window, particularly if you are mounting the panel in front of a plate glass window that has no molding of its own. Do this by nailing a separator strip, ½ to 1 inch deep, to the back of the wooden frame (see Figure 4b), top and bottom.

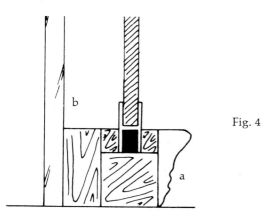

Fig. 4

Note: Special window molding is available at lumberyards. This may simplify the frame construction. In one popular style, for example, stopping molding is an integral part of the frame. You need only lay a bed of putty on the interior sides, lay the panel in, and set four strips against the panel (see Figure 5).

When you have mounted the panel in its frame, install the frame in the window opening, on the interior sill.

Whatever type of frame you construct for the panel, you should use H came rather than U came for the borders. As you can see, the outside (empty) channel of the came provides the depth with which to anchor the panel in the wooden frame. Moreover, the unused channel of the H came offers some leeway in fitting the panel into the frame; if you find that you have made your frame a little snug for the panel, you can slice some lead off the empty channel to whittle the panel down to size.

If you are installing a panel larger than 1½ by 2½ feet, you may want to reinforce it. One way is to join sections with special channels of zinc or aluminum (see Figure 6), if the design can be made in two or more segments.

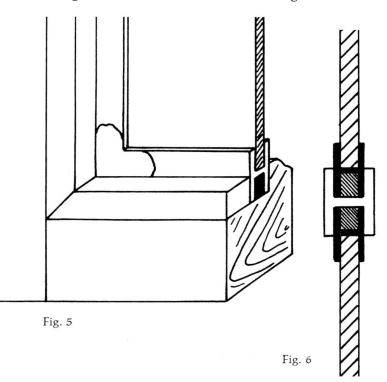

Fig. 5

Fig. 6

You can also attach reinforcing bars to the back of the panel with copper wires that have been soldered to the lead joints (this is fully explained in "Reinforcing Large Panels," pages 150–51). If your panel is particularly heavy or oversized, you may want to sink a longer reinforcing bar into both sides of the window frame. To do this, drill holes where the reinforcing rod hits the frame, and make the hole on one side slightly deeper than the hole on the other side (see Figure 7). Insert the rod into the deeper hole, then slide it over into the opposite hole and center the rod.

Twist the copper ties around the rod to hold it securely (see Figure 8).

In most installations, the stained glass

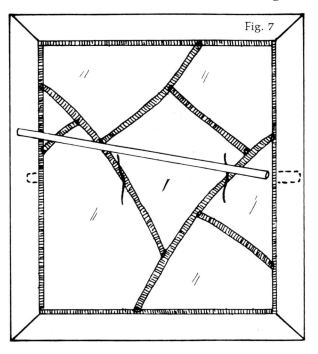

Fig. 7

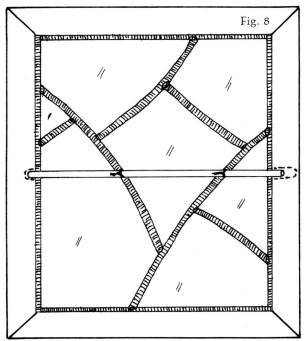

Fig. 8

panel will be mounted in front of the existing window, which will protect the stained glass. If you have mounted the stained glass panel in place of your actual window, you may want to protect it with an outer pane of clear glass. The easiest way to do this is to hang or install a storm window on the outside. If you value your panel highly, you can have wire-reinforced glass installed in the storm sash, but it may cast a shadow and detract from the beauty of your design.

To enjoy the stained glass panel at night, install a spot- or floodlight outside.

Backgammon Board

RECOMMENDED CONSTRUCTION: Copper foil
DIMENSIONS: About 17 by 23 inches
SPECIAL SUPPLIES: ¼-inch adhesive-backed copper foil
    16-gauge copper wire for two loops, each 2 inches long (optional)

Enlarging the design. On the book page, lightly connect the 1-inch marks that appear along the four sides of the design, joining opposite sides vertically and horizontally to create a grid of inch-square boxes over the design. If you don't want to mark the book, lay a sheet of tracing paper over the design and connect the inch marks to create a grid on the tracing paper.

On a large sheet of paper that will be your cartoon draw a corresponding grid with each of the boxes measuring 2½ inches square. Like the book-size grid, this enlarged grid will have seven horizontal and nine vertical boxes, and it will produce an enlarged design that is about 17 by 23 inches.

Now, box by box, transfer the design directly from the book—or through the gridded tracing paper that rests on the book page—into the corresponding box on the cartoon.

Tracing the design. Make a tracing sandwich of oak tag, brown wrapping paper, and the cartoon (on top), with sheets of carbon paper between the layers. Then trace the enlarged design from the cartoon to produce the cutting pattern on the oak tag and the assembly diagram on the brown paper. Before you disassemble the sandwich, mark the colors of each area of glass, following the Color Key. Also number each area of glass in what you expect will be the assembly sequence. Press down hard so the color code and numbers are transferred to the two drawings underneath.

Take the sandwich apart. Lay the cartoon in a shallow tray, set the assembly diagram aside, and cut the glass patterns out of the oak tag with a regular scissors or utility knife.

Cutting the glass. You can cut the pieces of glass individually from the oak tag patterns, or you can combine shapes that have related dimensions and are cut from the same type of glass. As you can see in Figure 1, various shapes are repeated, sometimes in the same color glass and sometimes in a different color glass. For uniformity of finished dimensions and fewer cuts, try to consolidate

medium blue (transparent)

medium green (transparent)

yellow/white (opalescent)

opaque white (milk glass)

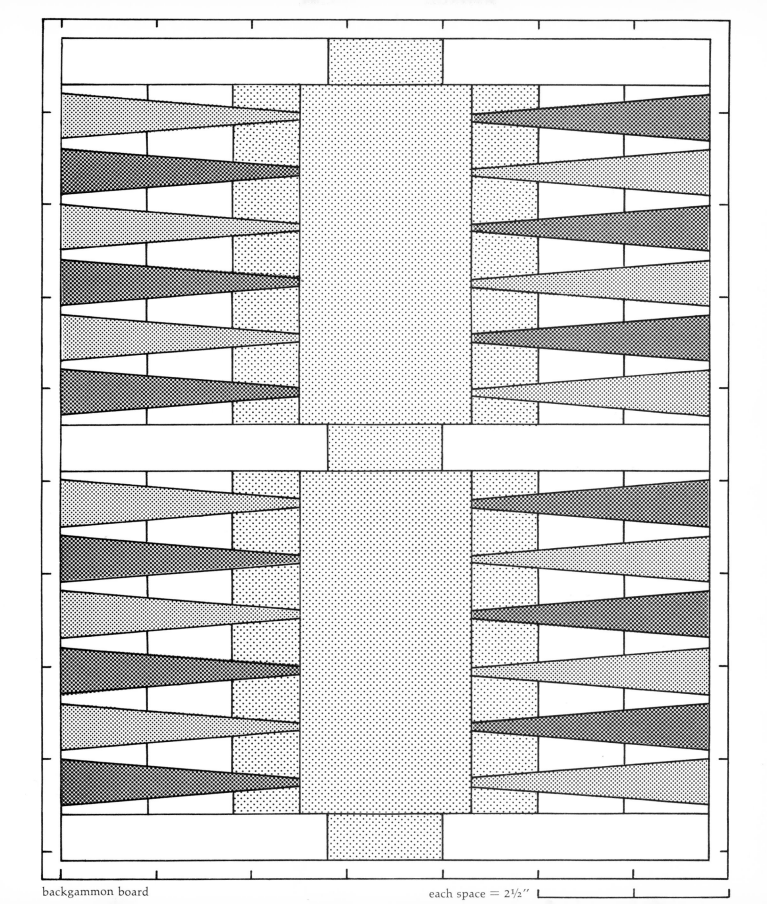

backgammon board

each space = 2½"

the cutting. For example, you can cut long strips of glass of the designated width (after enlarging the design), then lay one oak tag pattern on the glass strip (see Figure 2). Score and break off as many pieces as you need, using the same pattern as a cutting guide.

If the edges of the oak tag pattern start to get ragged, use another oak tag pattern of the same shape (you will have duplicates of every shape). If you make a bad cut, make another cut as close to the bad score as you can, discard the damaged piece of glass, and continue cutting pieces out of the long glass strip. Because there are so many duplicate and similar shapes, mark each piece of glass with the same number you assigned it in the assembly sequence. After grozing, lay each piece on the cartoon in its designated space.

Foiling the glass. Wrap each piece of glass in foil. After you have crimped and bur-

nished the foil, return the piece to its position on the cartoon. When all the pieces have been foiled and laid on the cartoon, you will be able to see the assembled project before sol-

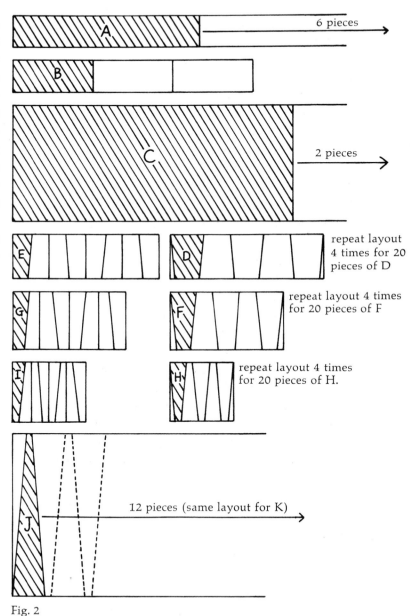

6 pieces

2 pieces

repeat layout 4 times for 20 pieces of D

repeat layout 4 times for 20 pieces of F

repeat layout 4 times for 20 pieces of H.

12 pieces (same layout for K)

Fig. 2

Fig. 1   backgammon board

dering, and to check the fit of each piece against the overall design and against its neighbors. Be sure the copper foil is clean for soldering.

Assembling the pieces. Pin or tape the assembly diagram on your worktable, and tack lathing strips at the bottom and left edge of the design. Transfer the foiled pieces from the cartoon to the assembly diagram, starting at the left corner. As you lay each piece in place, fit it snugly against its neighbor and hold it with horseshoe nails. As you build up the design, tack and retack the nails to hold successive pieces of glass. When you have completed the design, remove the nails and tack lathing strips at the top and right side to hold the panel at right angles.

Soldering. Flux and tack-solder the foiled pieces together at the seams.

Flux and tin all the copper foil surfaces on the face of the board. Work carefully, especially around the thin ends of the pointed pieces so you will not obscure any of the narrow points. Remove the lathing strips and turn the panel over.

Flux and tin all the exposed copper foil on the other side, then bead all the tinned seams, laying a neat rounded ridge of solder between all the pieces of glass and around the edges.

Turn the panel over and bead the first side. Finally, lay a neat beaded edge all around the rim of the panel.

Finishing the board. If you want to display the backgammon board between games—perhaps hang it in front of a window—make two loops from 16-gauge copper wire and solder them to one of the outer rims, a loop at each corner.

Wash the soldered seams and the glass. Apply a patina to the soldered seams and wash again.

Chess or Checker Board

DESIGN: page 228
RECOMMENDED CONSTRUCTION: Copper foil
DIMENSIONS: 10 inches by 10 inches
SPECIAL SUPPLIES: ¼-inch adhesive-backed copper foil
  16-gauge copper wire for two loops, each 2 inches long (optional)

Enlarging the design. On a large sheet of paper that will become your cartoon, draw a 10-inch square, using a triangle or T bar to get four right angles. Divide each side of the square into eighths and connect these marks on opposite sides to form sixty-four smaller squares—each should measure 1¼ inches square—inside the large square. This forms the sections of the chess or checker board. It also forms a grid by which you can transfer the design.

Working one box at a time, transfer the design from the book into the corresponding box on the cartoon.

Tracing the design. Make a tracing sandwich of oak tag, brown wrapping paper, and the cartoon (on top), with sheets of carbon paper between the layers. Then trace the enlarged design from the cartoon to produce the cutting pattern on the oak tag and the assembly diagram on the brown paper. Before you disassemble the sandwich, mark the colors of

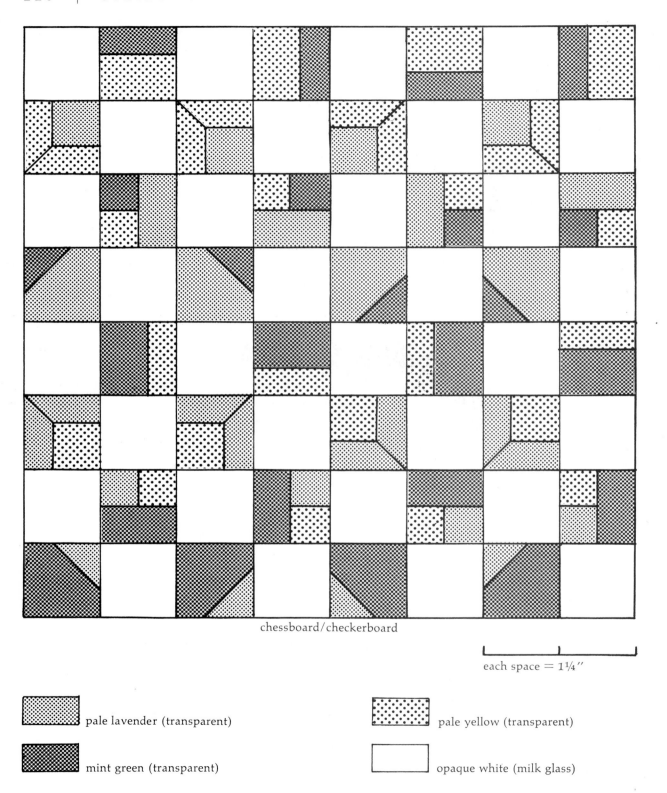

chessboard/checkerboard

each space = 1¼″

pale lavender (transparent)

pale yellow (transparent)

mint green (transparent)

opaque white (milk glass)

each area of glass, following the Color Key. Also number each area of glass in what you expect to be the assembly sequence. Press hard enough with your pen or pencil so the color code and numbers can be read on the two drawings underneath.

Take the sandwich apart. Lay the cartoon in a shallow tray, set the assembly diagram aside, and cut the glass patterns out of the oak tag, using a regular scissors or utility knife.

Cutting the glass. You can cut the pieces of glass individually from the oak tag patterns, or you can combine shapes that have related dimensions and are cut from the same type of glass. As you can see in Figure 1, various shapes are repeated, sometimes in the same glass and sometimes in different glass. For uniformity of finished dimensions and a lesser number of cuts, you can consolidate certain shapes (see Figure 2).

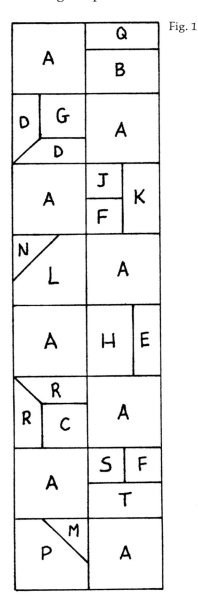

Fig. 1

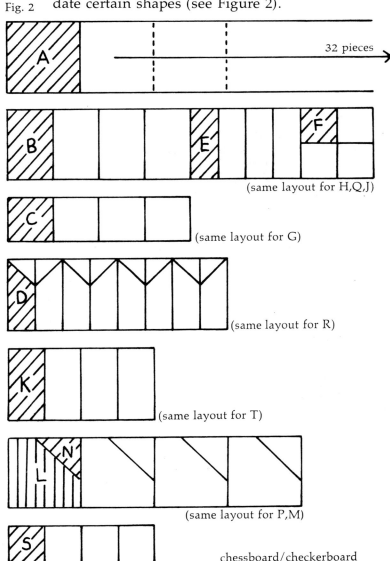

Fig. 2

(same layout for H,Q,J)

(same layout for G)

(same layout for R)

(same layout for T)

(same layout for P,M)

chessboard/checkerboard

32 pieces →

With this method, you cut long strips of glass of the designated width (after enlarging the design), then lay one oak tag pattern on the glass strip. Score and break off as many pieces of glass as you need, using the same pattern as a cutting guide.

If the edges of the pattern start to get ragged, use another oak tag pattern of the same shape (you will have duplicates of every shape). If you make a bad cut, simply make another cut as close to the bad score as you can, discard the damaged piece of glass, and continue cutting pieces out of the long glass strip. Because there are so many duplicate and similar pieces of glass, mark each piece with the same number you assign it in the assembly sequence. After you have grozed the glass, lay it on the cartoon in its designated space.

Foiling the glass. Wrap each piece of glass in foil. After crimping and burnishing the foil, return the piece to its position on the cartoon. When all the pieces have been foiled and laid on the cartoon, you will be able to see the assembled project before soldering, and to check the fit of each piece against the cartoon and against its neighbors. Be sure the foil is clean for soldering.

Assembling the pieces. Pin or tape the assembly diagram on your worktable, and tack lathing strips at the bottom and left edge of the design. Transfer the foiled pieces from the cartoon to the assembly diagram, starting at the left corner. As you lay each piece in place, fit it snugly against its neighbors and hold it in place with horseshoe nails. As you build up the design, tack and retack the nails to hold successive pieces of glass. When you have completed the design, remove the nails, then tack lathing strips at the top and right side to hold the panel at right angles.

Soldering. Flux and tack-solder the foiled pieces together at all the joints.

Flux and tin all the copper foil surfaces on the face of the board. Work carefully, especially around the small pieces so you will not obscure too much glass. Remove the lathing strips.

Turn the panel over. Flux and tin all the exposed copper foil on the other side, then bead all the tinned seams, laying a rounded ridge of solder between all the pieces of glass and around the edges.

Turn the panel over and bead the first side. Finally, lay a neat beaded edge all around the rim of the panel.

Finishing the board. If you want to display the board between games—perhaps hang it in a window—make two loops from 16-gauge copper wire and solder them to one of the outer rims, one at each corner.

Wash the soldered seams and the glass. Apply a patina, then wash again.

Fire Screen

RECOMMENDED CONSTRUCTION: Copper foil only

DIMENSIONS: Enlarging the design to four times its width and its height—to about 26 by 36 inches, will cover an average fireplace opening. If your fireplace is a different size, enlarge the design proportionately. You can use the design horizontally or vertically.

SPECIAL SUPPLIES: ¼-inch adhesive-backed copper foil

orange
(transparent)   yellow
(transparent)   red/white/orange
(opalescent)

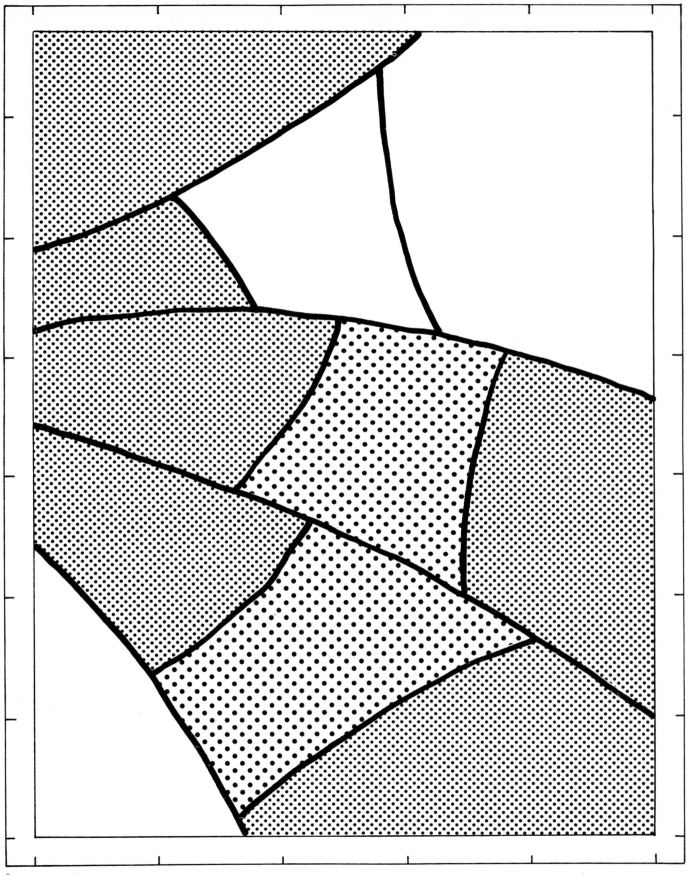

firescreen

Enlarging the design. On the book page, lightly connect the marks that appear along the four sides of the design, joining opposite sides vertically and horizontally to create a grid over the design. If you don't want to mark the book, lay a sheet of tracing paper over the design and connect the markings to create the grid on the tracing paper.

On a large sheet of paper that will be your cartoon, draw the outline of the finished fire screen, which is four times the width and the height of the design. Divide that outline into the same number of boxes as on the page-size grid—that is, seven horizontal and five vertical boxes.

Now box by box, transfer the design directly from the book—or through the gridded tracing paper that rests on the book page—into the corresponding box on the cartoon. Since the fire screen will be copper foiled, you do not need to duplicate the heavy lines.

Tracing the design. Make a tracing sandwich of oak tag, brown wrapping paper, and the cartoon (on top) with sheets of carbon paper between the layers. Then trace the enlarged design from the cartoon to produce the cutting pattern on the oak tag and the assembly diagram on the brown paper. Before you disassemble the sandwich, mark the colors of each area of glass, following the Color Key. Also number each area of glass in what you expect will be the assembly sequence. Press hard so the color code and numbers will appear on the two bottom drawings.

Take the sandwich apart. Lay the cartoon in a shallow tray, set the assembly diagram aside, and cut the glass patterns out of the oak tag, using a regular scissors or utility knife.

Cutting the glass. Cut the pieces of glass, using the oak tag patterns. After grozing each piece, lay it on the cartoon in its designated area.

Foiling the glass. Wrap each piece of glass in foil. After you have crimped and burnished the foil, return it to its position on the cartoon. When all the pieces of glass have been foiled and laid in position on the cartoon, you will be able to see the assembled project before soldering, and to check the fit of each piece against the overall design and against its neighbors. Be sure the copper is clean for soldering.

Assembling the pieces. Pin or tape the assembly diagram on your worktable, and tack lathing strips at the bottom and left edge of the design. Transfer the foiled pieces from the cartoon to the assembly diagram, starting at the left corner. As you lay each piece in place, fit it snugly against its neighbors and hold it with horseshoe nails. As you build up the design, tack and retack the nails to hold successive pieces of glass. When you have completed the design, remove the nails and tack lathing strips at the top and right side to hold the panel at right angles.

Soldering. Flux and tack-solder the foiled pieces together at all the joints.

Flux and tin all the copper foil surfaces on the face of the screen. Remove the lathing strips and turn the panel over.

Flux and tin all the exposed copper foil on the other side. Then bead all the tinned seams, laying a rounded ridge of solder between all pieces of glass and around the edge.

Turn the panel over again and bead the first side. Finally, lay a neat beaded edge around the rim of the panel.

Finishing the panel. Wash the soldered seams and the glass. Apply a patina to the soldered seams, and wash again.

Mounting the screen. A pair of andirons with special supports can hold the screen upright, or you can devise your own brace (see Figure 1). Bring the screen to an iron-worker—consult the Yellow Pages under "Iron Work" for custom-wrought iron fabricators—to have a brace made or to have your own andirons adapted.

Fig. 1

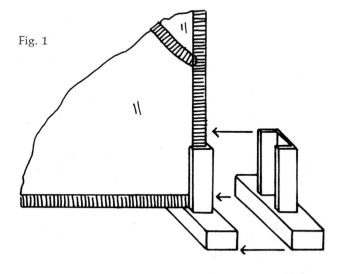

Box

DESIGN: page 234
RECOMMENDED CONSTRUCTION: Lead came
DIMENSIONS: Same as design
SPECIAL SUPPLIES: ¼-inch round lead for lid, 6 feet
    ¼-inch flat U came for edging, 6 feet
    right-angle came to join sides and bottom, 4 feet
    four ball feet, ⅝-inch size, nickel finish (see "Sources of Supplies")
    two hinges (see "Sources of Supplies")

Tracing the design. Trace the design from the book page onto a sheet of tracing paper; this will be your cartoon. Since the box will be leaded, duplicate the heavy lines between

each area of glass, using a marker ¹/₁₆ inch wide.

On another sheet of tracing paper, trace just the outline of the design; this will be the pattern for the bottom of the box. On this same paper, outline the other two patterns for the sides, and the front and back sections of glass (see Figure 1, page 236).

Make a tracing sandwich of oak tag, brown wrapping paper, and the cartoon, inserting carbon paper between the layers. Then trace the design onto the oak tag and the brown wrapping paper to create the cutting pattern and the assembly diagram. Duplicate the heavy lead lines on your tracing. While the sandwich is still assembled, mark the colors of each piece of glass on each color area, following the Color Key. Also number each area of glass and section of lead in what you expect will be the leading sequence, starting at the bottom left corner and fanning up and out. Press hard enough with pen or pencil so the color code and numbers appear on the assembly diagram and cutting pattern below.

Disassemble the tracing sandwich. Lay the cartoon in a shallow tray and set the assembly diagram aside. Cut the glass patterns out of the oak tag, using a pattern shears or double razor to remove the ¹/₁₆-inch allowance for the lead lines.

Lay another sheet of oak tag on your worktable and cover it with carbon paper. Over it lay the second tracing paper and transfer the outlines of the bottom of the box, and the patterns for the sides (see Figure 1). (It is not necessary to trace these outlines on brown paper for an assembly diagram; only the cutting patterns are needed.)

Remove the oak tag and cut the three rectangles out with a pattern shears or double razor.

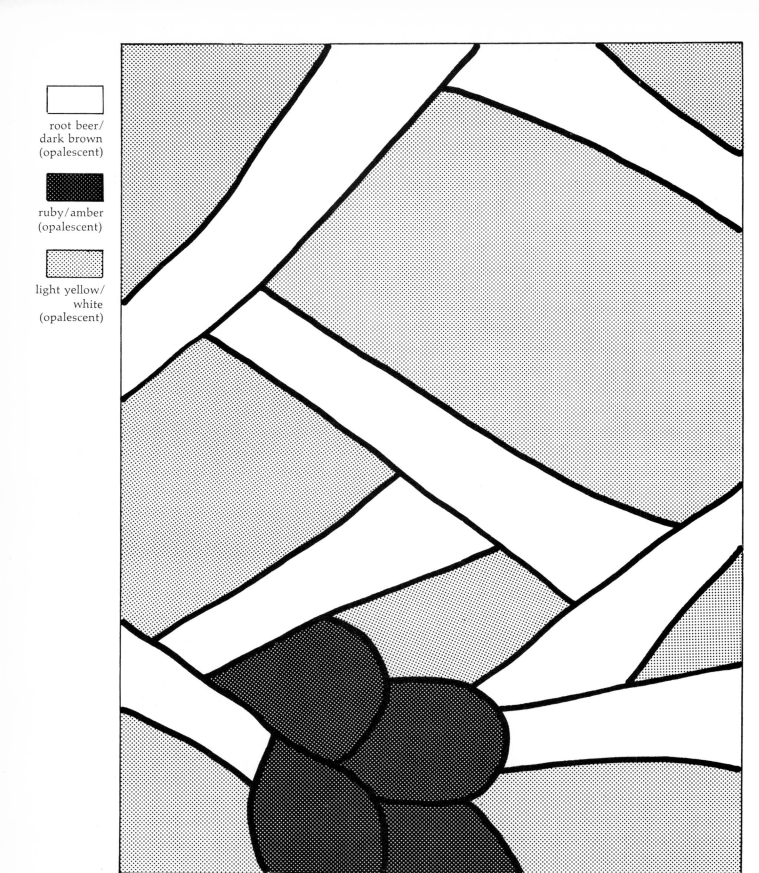

root beer/
dark brown
(opalescent)

ruby/amber
(opalescent)

light yellow/
white
(opalescent)

box

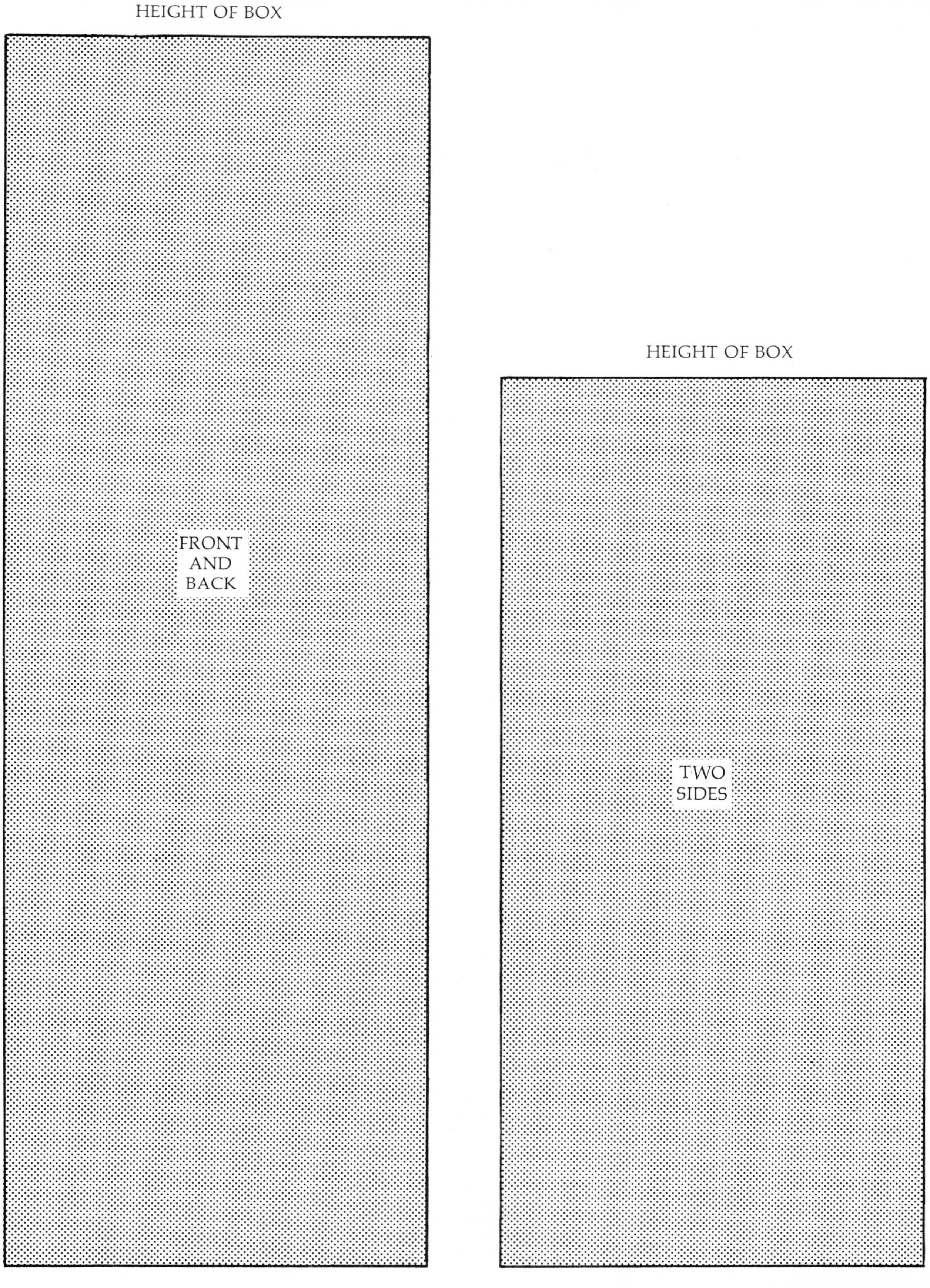

HEIGHT OF BOX

FRONT
AND
BACK

HEIGHT OF BOX

TWO
SIDES

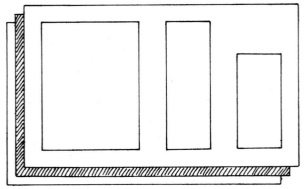

Fig. 1   box project

Cutting the glass. Cut the bottom of the box, using the pattern you just made. Then cut two side pieces from the smaller of the two remaining patterns, and a front and back section from the remaining pattern. You will now have five glass rectangles. Put them aside while you cut the glass pieces for the top of the box. As you cut and groze each piece, lay it on the cartoon in its designated area.

Leading up the top of the box. Set up your worktable with the assembly diagram, and lathing strips at the bottom and left side. Lead up the panel, following the sequence noted on the assembly diagram. Remember to use U came for the four borders, and slightly rounded came between the pieces.

Clean, flux, and solder the lead joints. Then turn the panel over and clean, flux, and solder the joints on the other side.

Putty the leading and clean both sides of the panel.

Assembling the box. Cut four pieces of right-angle came, each ⅛ inch shorter than the height of the box. Since the box is 3 inches high, each strip will measure about 2⅞ inches. Take one lead strip and slip one of its two channels over the edge of the front panel and slip the other channel over the adjoining

edge of a side panel; the panels will sit at right angles to each other. Center the lead so there is about ¹/₁₆ inch of glass on either side, then tape the lead and glass panels together with masking tape (see Figure 2).

Fig. 2

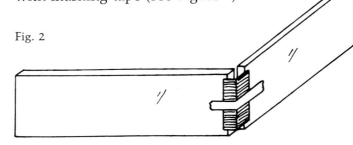

Join the other edge of the front panel to the other side of the box in the same way. You now have three sides of the box seated at right angles and taped together for stability. Now fit the remaining two strips of right-angle came on the edges of the back panel in the same way and join the back panel to the other three, taping to secure it (see Figure 3).

Fig. 3

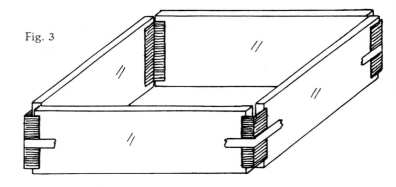

Cut four strips of right-angle lead came for the four edges of the bottom panel. Lay the bottom panel of glass on your worktable, raising it up on several thicknesses of cardboard because the angle of the lead strips prevents the came and the glass from lying flat. If one side of glass is better than the other, lay the better side face down; that side will eventually face up in the bottom of the box. One at a time, set the four edges of the glass into the right-angle lead strips (the empty channel of the right-angle came should point down). Trim the lead at each corner to form a miter. Then lightly solder the four corners, taking care only to solder the top surface of the right-angle came (see Figure 4).

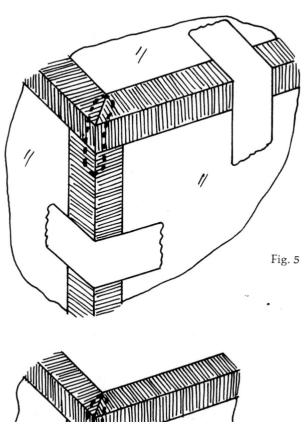

Fig. 5

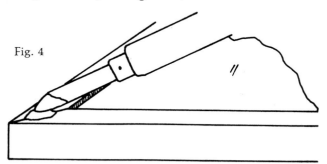

Fig. 4

Set the bottom panel of glass on top of the four side panels so that the box is upside down. Then seat the empty channels of the right-angle lead over the top edges of the glass sides, the back and the front panels. When you have fitted the corners neatly together and the five glass panels are at right angles to each other, secure the bottom panel to the other four with masking tape (see Figure 5). Then solder the corner joints, joining the upright strips to the corners (see Figure 5).

When the solder cools, turn the box over and solder the four inside corners at the bottom.

Cut and fit flat U came strips around the four remaining exposed edges of the box, which now sits like an open cube. Miter them neatly at the four corners, then solder them on their outside, inside, and flat surfaces (see Figure 6). When solder cools, remove all masking tape.

Finishing the box. Solder the four ball feet under the four corners of the bottom panel.

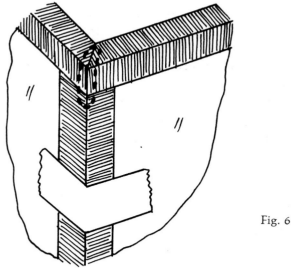

Fig. 6

Putty the leads and clean all surfaces.

Solder one half of each hinge carefully to the U came edge of the back panel. If the hinge protrudes over the lead strip and onto the glass, you may have to cut that part of the hinge away. Hold the hinge with small pliers and work carefully so that hot solder doesn't fall into and jam the movable part of the hinge (see Figure 7).

Fit the other half of each hinge to the back of the lid, and solder them in the same way.

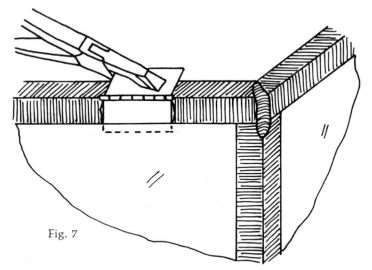

Fig. 7

Note: Different hinges work in different ways. Some are attached to the inside surfaces of the panels, some to the outside. Some types—such as a movable rod-and-tube hinge—run along the entire length of the surface to be hinged and are occasionally attached to the narrow top edge. Explain your needs at a crafts supply store and you will receive guidance.

Mirror

RECOMMENDED CONSTRUCTION: Copper foil. The mirror can also be leaded.

DIMENSIONS: Twice as wide and as high as the design—about 13 by 17 inches—or any other size.

SPECIAL SUPPLIES: ¼-inch adhesive-backed copper foil

16-gauge copper wire for two loops, each 2 inches long
adhesive-backed felt for mirror
thin wire or nylon thread for hanging

Enlarging the design. On the book page, lightly connect the markings that appear along the four sides of the design, joining opposite sides vertically and horizontally to create a grid over the mirror design. If you don't want to mark the book, lay a sheet of tracing paper over the design and connect the markings to create the grid on the tracing paper.

On a large sheet of paper that will be your cartoon, draw a rectangle twice as wide and twice as high as that on the design page. Divide it into the same number of boxes— that is, seven horizontal and nine vertical—to create a corresponding grid with larger boxes. Now, box by box, transfer the design directly from the book—or through the gridded tracing paper that rests on the book page—into the corresponding box on the cartoon. Since the mirror will be copper foiled, you do not need to duplicate the heavy lead lines.

Tracing the design. Make a tracing sandwich of oak tag, brown wrapping paper, and the cartoon (on top), with sheets of carbon paper between the layers. Then trace the enlarged design from the cartoon to produce the cutting patterns on the oak tag and the assembly diagram on the brown paper. Before you disassemble the sandwich, mark the colors of each area of glass, following the Color Key.

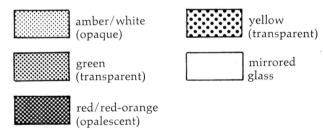

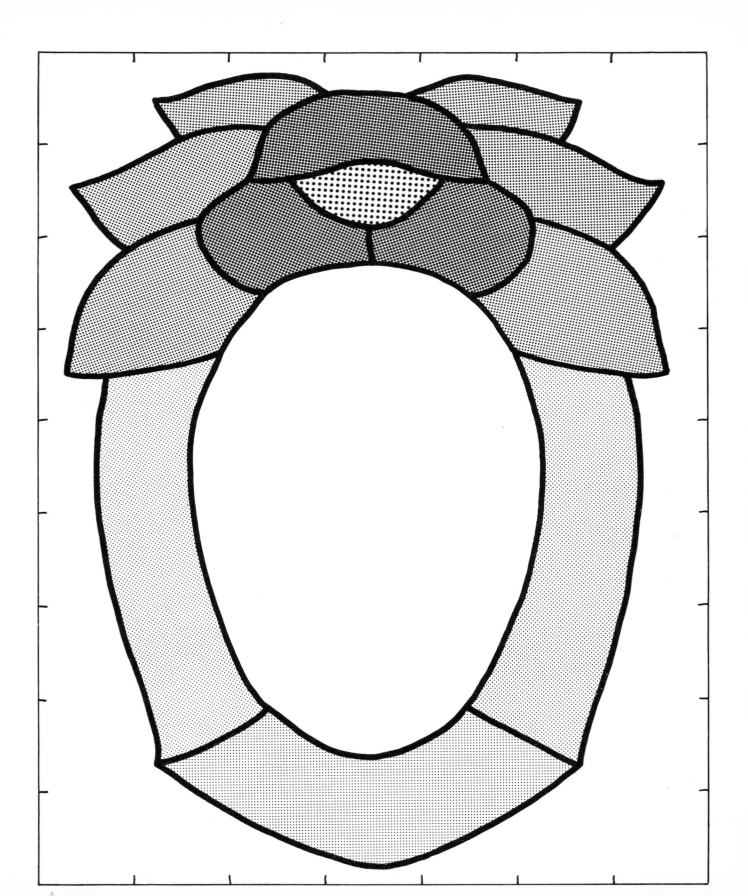

Also number each area of glass in what you expect will be the assembly sequence. Press hard enough with pen or pencil so the color code and numbers can be read on the oak tag and brown paper.

Take the sandwich apart. Lay the cartoon in a shallow tray, set the assembly diagram aside, and cut the glass patterns out of the oak tag with a regular scissors or utility knife.

Cutting the glass. Cut the pieces of glass from the oak tag patterns. After grozing each piece, lay it on the cartoon in its designated space. You can cut the mirror just like the other pieces of glass.

Foiling the glass. Wrap each piece of glass in foil. After crimping and burnishing the foil, return each piece to its place on the cartoon. When all the pieces, including the mirror, have been foiled and laid on the cartoon, you will be able to see the assembled project before soldering, and to check the fit of each piece against the overall design and against its neighbors. Be sure the copper is clean for soldering.

Assembling the pieces. Pin or tape the assembly diagram on the worktable. Transfer the foiled pieces from the cartoon to the assembly diagram, starting with the mirror and working outward. As you build up the design, hold each piece in place with horseshoe nails.

Soldering. Flux and tack-solder the foiled pieces together at all the joints, using water-based zinc chloride flux, which will not mar the mirror backing. Remove the nails that hold the sections together.

Flux and tin all the copper foil surfaces on the face of the mirror. Turn the project over, and flux and tin all the exposed copper foil surfaces on the back. Then bead all the tinned seams, laying a neat rounded ridge of solder

between all the pieces of glass, around the mirror, and around the edges.

Turn the panel over and bead the first side. Finally, lay a beaded edge around the rim of the mirror.

Attaching loops. Form the copper wire into two semicircular loops with outstretched feet, and solder each to the back of the mirror at a joint (see Figure 1).

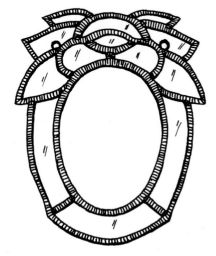

Fig. 1

Finishing the mirror. Wash the soldered seams, the glass, and the mirror. If desired, apply a patina to the soldered seams—keep it off the mirror—and wash again.

Cut adhesive-backed felt to fit the back of the mirror section to protect its coating, and apply it.

Attach wire or nylon thread through the soldered loops for hanging the mirror.

Clock

DESIGN: page 242

RECOMMENDED CONSTRUCTION: Lead came

DIMENSIONS: Same as design

SPECIAL SUPPLIES: ¼-inch round came for leading circular face of the clock, 1 foot

¼-inch flat came for leading remainder of clock design, 6 feet

¼-inch flat U came for edging at back, 3 feet

right-angle lead to join face, sides, and bottom of clock, 4 feet

battery-operated transistorized clock movement with hands (see "Sources of Supplies")

four nickel-finished brass ball feet, ⅜-inch diameter (see "Sources of Supplies")

Tracing the design. Trace the design from the book page onto a large sheet of tracing paper; this will be your cartoon. Since this clock will be leaded, duplicate the heavy lines between each glass area, using a marker ¹⁄₁₆ inch wide.

On another sheet of tracing paper outline the other two patterns; these are for the two side sections and for the top and bottom of the clock.

Make a tracing sandwich of oak tag, brown wrapping paper, and the cartoon (on top), inserting carbon paper between the layers. Then trace the design onto the oak tag and brown paper to create the cutting pattern and assembly diagram. Duplicate the heavy lead lines on your tracings.

While the sandwich is still assembled, mark the colors of each area of glass, following the Color Key. Also number each area of glass and section of lead in what you expect will be the leading sequence (a leading-up sequence is shown in Figure 95, Part II). Press hard enough with pen or pencil so the color code and numbers can be read on the assembly diagram and cutting pattern.

Take the tracing sandwich apart. Lay the cartoon in a shallow tray and set the assembly diagram aside. Cut the glass patterns out of the oak tag, using a pattern shears or double razor to remove the ¹⁄₁₆-inch allowance for the lead lines.

Lay another sheet of oak tag on your worktable and cover it with carbon paper. Over it lay the second tracing paper, then trace the outlines for the sides of the clock and the top and bottom. (It is not necessary to trace these patterns on brown paper for an assembly diagram; only the cutting patterns are needed.)

Remove the oak tag and cut the two rectangles out with a pattern shears or a double razor.

Cutting the glass. Using the smaller of the two rectangular patterns, cut the top and bottom pieces of glass for the clock; cut the side pieces using the other rectangle. Put these four pieces of glass aside while you cut the glass for the face of the clock. As each piece is cut and grozed, lay it on the cartoon in its designated area so you can keep track of each piece.

With a carbide drill make a small hole in the center of the clock face for attaching the clock movement and the hands of the clock. (The mechanism won't show through the opaque glass.)

Leading up the clock face. For this project you will have to set up the worktable a little differently, because the right-angle lead strips that border the clock design won't lie flat on the table. First nail lathing strips for the bottom and left sides of the design. Then, for the bottom and left borders, install right-angle lead cames, mitering the corner where they meet (see Figure 1a, page 243). You must raise the work area so that the glass will be at the same level as the channel into which

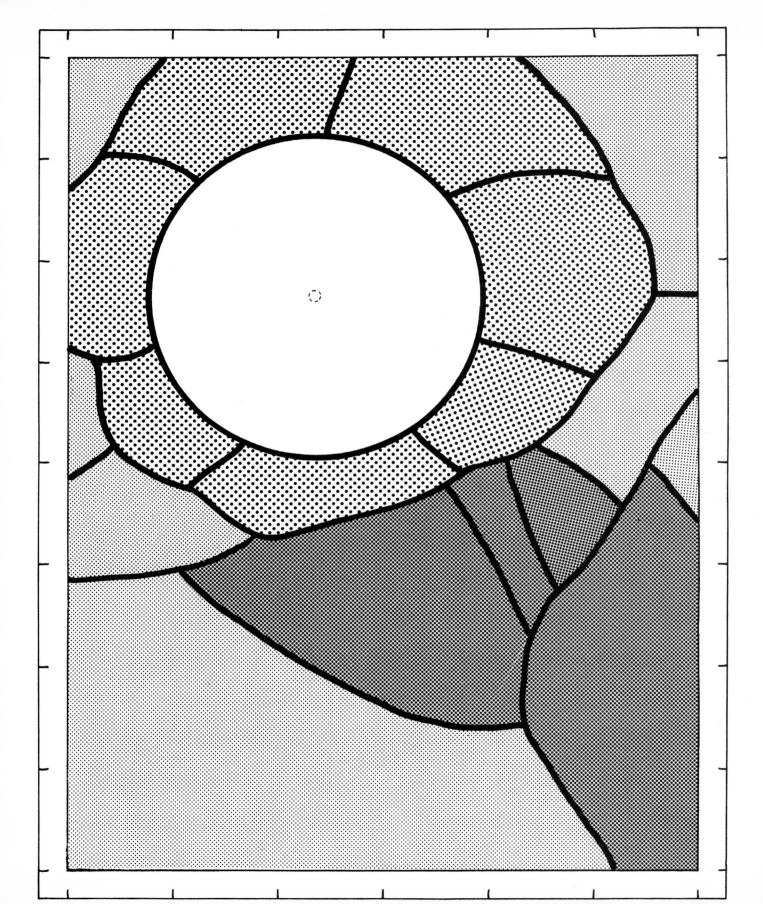

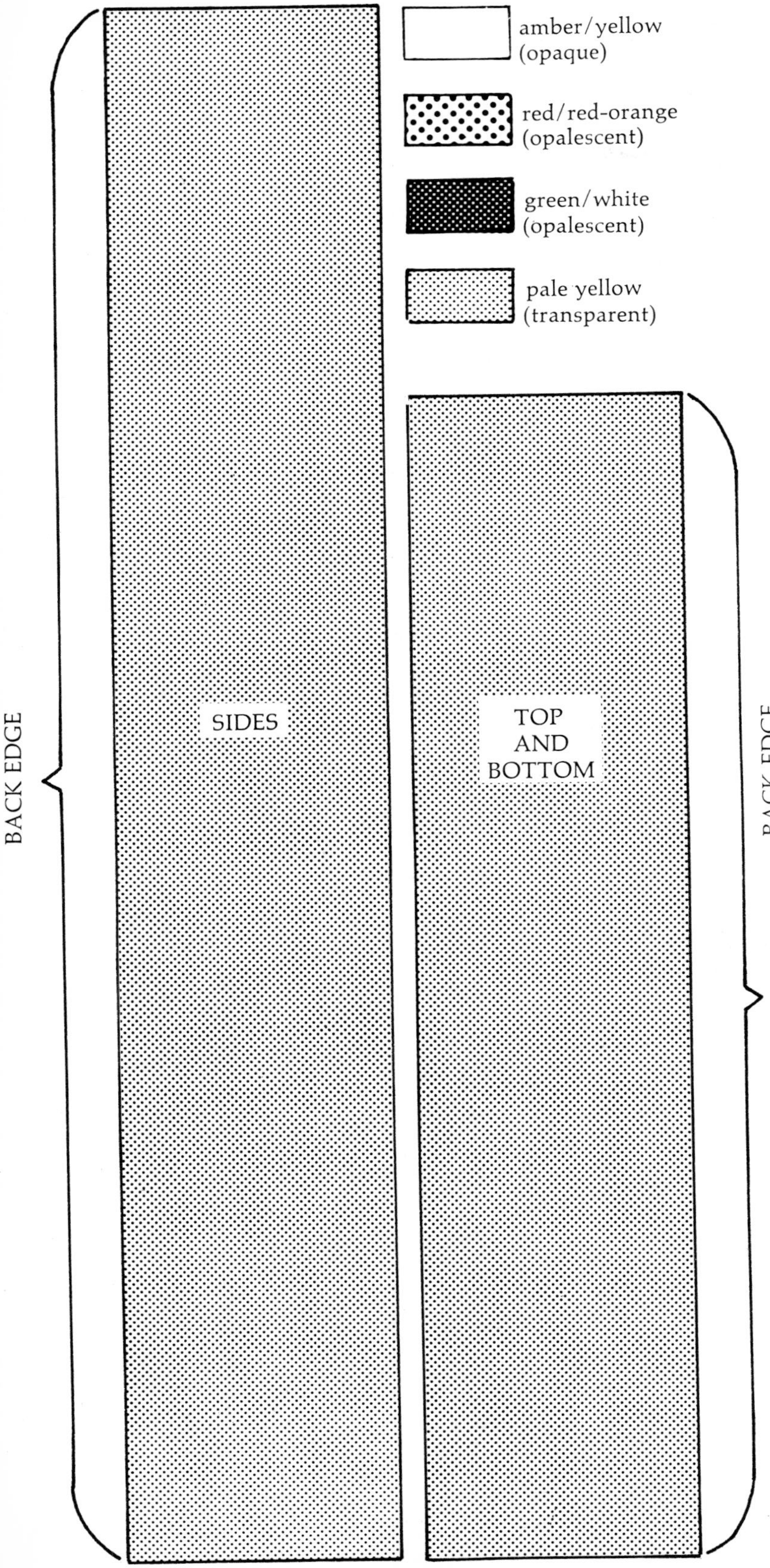

amber/yellow
(opaque)

red/red-orange
(opalescent)

green/white
(opalescent)

pale yellow
(transparent)

SIDES

TOP
AND
BOTTOM

BACK EDGE

BACK EDGE

Fig. 1

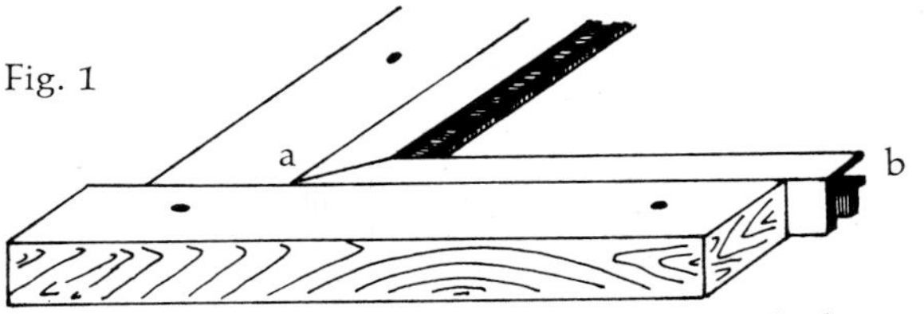

a

b

clock project

Fig. 2

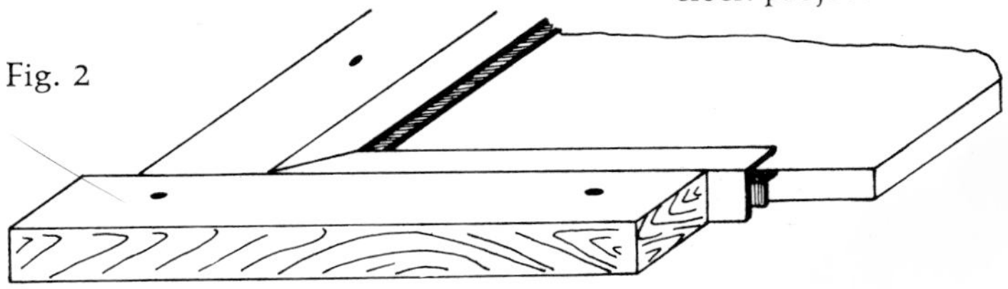

Fig. 3

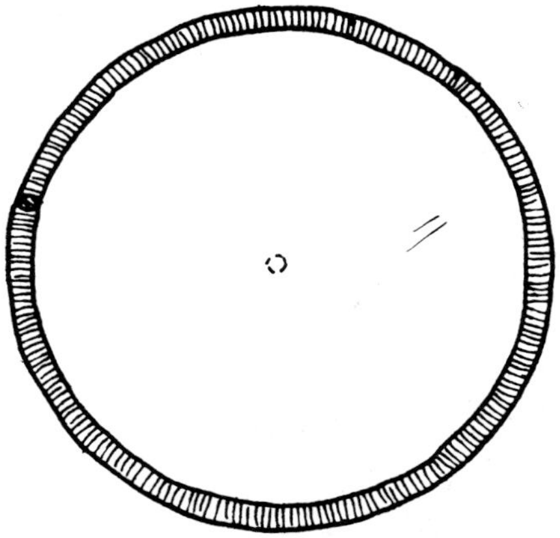

it fits (see Figure 1b). This is easily done with a piece of composition board—it will be about ¼ inch thick—cut to the size of the design (see Figure 2), or with several pieces of stacked cardboard.

Tape or tack the assembly diagram to the work surface and lead up the design according to the leading layout you marked on it.

When you are ready to lead up the round face of the clock, wrap the circular glass in the strip of round came, rather than the flat came you have been using. Cut and solder the lead ends together before setting it into the panel (see Figure 3). Place the leaded circle into the layout so its soldered joint touches any one of the leads that run into it; this will eliminate an extra joint.

Finish leading up the entire panel, then

install the border leads on the top and right side, using right-angle came and mitering the corners. (All the steps in leading up this design are illustrated in Figures 95–106, Part II.)

Clean, flux, and solder all the lead joints. When the solder cools, turn the panel over carefully and clean, flux, and solder the joints on the other side.

Putty the leading and clean both sides of the panel.

Assembling the clock. Cut four pieces of right-angle lead came, each ⅛ inch shorter than the depth of the clock. Since the clock is 1½ inches deep, each lead strip will measure 1⅜ inches. Take one of the lead strips and slip one of its two channels over the short edge of the top glass panel, and the other channel over the short edge of one of the side panels; the panels will sit on edge at right angle to each other (see Figure 4). Center the lead so there is about 1/16 inch of glass on either side of it, then tape the lead and glass panels together with masking tape (see Figure 4).

Join the other side panel to the top in the same way. You now have three sides of the clock seated at right angles and taped together for stability. Now fit the remaining two strips of right-angle lead on the bottom panel in the same way and join the bottom to the other three pieces, taping to secure it (see Figure 5).

With the four pieces of glass taped together and lying on edge, cut and fit flat U came around those exposed edges; miter the leads neatly at the four corners, then solder them (see Figure 6). When the joints cool, turn the glass rectangle over carefully, with the masking tape still in place, so the opposite edges of the glass are now exposed.

Set the leaded-up clock face over these exposed edges. Carefully seat the empty flanges of its right-angle border leads over the exposed edges of the housing. When you have fitted the corners neatly together and the five glass panels are all at right angles to each other, secure the face of the clock to the other four panels with masking tape. Then carefully solder the corner joints (see Figure 7).

Putty and clean all leaded glass.

Fig. 4

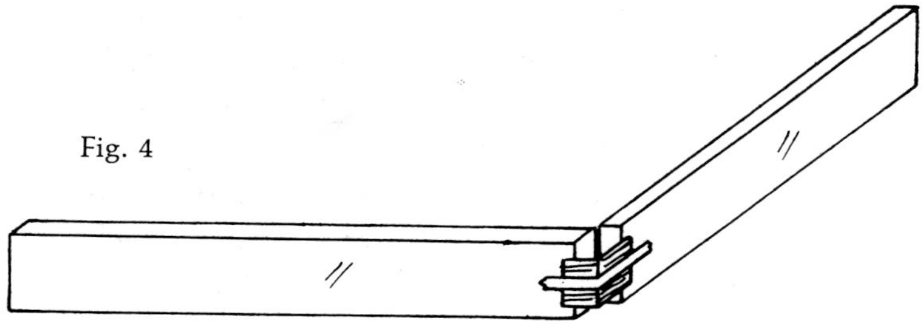

Fig. 5

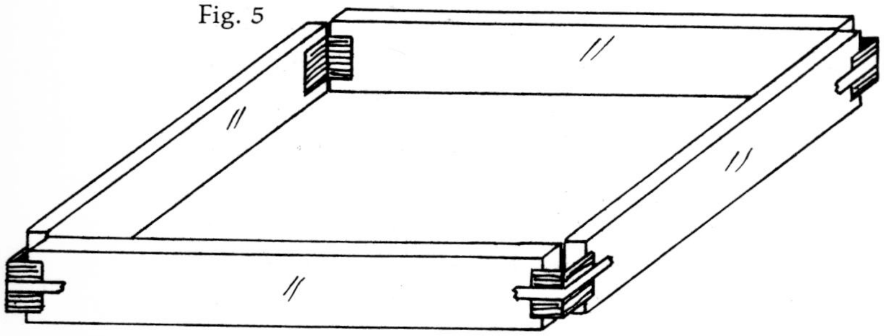

Fig. 6

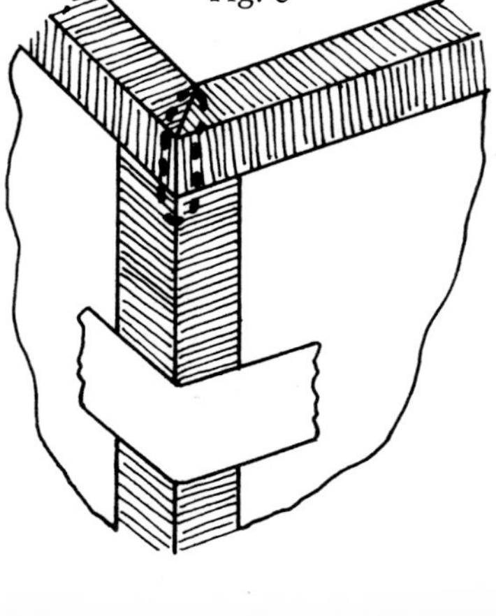

Fig. 7

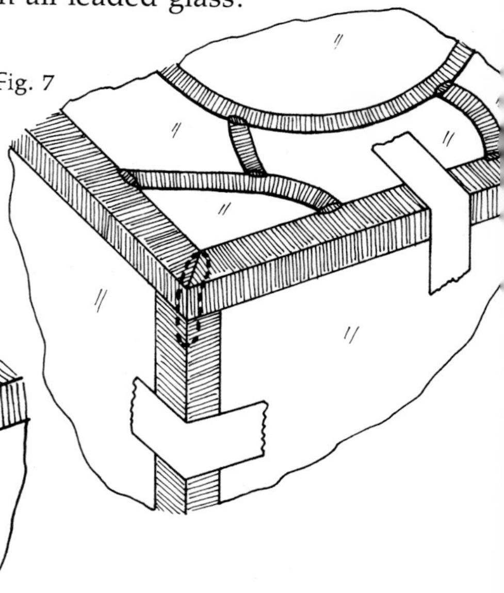

Finishing the clock. Turn the clock housing upside down and solder the four ball feet at the four corners of the base.

Install the clock mechanism according to the manufacturer's instructions.

Note: As assembled above, the back of the clock is exposed, which will not make any difference if you set it against a wall. However, if you display the clock on a freestanding table, you may want to provide a hinged back panel. If so, cut the back panel from the outline of the clock design, and edge it with U came. Solder hinges to one side and a copper hook and loop to the opposite side. You can follow the instructions for assembling the lid of the box (on page 237), substituting the back panel for the box lid.

Wall Light

DESIGN: page 246
RECOMMENDED CONSTRUCTION: Lead came
DIMENSIONS: About 30 inches wide and 8 inches high (three times the width and height of the design)
SPECIAL SUPPLIES: ¼-inch round lead came for design, 2 feet
ㅤㅤ¼-inch flat U came for edging, 7 feet
ㅤㅤribbon came, ¼ inch wide, 4 feet
ㅤㅤ18-gauge copper wire, 18 inches long
ㅤㅤtwo angle irons, each with a projection of about 4 inches for wall mounting
ㅤㅤ24-inch wall-mount fluorescent fixture and bulb

Enlarging the design. On the book page, lightly connect the marks that appear along the four sides of the design, joining opposite sides vertically and horizontally to create a grid over the design. If you don't want to mark the book, lay a sheet of tracing paper over the design and connect the markings to create the grid on the tracing paper.

On a large piece of paper that will be your cartoon, outline the dimensions of the light panel, which is three times the width and the height of the design. Divide that outline into the same number of boxes as on the page-size grid—that is, four boxes vertically and fifteen horizontally.

Box by box, transfer the design directly from the book—or through the gridded tracing paper that rests on the book page—into the corresponding box on the cartoon. Since this project will be leaded, duplicate the heavy lines separating the central glass from the two sides. Also include the dotted lines.

Tracing the design. Make a tracing sandwich of oak tag, brown wrapping paper, and the cartoon (on top), with sheets of carbon paper between the layers. Then trace the enlarged design from the cartoon to produce the cutting pattern on the oak tag and the assembly diagram on the wrapping paper. Duplicate the heavy lead lines as you trace. Note the dotted lines as well; they are needed on the assembly diagram. Before you disassemble the sandwich, mark the colors of each piece of glass, following the Color Key.

Take the tracing sandwich apart. Lay the cartoon in a shallow tray, set the assembly diagram aside, and cut the glass patterns out of the oak tag, using a pattern shears or double razor to remove the 1/16-inch lead line allowance. There are only three pieces of glass in this project; for cutting, ignore the dotted lines, which designate the later placement of flat lead over the glass and not the joining of several pieces of glass.

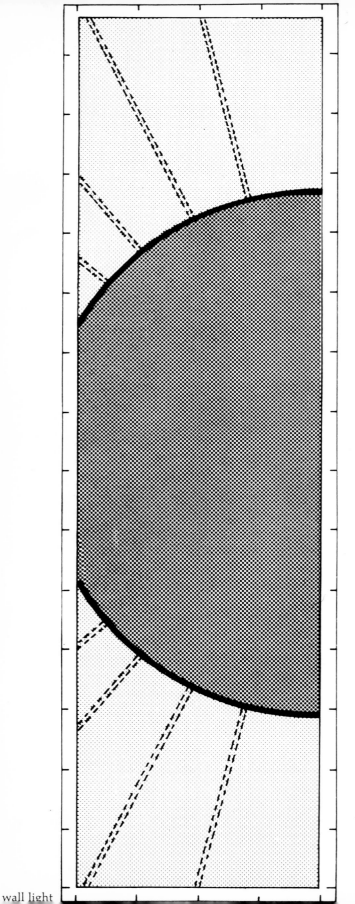

Cutting the glass. Cut the glass, using the oak tag patterns. Even though there are only three pieces of glass, mark the right and left pieces, which are mirror images of each other, so you don't confuse them.

Leading up the panel. Set up your worktable with the assembly diagram and lathing strips at the bottom and left side. Lead up the panel, using U came on the four outside edges and round came to frame the center piece of glass.

After the three pieces have been leaded and the U came border leads installed, cut the eight lengths of ribbon came that simulate the rays of the sun. Fit them in tightly between the border and the interior leads.

Clean, flux, and solder all the lead joints, including the ribbon came joints.

Turn the panel over carefully, and clean, flux, and solder the joints on the other side. The ribbon came, of course, does not appear on the back of the panel. Make sure the soldering at the four corners—front and back—is flat and neat.

Finishing the project. On the back of the panel, reinforce the large central piece of glass

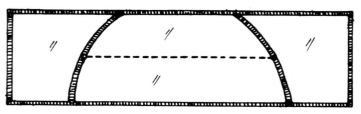

Fig. 1   bedlight

with 18-gauge copper wire across the back. Solder each end of the wire to the leads on either side of the glass (see Figure 1).

Solder each mounting iron to the heavy leading on the back of the panel (see Figure

bright yellow (transparent)   ruby/amber (opalescent)

2). If the irons have screw holes in them at this end, ignore them and solder over the holes.

Putty the leading and clean both sides of the panel.

Installing the light. Install the wall-mount fluorescent fixture on the wall where desired.

Center the finished panel over the light fixture and attach the wall end of the mounting irons with toggle bolts or molly screws for maximum weight bearing (see Figure 3).

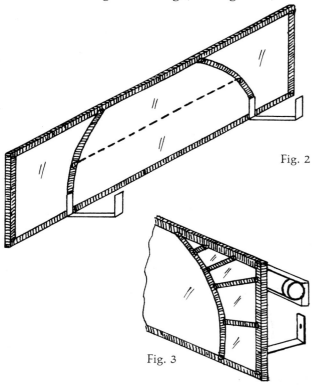

Fig. 2

Fig. 3

Note: If you want to enclose the wall light on the two sides, top, and/or bottom, simply measure the dimensions of your finished panel and its precise extension from the wall and cut the additional panels accordingly. Then use right-angle lead instead of U came on any edge that will be perpendicular to another piece of glass, and follow the instructions for assembling the box (page 236).

Window Shade Pull

DESIGN: From the "Design Workbook," bottom of page 194
RECOMMENDED CONSTRUCTION: Copper foil. The shade pull can also be leaded.
DIMENSIONS: Same as design
SPECIAL SUPPLIES: ¼-inch adhesive-backed copper foil
    20-gauge copper wire for loop, 2 inches long
    nylon thread for hanging

Tracing the design. Trace the design from the book (bottom of page 194 in the "Design Workbook") onto a sheet of tracing paper; this will be your cartoon. Since the pull will be copper foiled, trace through the center of the heavy lead lines with a pen or thin pencil. (If you want to assemble the pull with lead came, duplicate the heavy lines between each area of glass with a thick marker.)

Make a tracing sandwich of oak tag, brown wrapping paper, and the cartoon (on top), inserting carbon paper between the layers. Then trace the design onto the oak tag and the wrapping paper to create the cutting pattern and assembly diagram. (If you are going to lead up the rose, duplicate the heavy lead lines on your tracings.)

While the sandwich is still assembled, mark the colors of each area of glass, following the Color Key. Also number each area of glass in what you expect will be the assembly sequence. Press hard enough with your pen or pencil so that the color code and numbers can be read on the assembly diagram and cutting patterns.

Take the tracing sandwich apart. Lay the cartoon in a shallow tray and set the assembly diagram aside. Cut the glass patterns out of the oak tag, using a regular scissors or utility knife. (If you are leading the design, cut the patterns out with a pattern shears or double razor to remove the 1/16-inch allowance for the lead.)

Cutting the glass. Cut the pieces of glass from the oak tag patterns. After you have grozed each piece, lay it on the cartoon in its designated area.

Foiling the glass. Wrap each piece of glass in foil. After crimping and burnishing the foil, return each piece to its place on the cartoon. When all the pieces of glass have been foiled, you will be able to see the assembled design before soldering it, and to check the fit of each piece against the cartoon and against its neighbors. Be sure the copper foil is clean for soldering.

Assembling the pieces. Pin or tape the assembly diagram on your worktable. Transfer the foiled pieces from the cartoon, starting with the large petal near the top of the rose, then working outward. As you lay each successive piece in place, fit it snugly against its neighbor and hold it in place with horseshoe nails. As you build up the design, tack and retack the nails.

Soldering. Flux and tack-solder the foiled pieces together at all the joints. Remove the nails that hold the pieces of glass.

Flux and tin all the copper-foiled surfaces on the face of the pull. Turn the pull over, and flux and tin all the exposed copper foil surfaces on the other side. Then bead the tinned seams.

Turn the piece over and bead the first side. Finally, lay a neat beaded edge all around the rim of the rose.

Attaching the loop. Form the copper wire into a semicircular loop with outstretched feet, then solder it to the top of the rose (see Figure 1).

Finishing the pull. Wash the soldered seams and the glass. Apply a patina to the copper, if desired, and wash the piece again.

Hang the pull from a window shade with nylon thread (as illustrated in Figure 171, Part III).

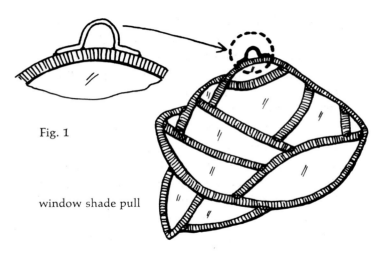

Fig. 1

window shade pull

Strawberry Pin

DESIGN: From the Design Workbook, page 190

RECOMMENDED CONSTRUCTION: Copper foil. The pin can also be leaded.

DIMENSIONS: Half as wide and as high as the design

SPECIAL SUPPLIES: ¼-inch adhesive-backed copper foil

pin back, 1¼ inches long (see "Sources of Supplies")

Reducing the design. On a sheet of tracing paper outline an 8-inch square, then divide each side of the square into eighths and connect the lines on opposite sides to form a grid of sixty-four 1-inch squares within the large outline.

On another sheet of paper that will be your cartoon, draw a 4-inch square, and divide it in the same way into sixty-four squares. Like the tracing paper grid, this grid will have eight horizontal and eight vertical squares, but these boxes will be ½-inch rather than 1-inch squares, and they will produce a design that is half the width and the height of the original.

Place the tracing paper grid over the double strawberry design on page 190. Working one box at a time, transfer the design from the book into the corresponding box on the cartoon; you will be able to see through the tracing paper resting on the design. (If you want to assemble the pin with lead came, duplicate the heavy lines between each area of glass with a thick marker.)

Tracing the design. Make a tracing sandwich of oak tag, brown wrapping paper, and the cartoon (on top), inserting carbon paper between the layers. Then trace the reduced design onto the oak tag and the brown paper to create the cutting pattern and the assembly diagram. (If you are going to lead up the pin, duplicate the heavy lead lines on your tracings.)

Before you disassemble the sandwich, mark the colors of each glass area, following the Color Key. Also number each area of glass

in what you expect will be the assembly sequence. Press hard enough with your pen or pencil so that the color code and numbers can be read on the assembly diagram and cutting pattern.

Take the sandwich apart. Lay the cartoon in a shallow tray and set the assembly diagram aside. Cut the glass patterns out of the oak tag, using a regular scissors or mat knife. (If you are leading the design, cut the patterns out with a pattern shears or double razor to remove the 1/16-inch allowance for the lead lines.)

Cutting the glass. Cut the pieces of glass from the oak tag patterns. After you have grozed each piece, lay it on the cartoon in its designated space. To keep track of the leaf and strawberry sections, you may find it helpful to number each piece of glass according to the sequence of numbers now noted on the cartoon.

Foiling the glass. Wrap each piece of glass in foil. After crimping and burnishing the foil, return each piece to the cartoon. When all the pieces of glass have been foiled, you will be able to see the assembled design before soldering it, and to check the fit of each piece against the cartoon and against its neighbors. Be sure the copper foil is clean for soldering.

Assembling the pieces. Pin or tape the assembly diagram on your worktable. Transfer the foiled pieces from the cartoon, starting with a piece near the center of the design, then working outward. As you lay each successive piece in place, fit it snugly against its neighbor and hold it securely with horseshoe nails. As you build up the design, tack and retack the nails.

Soldering. Flux and tack-solder the foiled pieces together at all joints. Remove the nails that hold the glass.

Fig. 1

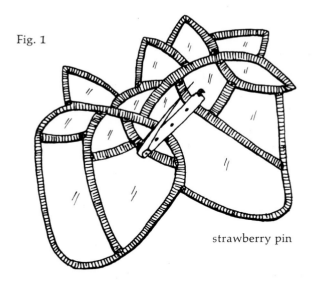

strawberry pin

Flux and tin all the copper-foiled surfaces on the face of the pin. Turn the pin over, and flux and tin all the exposed copper foil on the back. Then bead all tinned seams, laying a rounded ridge of solder between all the pieces of glass.

Turn the pin over and bead the first side. Finally, lay a beaded edge all around the rim of the pin.

Attaching the pin back. Brush flux on the pin back, and solder it to one side of the piece along a soldered seam or across several seams (see Figure 1).

Finishing the pin. Wash the soldered seams and the glass. Apply a patina to the copper, if desired, and wash the piece again.

Sources of Supplies

Supplies for stained glass work are listed in your Yellow Pages under Glass, Stained and Leaded. You may also be able to locate supplies at glaziers and craft stores. If you can't find the equipment you need locally, the following mail order sources carry a variety of supplies for stained glass work. Some of these sources have catalogs, for which there is sometimes a charge. Some require a minimum order. Some will send samples of glass and lead came. For current information, write them directly.

General Equipment, Including Tools and Supplies

Allcraft Tool & Supply Co., 100 Frank Road,
  Hicksville, N.Y. 11801
American Metalcraft Co., 4100 Belmont Ave.,
  Chicago, Ill. 60641
Arts & Crafts Colony, 4132 N. Tamiami Trail,
  Sarasota, Fla. 33580
S. A. Bendheim Co., Inc., 122 Hudson St.,
  New York, N.Y. 10013
Bienenfeld Industries, Inc., 1539 Covert St.,
  Brooklyn, N.Y. 11227
Boin Arts & Crafts Co., 87 Morris St.,
  Morristown, N.J. 07960
Cline Glass Co., 1135 S.E. Grand St.,
  Portland, Oreg. 97214
Coran–Sholes Industries, 509 E. Second St.,
  S. Boston, Mass. 02127
Glass Masters Guild, 621 Avenue of the Americas,
  New York, N.Y. 10011
New Renaissance Glass Works, 5151 Broadway,
  Oakland, Calif. 94611
New York Art Glass, 920 Broadway,
  New York, N.Y. 10010
Occidental Associates, 410 Occidental South,
  Seattle, Wash. 98104
Pilgrims' Pride, P.O. Box 47,
  Roslyn, Pa. 19001

San Francisco Stained Glass Works, 3463 16th St.,
  San Francisco, Calif. 94114
Sax Arts & Crafts, 207 N. Milwaukee St.,
  Milwaukee, Wis. 53202
Saylescrafts, Inc., 171 Main St.,
  Nyack, N.Y. 10960
Sommer & Maca Co., 5501 West Ogden Ave.,
  Chicago, Ill. 60650
The Stained Glass Club, P.O. Box 244,
  Norwood, N.J. 07648
Henry Westpfal & Co., Inc., 4 E. 32 St.,
  New York, N.Y. 10016
Whittemore–Durgin Glass Co., Box 2065,
  Hanover, Mass. 02339

Glass

S. A. Bendheim Co., Inc., 122 Hudson St.,
  New York, N.Y. 10013
Bienenfeld Industries, Inc., 1539 Covert St.,
  Brooklyn, N.Y. 11227
Blenko Glass Co., Milton,
  W. Va. 25541
Boin Arts & Crafts Co., 87 Morris St.,
  Morristown, N.J. 07960
Cline Glass Co., 1135 S.E. Grand St.,
  Portland, Oreg. 97214
Coran–Sholes Industries, 509 E. Second St.,
  S. Boston, Mass. 02127
Glass Masters Guild, 621 Avenue of the Americas,
  New York, N.Y. 10011
New York Art Glass, 920 Broadway,
  New York, N.Y. 10010. Antique only.
Occidental Associates, 410 Occidental South,
  Seattle, Wash. 98104
Pilgrims' Pride, P.O. Box 47,
  Roslyn, Pa. 19001
The Stained Glass Club, P.O. Box 244,
  Norwood, N.J. 07648
Whittemore–Durgin Glass Co., Box 2065,
  Hanover, Mass. 02339

Copper Foil and Wire Only

Conklin Brass & Copper, Inc., 324 West 23 St.,
New York, N.Y. 10011
Paragon Industries, Inc., Box 10133,
Dallas, Tex. 75207

Lead Came and Solder Only

Gardiner Metal Co., 4820 S. Campbell Ave.,
Chicago, Ill. 60632
White Metal Rolling & Stamping Corp., 80 Moultrie St., Brooklyn, N.Y. 11222

Zinc Came

Chicago Metallic Corp., 4849 S. Austin Ave.,
Chicago, Ill. 60638

Reinforcing Steel Bars

Chicago Metallic Corp., 4849 S. Austin Ave.,
Chicago, Ill. 60638
Glass Masters Guild, 621 Avenue of the Americas,
New York, N.Y. 10011
New York Art Glass, 920 Broadway,
New York, N.Y. 10010
Pilgrims' Pride, P.O. Box 47,
Roslyn, Pa. 19001
White Metal Rolling & Stamping Corp., 80 Moultrie St., Brooklyn, N.Y. 11222

Miscellaneous Supplies and Findings (hinges, pin backs, etc.)

Allcraft Tool & Supply Co., 100 Frank Road,
Hicksville, N.Y. 11801
American Metalcraft Co., 4100 Belmont Ave.,
Chicago, Ill. 60641
Glass Masters Guild, 621 Avenue of the Americas,
New York, N.Y. 10011. Hinges, ball feet,
solder-coated wire for hooks and catches.
New Renaissance Glass Works, 5151 Broadway,
Oakland, Calif. 94611
New York Art Glass, 920 Broadway,
New York, N.Y. 10010
Pilgrims' Pride, P.O. Box 47,
Roslyn, Pa. 19001
Sax Arts & Crafts, 207 N. Milwaukee St.,
Milwaukee, Wis. 53202. Pin backs, hinges.
Saylescrafts, Inc., 171 Main St.,
Nyack, N.Y. 10960. Battery-operated clock
mechanism.

Tiffany-Type Lamp Kits, Lamp Shade Molds, Lamp Parts

S. A. Bendheim Co., Inc., 122 Hudson St.,
New York, N.Y. 10013
Cline Glass Co., 1135 S.E. Grand St.,
Portland, Oreg. 97214
Coran–Sholes Industries, 509 E. Second St.,
S. Boston, Mass. 02127
Glass Masters Guild, 621 Avenue of the Americas,
New York, N.Y. 10011
New Renaissance Glass Works, 5151 Broadway,
Oakland, Calif. 94611
New York Art Glass, 920 Broadway,
New York, N.Y. 10010
Pilgrims' Pride, P.O. Box 47,
Roslyn, Pa. 19001
San Francisco Stained Glass Works, 3463 16th St.,
San Francisco, Calif. 94114
The Stained Glass Club, P.O. Box 244,
Norwood, N.J. 07648
Whittemore–Durgin Glass Co., Box 2065,
Hanover, Mass. 02339

Glossary

AMBULATORY. The aisle circling the eastern end of a church, behind the altar.

ANNEALING. The process of heating, then gradually cooling glass in a kiln to avoid internal stress. Rapidly cooled glass will crack.

ANTIQUE GLASS. Handblown glass made to resemble old glass and manufactured in much the same way. It has irregularities, bubbles, streaks, ripples, and varying thicknesses, all of which provide interest and beauty as light passes through and creates refractions.

APSE. The projecting end of a church, commonly at the east.

BEADING. Laying an edge of solder over a tinned copper foil seam.

BUTT JOINT. An intersection in which two pieces of lead came fit next to each other, rather than one overlapping or notching the other.

CAME. A grooved length of metal—commonly lead—that holds individual sections of glass in its channels.

CANOPY. An architectural space or niche painted on glass to enclose a figure or a scene. It was popular beginning in the fourteenth century.

CARTOON. A full-size design.

CATHEDRAL GLASS. Mechanically rolled glass made in a variety of textures, including smooth.

CLERESTORY. The upper part of a church, with windows.

DECORATED. A style of English Gothic architecture, characterized by geometric tracery, that flourished in the early fourteenth century.

DIAPER PATTERN. A geometric design of rectangles or lozenge shapes.

DOUBLE GLAZING. The technique of using two pieces of glass, one on top of the other, to create a new color or texture. They can be soldered together with wide copper foil, set into a double-grooved lead strip, or into two single strips that are then joined.

EPOXY. Resin mixed with hardener to form a plastic adhesive that is used for embedding slab glass.

FACETED GLASS. Thick slabs of glass that are chipped, or faceted, along their edges, then set into epoxy or concrete.

FAVRILE GLASS. Iridescent glass made and patented by Tiffany in the late nineteenth century.

FIRING. Heating glass in a kiln to fuse the glass and its painted design.

FLAMBOYANT. A French Gothic style, characterized by flamelike forms, that flourished in the fifteenth century.

FLASHED GLASS. Usually clear glass with a thin layer of color on one side that can be etched or sandblasted away to reveal the underlying glass. It is usually used for signs, for lettering, and for pictorial details.

FLUX. A material, often liquid, that removes oxides from metal and helps solder flow and form a strong joint between the pieces to be soldered.

FOILING. The process of wrapping the edges of cut glass with adhesive-backed copper foil.

GLAZING. The process of assembling and leading up a glass project.

GRISAILLE. A panel of clear or light-colored glass painted with geometric or foliate designs in black or brown paint that creates a greenish-gray appearance.

GROZE. To snap off irregular glass edges with a grozing pliers.

LEADING, LEADING UP. The process of assembling cut glass sections with strips of lead came and soldering them at the joints.

LEAD JOINTS. The intersections where two strips of lead came meet, which are soldered. There are two types of joints: butt and overlapping.

LIGHTS. The window opening between the mullions.

MATT. A thin coat of enamel laid evenly over the surface of the glass.

MEDALLION WINDOW. A medieval window, primarily of the twelfth and thirteenth centuries, made up of repeated geometric shapes showing different scenes of a Biblical narrative.

MULLIONS. The vertical division between two adjacent windows, or within one window to divide it into smaller sections.

OCCHIO (plural, *occhi*). An Italian eye window.

OCULUS, or eye window. A round window, often placed in the west façade of European churches, that has no stone tracery.

OPALESCENT GLASS. Non-transparent, milky, iridescent glass that usually has two or more colors in it.

PATINA. A surface treatment of lead or copper foil by acids or exposure to simulate age.

PATTERN. A piece of paper cut to the exact size for a section of glass and used as a guide for cutting the glass.

PERPENDICULAR. Style of English Gothic architecture, characterized by vertical lines and tracery, that flourished in the late fourteenth and fifteenth centuries.

POT METAL. Antique glass colored throughout with one color.

QUARRIES. Glass diamonds or rectangles often leaded together in a diagonal lattice pattern.

SCORING. Scratching the surface of the glass with a glass cutter so that the glass will break along that line.

SILVER STAIN. Silver salts that produce shades of yellow when painted and fired on glass.

SLAB GLASS, or *dalles*, or *dalle-de-verre*. Thick slabs of glass made by casting; usually about 8 by 12 by ¾ or 1 inches.

SOLDER. A metal alloy, usually tin and lead, melted to form a joint between two pieces of metal.

STIPPLING. The technique of producing tiny dots in an area of matt paint so the light comes through and defines pictorial details. It is done with a stub-ended stippling brush.

TINNING. Laying a thin coat of solder over copper foil, or over the tip of a soldering iron.

TRACERY. The decorative stonework above the window opening. It takes different shapes in different styles of architecture.

TRANSLUCENT GLASS. Semi-transparent glass that lets light through but does not permit clear visibility of objects on the other side.

TRANSPARENT GLASS. Glass that lets light through while permitting clear visibility of objects on the other side.

Bibliography

ADAMS, HENRY. *Mont-Saint-Michel and Chartres.* New York: Doubleday-Anchor Books, 1959.

ARNOLD, HUGH. *Stained Glass of the Middle Ages in England and France.* London: A & C Black, 1925.

AUBERT, MARCEL. *French Cathedral Windows of the Twelfth and Thirteenth Centuries.* New York and Toronto: Oxford Univ. Press, 1939.

CLOW, BARBARA and GERRY. *Stained Glass, A Basic Manual.* Boston: Little, Brown, 1976.

CONNICK, CHARLES J. *Adventures in Light and Color: An Introduction to the Stained Glass Craft.* New York: Random House, 1937.

DAY, LEWIS FOREMAN. *Stained Glass.* London: Chapman & Hall, 1903.

————. *Windows: A Book about Stained and Painted Glass.* New York: Scribner's, 1909.

DIVINE, J.A.F., and G. BLACHFORD. *Stained Glass Craft.* New York: Dover, 1972.

DUNCAN, ALASTAIR. *Leaded Glass: A Handbook of Technique.* New York: Watson-Guptill, 1975.

ERIKSON, ERIK. *Step-by-Step Stained Glass.* New York: Golden Press, 1974.

FRENCH, JENNIE. *Glass-Works: The Copper Foil Technique of Stained Glass.* New York: Van Nostrand Reinhold, 1974.

FREUND, MIRIAM K. *Jewels for a Crown: The Story of the Chagall Windows.* New York: McGraw-Hill, 1963.

GAUDIN, FÉLIX. *Le Vitrail du XIIe Siècle au XVIIIe Siècle en France.* Les Arts Décoratifs. Paris: Flammarion, 1928.

GOBILLET, RENÉ. *The Cathedral of Chartres—Its Influence on the Art of Glass.* New York: Loire Imports, 1962.

GRODECKI, LOUIS. *The Stained Glass of French Churches.* Paris: Les Éditions du Chêne, 1948.

HARRISON, FREDERICK. *The Painted Glass of York.* New York: Macmillan, 1927.

HILL, ROBERT and JILL, and HANS ALBERSTADT.

Stained Glass: Music for the Eye. San Francisco: Scrimshaw Press, 1976.

ISENBERG, ANITA and SEYMOUR. *How to Work in Stained Glass.* Radnor, Pa.: Chilton, 1972.

JOHNSON, JAMES R. *The Radiance of Chartres.* London: Phaidon Press, 1964.

JUDSON, WALTER W. *Stained Glass.* New York: Galahad, 1972.

KOCH, ROBERT. *Louis Comfort Tiffany, 1848–1933.* New York: Museum of Contemporary Crafts, 1958.

————. *Louis C. Tiffany, Rebel in Glass.* New York: Crown, 1964.

LE COUTEUR, J. D. *English Medieval Painted Glass.* London: S.P.C.K., 1926.

LEE, LAWRENCE. "Modern Secular Stained Glass." *Architectural Design,* May, 1951.

————. *Stained Glass.* New York: Oxford Univ. Press, 1967.

LEE, LAWRENCE, et al. *Stained Glass.* Photographs by Sonia Halliday and Laura Lushington. New York: Crown, 1976.

LEE, RUTH WEBB. *Nineteenth-Century Art Glass.* New York: M. Barrows, 1952.

LEYMARIE, JEAN. *Marc Chagall, The Jerusalem Windows.* Trans. Elaine Desautels. New York: George Braziller, 1976 ed.

LLOYD, JOHN GILBERT. *Stained Glass in America.* Jenkintown, Pa.: Foundation, 1963.

MARCHINI, G. *Italian Stained Glass Windows.* New York: Harry N. Abrams, 1956.

METCALF, ROBERT and GERTRUDE. *Making Stained Glass.* New York: McGraw-Hill, 1973.

NEUSTADT, EGON. *The Lamps of Tiffany.* New York: Fairfield Press, 1970.

PANOFSKY, ERWIN. *Gothic Architecture and Scholasticism.* New York: World, 1957.

PFAFF, KONRAD. *Ludwig Schaffrath.* Trans. Rozemarijn van der Horst. Krefeld, Germany: Scherpe Verlag Krefeld, 1977.

PIPER, JOHN. *Stained Glass: Art or Anti-Art.* New York: Van Nostrand Reinhold, 1968.

QUAGLIATA, NARCISSUS. *Stained Glass from Mind to Light.* San Francisco: Mattole Press, 1976.

———. "Art in Architecture," *Glass*, October, 1977, pp. 26–45.

RACKHAM, BERNARD. *A Guide to the Collections of Stained Glass.* London: H.M.S.O., 1936.

———. *The Ancient Glass of Canterbury Cathedral.* London: Lund, Humphries, 1949.

READ, HERBERT E. *English Stained Glass.* London and New York: Putnam, 1926.

———, and JOHN BAKER. *English Stained Glass.* New York: Harry N. Abrams, 1960.

REYNTIENS, PATRICK. *Technique of Stained Glass.* New York: Watson-Guptill, 1967.

RIGAN, OTTO B. *New Glass.* San Francisco: San Francisco Book Company, 1976.

RORIMER, JAMES J. "Recent Reinstallations of Medieval Art," *The Metropolitan Museum of Art Bulletin*, December 1947–January 1948, pp. 199–204.

SEWTER, A. CHARLES. *The Stained Glass of William Morris and His Circle.* New Haven: Yale Univ. Press, 1974.

SHERRILL, CHARLES H. *Stained Glass Tours in England.* London: J. Lane, 1909.

———. *Stained Glass Tours in France.* New York: Dodd, 1922.

———. *Stained Glass Tours in Germany, Austria, and the Rhineland.* New York: Dodd, Mead, 1927.

———. *Stained Glass Tours in Italy.* London: J. Lane, 1913.

———. *Stained Glass Tours in Spain and Flanders.* New York: Dodd, Mead, 1924.

SIMSON, OTTO VON. *The Gothic Cathedral.* Bollingen Series XLVIII. Princeton: Princeton Univ. Press, 1974.

SOWERS, ROBERT. *Stained Glass: An Architectural Art.* New York: Universe, 1965.

———. *The Lost Art.* Problems of Contemporary Art, No. 7. New York: George Wittenborn, 1954.

"The Stained Glass Theories of Viollet-le-Duc," *The Art Bulletin*, June, 1963, p. 123.

"Stained-Glass Windows," *The Metropolitan Museum of Art Bulletin*, December 1971–January 1972.

THEOPHILUS (RUGERUS). *The Various Arts.* Trans. C. R. Dodwell. London: Thomas Nelson, 1961.

LE VITRAIL FRANÇAIS. Musée des Arts Décoratifs. Paris: Editions des Deux Mondes, 1958.

VITRAUX DE FRANCE. Paris: Musée des Arts Décoratifs, 1953.

WESTLAKE, NAT. *A History of Design in Painted Glass.* London: J. Parker, 1881–94.

WHALL, CHRISTOPHER W. *Stained Glass Work.* London: Sir Isaac Pitman & Sons, 1920.

WOODFORDE, CHRISTOPHER. *English Stained and Painted Glass.* Oxford: Oxford Univ. Press, 1954.

Index